UTAH TRAILS

NORTHERN REGION

Printed in Korea

Cover photos
Clockwise from bottom left: Brown's Park Trail, Rainbow and Island Park Trail, Rainbow and Island Park Trail

Rear cover photos
From left: Wendover to Lucin Trail, Left Hand Fork Canyon Trail

UTAH TRAILS

NORTHERN REGION

PETER MASSEY
JEANNE WILSON
ANGELA TITUS

APC
PUBLISHING

Acknowledgements

Many people and organizations have made major contributions to the research and production of this book. We owe them all special thanks for their assistance.

We would also like to thank the many people at the Bureau of Land Management offices throughout Utah, who spent countless hours assisting us. In particular, we would like to thank Dennis Willis, outdoor recreational planner at the Price Field Office, and Blaine Miller, archaeologist at the Price Field Office.

Staff at many offices of the National Forest Service also provided us with valuable assistance, particularly the offices in Price, Ferron, Teasdale, and Richfield.

We received a great deal of assistance from many other people and organizations. We would like to thank the Utah State Historical Society, the Denver Public Library Western History Department, Kari Murphy at the Moab to Monument Valley Film Commission, and the Moab Historical Society. Mrs. Betty Smith of Green River, Utah, was most helpful in providing information about Smith's Cabin.

Publisher's Note: Every effort has been taken to ensure that the information in this book is accurate at press time. Please visit our website to advise us of any changes or corrections you find. We also welcome recommendations for new 4WD trails or other suggestions to improve the information in this book.

APC PUBLISHING

APC Publishing
Parker, Colorado
Phone: 800-660-5107
Fax: 303-688-4388
4WDbooks.com

Contents

Sidebars

Before You Go

Why a 4WD Does It Better

The design and engineering of 4WD vehicles provide them with many advantages over normal cars when you head off the paved road:

- improved distribution of power to all four wheels;
- a transmission transfer case, which provides low-range gear selection for greater pulling power and for crawling over difficult terrain;
- high ground clearance;
- less overhang of the vehicle's body past the wheels, which provides better front and rear clearance when crossing gullies and ridges;
- large-lug, wide-tread tires;
- rugged construction (including underbody skid plates on many models).

If you plan to do off-highway touring, all of these considerations are important, whether you are evaluating the capabilities of your current 4WD or are looking to buy one; each is considered in detail in this chapter.

In order to explore the most difficult trails described in this book, you will need a 4WD vehicle that is well rated in each of the above features. If you own a 2WD sport utility vehicle, a lighter car-type SUV, or a 2WD pickup truck, your ability to explore the more difficult trails will depend on conditions and your level of experience.

A word of caution: Whatever type of 4WD vehicle you drive, understand that it is not invincible or indestructible. Nor can it go everywhere. A 4WD has a much higher center of gravity and weighs more than a car, and so has its own consequent limitations.

Experience is the only way to learn what your vehicle can and cannot do. Therefore, if you are inexperienced, we strongly recommend that you start with trails that have lower difficulty ratings. As you develop an understanding of your vehicle and of your own taste for adventure, you can safely tackle the more challenging trails.

One way to beef up your knowledge quickly, while avoiding the costly and sometimes dangerous lessons learned from on-the-road mistakes, is to undertake a 4WD course taught by a professional. Look in the Yellow Pages for courses in your area.

Using This Book

Route Planning

The regional map on pages 22 and 23 provides a convenient overview of the trails in the northern portion of the state. Each 4WD trail is shown, as are major highways and towns, helping you to plan various routes by connecting a series of 4WD trails and paved roads.

As you plan your overall route, you will probably want to utilize as many 4WD trails as possible. However, check the difficulty rating and time required for each trail before finalizing your plans. You don't want to be stuck 50 miles from the highway—at sunset and without camping gear, since your trip was supposed to be over hours ago—when you discover that your vehicle can't handle a certain difficult passage.

Difficulty Ratings

We utilize a point system to provide a guide rating the difficulty of each trail. Any such system is subjective, and your experience of the trails will vary depending on your skill and the road conditions at the time. Indeed, particularly in Utah, any amount of rain makes the trails much more difficult, if not completely impassable.

We have rated the 4WD trails on a scale of 1 to 10—1 being passable for a normal passenger vehicle in good conditions and 10 requiring a heavily modified vehicle and an experienced driver who expects to encounter vehicle damage. Because this book is designed for owners of unmodified 4WD vehicles—who we assume do not want to damage their vehicles—most of the trails are rated 5 or lower. A few trails are included that rate as high as 7, while those rated 8 to 10 are beyond the scope of this book.

This is not to say that the moderate-rated trails are easy. We strongly recommend that inexperienced drivers not tackle trails rated at 4 or higher until they have undertaken a number of the lower-rated ones, so that they can gauge their skill level and prepare for the difficulty of the higher-rated trails.

In assessing the trails, we have always assumed good road conditions (dry road surface, good visibility, and so on). The factors influencing our ratings are as follows:

- obstacles such as rocks, mud, ruts, sand, slickrock, and stream crossings;
- the stability of the road surface;
- the width of the road and the vehicle clearance between trees or rocks;
- the steepness of the road;
- the margin for driver error (for example, a very high, open shelf road would be rated more difficult even if it was not very steep and had a stable surface).

The following is a guide to the ratings.

Rating 1: The trail is graded dirt but suitable for a normal passenger vehicle. It usually has gentle grades, is fairly wide, and has very shallow water crossings (if any).

Rating 2: High-clearance vehicles are preferred but not necessary. These trails are dirt roads, but they may have rocks, grades, water crossings, or ruts that make clearance a concern in a normal passenger vehicle. The trails are fairly wide, so that passing is not a concern, and mud is not a concern under normal weather conditions.

Rating 3: High-clearance 4WDs are preferred, but any high-clearance vehicle is acceptable. Expect a rough road surface; mud and sand are possible but will be easily passable. You may encounter rocks up to 6 inches in diameter, a loose road surface, and shelf roads, though these will be wide enough for passing or will have adequate pull-offs.

Rating 4: High-clearance 4WDs are recommended, though most stock SUVs are acceptable. Expect a rough road surface with rocks larger than 6 inches, but there will be a reasonable driving line available. Patches of mud are possible but can be readily negotiated; sand may be deep and require lower tire pressures. There may be stream crossings up to 12 inches deep, substantial sections of single-lane shelf road, moderate grades, and sections of moderately loose road surface.

Rating 5: High-clearance 4WDs are required. These trails have a rough, rutted surface, rocks up to nine inches, mud and deep sand that may be impassable for inexperienced drivers, and stream crossings up to 18 inches deep. Certain sections may be steep enough to cause traction problems, and you may encounter very narrow shelf roads with steep drop-offs and tight clearance between rocks or trees.

Rating 6: These trails are for experienced four-wheel drivers only. They are potentially dangerous, with large rocks, ruts, or terraces that may need to be negotiated. They may also have stream crossings at least 18 inches deep, involve rapid currents, unstable stream bottoms, or difficult access; steep slopes, loose surfaces, and narrow clearances; and very narrow shelf roads with steep drop-offs and possibly challenging road surfaces.

Rating 7: Skilled, experienced four-wheel drivers only. These trails include very challenging sections with extremely steep grades, loose surfaces, large rocks, deep ruts, and/or tight clearances. Mud or sand may necessitate winching.

Rating 8 and above: Stock vehicles are likely to be damaged and may find the trail impassable. Highly-skilled, experienced four-wheel drivers only.

Scenic Ratings

If rating the degree of difficulty is subjective, rating scenic beauty is guaranteed to lead to arguments. Utah contains a spectacular variety of scenery—from its grand canyons and towering mountains and buttes to its seemingly endless desert country. We love the wide-open remoteness of many areas of Utah, but realize they are not to everyone's liking. Nonetheless, we have tried to provide some guide to the relative scenic quality of the various trails. The ratings are based on a scale of 1 to 10.

Remoteness Ratings

Many of the trails in Utah are in remote country; sometimes the trails are seldom traveled, and the likelihood is low that another vehicle will appear within a reasonable time to assist you if you get stuck or break down. We have included a ranking for remoteness of +0 through +2. Summer temperatures can make a breakdown in the more remote areas a life-threatening experience. Prepare carefully before tackling the higher-rated, more remote trails (see Special Preparations for Remote Travel, page 11). For trails with a high remoteness rating, consider traveling with a second vehicle.

Estimated Driving Times

In calculating driving times, we have not allowed for stops. Your actual driving time may be considerably longer depending on the number and duration of the stops you make. Add more time if you prefer to drive more slowly than good conditions allow.

Current Road Information

All the 4WD trails described in this book may become impassable in poor weather conditions. Storms can alter roads, remove tracks, and create impassable washes. Most of the trails described, even easy 2WD trails, can quickly become impassable even to 4WD vehicles after only a small amount of rain. For each trail, we have provided a phone number for obtaining current information about conditions.

Abbreviations

The route directions for the 4WD trails use a series of abbreviations as follows:

SO	CONTINUE STRAIGHT ON
TL	TURN LEFT
TR	TURN RIGHT
BL	BEAR LEFT
BR	BEAR RIGHT
UT	U-TURN

Using Route Directions

For every trail, we describe and pinpoint (by odometer reading) nearly every significant feature along the route—such as intersections, streams, washes, gates, cattle guards, and so on—and provide directions from these landmarks. Odometer readings will vary from vehicle to vehicle, so you should allow for slight variations. Be aware that trails can quickly change in the desert. A new trail may be cut around a washout, a faint trail can be graded by the county, or a well-used trail may fall into disuse. All these factors will affect the accuracy of the given directions.

If you diverge from the route, zero your trip meter upon your return and continue along the route, making the necessary adjustment to the point-to-point odometer readings. In the directions, we regularly reset the odometer readings—at significant landmarks or popular lookouts and spur trails—so that you won't have to recalculate for too long.

Most of the trails can be started from either end, and the route directions include both directions of travel; reverse directions are printed in green below the main directions. When traveling in reverse, read from the bottom of the table and work up.

Route directions include cross-references whenever two 4WD trails included in this book connect; this allows for an easy change of route or destination.

Each trail includes periodic latitude and longitude readings to facilitate using a global positioning system (GPS) receiver. These readings may also assist you in finding your location on the maps. The GPS coordinates were taken using the NAD 1927 datum and are in the format dd°mm.mm'. When loading coordinates into your GPS receiver, you may wish to include only one decimal place, since in Utah, the third decimal place equals only about 2 yards and the second less than 20 yards.

Map References

We recommend that you supplement the information in this book with more-detailed maps. For each trail, we list the sheet maps and road atlases that provide the best detail for the area. Typically, the following references are given:

- Bureau of Land Management Maps

■ U.S. Forest Service Maps

■ *Utah Atlas & Gazetteer,* 10th ed. (Freeport, Maine: Garmin Ltd., 2017)—Scale 1:235,000,

■ *Utah Road and Recreation Atlas,* 7th ed. (Medford, Oregon: Benchmark Maps, 2017)—Scale 1:250,000,

■ Terrain Navigator Pro Topo Maps—Scale 1:100,000 and 1:24,000,

■ *Trails Illustrated* Topo Maps; National Geographic Maps—Various scales, but all contain good detail.

We recommend the *Trails Illustrated* series of maps as the best for navigating these trails. They are reliable, easy to read, and printed on nearly indestructible plastic paper. However, this series covers only a few of the 4WD trails described in this book.

The DeLorme Atlas has the advantage of providing you with maps of the state at a reasonable price. Although its 4WD trail information doesn't go beyond what we provide, it is useful if you wish to explore the hundreds of side roads.

U.S. Forest Service maps lack the topographic detail of the other sheet maps and, in our experience, are occasionally out of date. They have the advantage of covering a broad area and are useful in identifying land use and travel restrictions. These maps are most useful for the longer trails.

The Terrain Navigator series of maps published on DVD or via download by Maptech are also very useful. These maps contain an amazing level of detail because they include the entire set of U.S. Geological Survey topographical maps of Utah at both the 1:24,000 scale and the 1:100,000 scale. These maps offer many advantages over normal maps:

■ GPS coordinates for any location can be found and loaded into your GPS receiver. Conversely, if you have your GPS coordinates, your location on the map can be pinpointed instantly.

■ Towns, rivers, passes, mountains, and many other sites are indexed by name so that they can be located quickly.

■ 4WD trails can be marked and profiled for elevation changes and distances from point to point.

■ Customized maps can be printed out.

■ The DVDs can be used with a laptop computer and a GPS receiver in your vehicle to monitor your location on the map and navigate directly from the display.

All these maps should be available through good map stores.

Backcountry Driving Rules, Preparations, and Permits

Four-wheel driving involves special driving techniques and road rules. This section is an introduction for 4WD beginners.

4WD Road Rules

To help ensure that these trails remain open and available for all four-wheel drivers to enjoy, it is important to minimize your impact on the environment and not be a safety risk to yourself or anyone else. Remember that the 4WD clubs in Utah fight a constant battle with the U.S. Forest Service (USFS) and the Bureau of Land Management (BLM) to retain the access that currently exists.

The fundamental rule when traversing the 4WD trails described in this book is to use common sense. In addition, special road rules for 4WD trails apply:

■ Vehicles traveling uphill have the right of way.

■ If you are moving more slowly than the vehicle behind you, pull over to let the other vehicle by.

■ Park out of the way in a safe place. Blocking a track may restrict access for emergency vehicles as well as for other recreationalists. Set the parking brake—don't rely on leaving the transmission in park. Manual transmissions should be left in the lowest gear.

Tread Lightly!

Remember the rules of the Tread Lightly! program:

■ Be informed. Obtain maps, regulations, and other information from the forest service or from other public land agencies.

Learn the rules and follow them.

- Resist the urge to pioneer a new road or trail or to cut across a switchback. Stay on constructed tracks and avoid running over young trees, shrubs, and grasses, damaging or killing them. Don't drive across alpine tundra; this fragile environment can take years to recover.
- Stay off soft, wet roads and 4WD trails readily torn up by vehicles. Repairing the damage is expensive, and quite often authorities find it easier to close the road rather than repair it.
- Travel around meadows, steep hillsides, stream banks, and lake shores that are easily scarred by churning wheels.
- Stay away from wild animals that are rearing young or suffering from a food shortage. Do not camp close to the water sources of domestic or wild animals.
- Obey gate closures and regulatory signs.
- Preserve America's heritage by not disturbing old mining camps, ghost towns, or other historical features. Leave historic sites, Native American rock art, ruins, and artifacts in place and untouched.
- Carry out all your trash, and even that of others.
- Stay out of designated wilderness areas. They are closed to all vehicles. It is your responsibility to know where the boundaries are.
- Get permission to cross private land. Leave livestock alone. Respect landowners' rights.

Report violations of these rules to help keep these 4WD trails open and to ensure that others will have the opportunity to visit these backcountry sites. Many groups are actively seeking to close these public lands to vehicles, thereby denying access to those who are unable, or perhaps merely unwilling, to hike long distances. This magnificent countryside is owned by, and should be available to, all Americans.

Special Preparations for Remote Travel

Due to the remoteness of some areas in Utah and the very high summer temperatures, you should take some special precautions to ensure that you don't end up in a life-threatening situation:

- When planning a trip into the desert, always inform someone as to where you are going, your route, and when you expect to return. Stick to your plan.
- Carry and drink at least one gallon of water per person per day of your trip. (Plastic gallon jugs are handy and portable.)
- Be sure your vehicle is in good condition with a sound battery, good hoses, spare tire, spare fan belts, necessary tools, and reserve gasoline and oil. Other spare parts and extra radiator water are also valuable. If traveling in pairs, share the common spares and carry a greater variety.
- Consider taking a satellite phone, which will always be in range and can be rented at reasonable price.
- Keep an eye on the sky. Flash floods can occur in a wash any time you see thunderheads—even when it's not raining a drop where you are.
- If you are caught in a dust storm while driving, get off the road and turn off your lights. Turn on the emergency flashers and back into the wind to reduce windshield pitting by sand particles.
- Test trails on foot before driving through washes and sandy areas. One minute of walking may save hours of hard work getting your vehicle unstuck.
- If your vehicle breaks down, stay near it. Your emergency supplies are there. Your car has many other items useful in an emergency. Raise your hood and trunk lid to denote "help needed." Remember, a vehicle can be seen for miles, but a person on foot is very difficult to spot from a distance.
- When you're not moving, use available shade or erect shade from tarps, blankets, or seat covers—anything to reduce the direct rays of the sun.
- Do not sit or lie directly on the ground. It may be 30 degrees hotter than the air.
- Leave a disabled vehicle only if you are positive of the route and the distance to help. Leave a note for rescuers that gives the time you left and the direction you are taking.

■ If you must walk, rest for at least 10 minutes out of each hour. If you are not normally physically active, rest up to 30 minutes out of each hour. Find shade, sit down, and prop up your feet. Adjust your shoes and socks, but do not remove your shoes—you may not be able to get them back on swollen feet.

■ If you have water, drink it. Do not ration it.

■ If water is limited, keep your mouth closed. Do not talk, eat, smoke, drink alcohol, or take salt.

■ Keep your clothing on, despite the heat. It helps to keep the body temperature down and reduces your dehydration rate. Cover your head. If you don't have a hat, improvise a head covering.

■ If you are stalled or lost, set signal fires. Set smoky fires in the daytime and bright ones at night. Three fires in a triangle denote "help needed."

■ A roadway is a sign of civilization. If you find a road, stay on it.

■ If hiking in the desert, equip each person, especially children, with a police-type whistle. It makes a distinctive noise with little effort. Three blasts denote "help needed."

■ To avoid poisonous creatures, put your hands or feet only where your eyes can see. One insect to be aware of in Utah is the Africanized honeybee. Though indistinguishable from its European counterpart, these bees are far more aggressive and can be a threat. They have been known to give chase of up to a mile and even wait for people who have escaped into the water to come up for air. The best thing to do if attacked is to cover your face and head with clothing and run to the nearest enclosed shelter. Keep an eye on your pet if you notice a number of bees in the area, as many have been killed by Africanized honeybees.

■ Avoid unnecessary contact with wildlife. Some mice in Utah carry the deadly hantavirus, a pulmonary syndrome fatal in 60 to 70 percent of human cases. Fortunately the disease is very rare but caution is still advised. Other rodents may transmit bubonic plague, the same epidemic that killed one-third of Europe's population in the 1300s. Be especially wary near sick animals and keep pets, especially cats, away from wildlife and their fleas. Another creature to watch for is the western black-legged tick, the carrier of Lyme disease. Wearing clothing that covers legs and arms, tucking pants into boots, and using insect repellent are good ways to avoid fleas and ticks.

Obtaining Permits

Backcountry permits, which usually cost a fee, are often required for certain activities on public lands in Utah, whether the area is a national park, state park, national monument, Indian reservation, or BLM land.

Restrictions may require a permit for all overnight stays, which can include backpacking and 4WD or bicycle camping. Permits may also be required for day use by vehicles, horses, hikers, or bikes in some areas.

When possible, we include information about fees and permit requirements and where permits may be obtained, but these regulations change constantly. If in doubt, check with the most likely governing agency.

Assessing Your Vehicle's Off-Road Ability

Many issues come into play when evaluating your 4WD vehicle, though most of the 4WDs on the market are suitable for even the roughest trails described in this book. Engine power will be adequate in even the least powerful modern vehicle. However, some vehicles are less suited to off-highway driving than others, and some of the newest, carlike sport utility vehicles (SUVs) simply are not designed for off-highway touring. The following information should allow you to identify the good, the bad, and the ugly.

Differing 4WD Systems

All 4WD systems have one thing in common: The engine provides power to all four wheels rather than to only two, as is typical in most standard cars. However, there are a number of differences in the way power is applied to the wheels.

The other feature that distinguishes nearly all 4WDs from normal passenger vehicles is that the gearboxes have high and low ratios that effectively double the number of gears. The high range is comparable to the range on a passenger car. The low range provides lower speed and more power, which is useful when towing heavy loads, driving up steep hills, or crawling over rocks. When driving downhill, the 4WD's low range increases engine braking.

Various makes and models of SUVs offer different drive systems, but these differences center on two issues: the way power is applied to the other wheels if one or more wheels slip, and the ability to select between 2WD and 4WD.

Normal driving requires that all four wheels be able to turn at different speeds; this allows the vehicle to turn without scrubbing its tires. In a 2WD vehicle, the front wheels (or rear wheels in a front-wheel-drive vehicle) are not powered by the engine and thus are free to turn individually at any speed. The rear wheels, powered by the engine, are only able to turn at different speeds because of the differential, which applies power to the faster-turning wheel.

This standard method of applying traction has certain weaknesses. First, when power is applied to only one set of wheels, the other set cannot help the vehicle gain traction. Second, when one powered wheel loses traction, it spins, but the other powered wheel doesn't turn. This happens because the differential applies all the engine power to the faster-turning wheel and no power to the other wheels, which still have traction. All 4WD systems are designed to overcome these two weaknesses. However, different 4WDs address this common objective in different ways.

Full-Time 4WD. For a vehicle to remain in 4WD all the time without scrubbing the tires, all the wheels must be able to rotate at different speeds. A full-time 4WD system allows this to happen by using three differentials. One is located between the rear wheels, as in a normal passenger car, to allow the rear wheels to rotate at different speeds. The second is located between the front wheels in exactly the same way. The third differential is located between the front and rear wheels to allow different rotational speeds between the front and rear sets of wheels. In nearly all vehicles with full-time 4WD, the center differential operates only in high range. In low range, it is completely locked. This is not a disadvantage because when using low range the additional traction is normally desired and the deterioration of steering response will be less noticeable due to the vehicle traveling at a slower speed.

Part-Time 4WD. A part-time 4WD system does not have the center differential located between the front and rear wheels. Consequently, the front and rear drive shafts are both driven at the same speed and with the same power at all times when in 4WD.

This system provides improved traction because when one or both of the front or rear wheels slips, the engine continues to provide power to the other set. However, because such a system doesn't allow a difference in speed between the front and rear sets of wheels, the tires scrub when turning, placing additional strain on the whole drive system. Therefore, such a system can be used only in slippery conditions; otherwise, the ability to steer the vehicle will deteriorate and the tires will quickly wear out.

Some vehicles, such as Jeeps with Selec-trac™ and Mitsubishi Monteros with Active Trac 4WD™ offer both full-time and part-time 4WD in high range.

Manual Systems to Switch Between 2WD and 4WD. There are three manual systems for switching between 2WD and 4WD. The most basic requires stopping and getting out of the vehicle to lock the front hubs manually before selecting 4WD. The second requires you to stop, but you change to 4WD by merely throwing a lever inside the vehicle (the hubs lock automatically). The third allows shifting between 2WD and 4WD high range while the vehicle is moving. Any 4WD that does not offer the option of driving in 2WD must have a full-time 4WD system.

Automated Switching Between 2WD and 4WD. Advances in technology are leading to greater automation in the selection of two- or four-wheel drive. When operating in high range, these high-tech systems use sensors to monitor the rotation of each wheel. When any slippage is detected, the vehicle switches the proportion of power from the wheel(s) that is slipping to the wheels that retain grip. The proportion of power supplied to each wheel is therefore infinitely variable as opposed to the original systems where the vehicle was either in two-wheel drive or four-wheel drive.

In recent years, this process has been spurred on by many of the manufacturers of luxury vehicles entering the SUV market—Mercedes, BMW, Cadillac, Lincoln, and Lexus have joined Range Rover in this segment.

Manufacturers of these higher-priced vehicles have led the way in introducing sophisticated computer-controlled 4WD systems. Although each of the manufacturers has its own approach to this issue, all the systems automatically vary the allocation of power between the wheels within milliseconds of the sensors' detecting wheel slippage.

Limiting Wheel Slippage

4WDs employ various systems to limit wheel slippage and transfer power to the wheels that still have traction. These systems may completely lock the differentials, or they may allow limited slippage before transferring power back to the wheels that retain traction.

Lockers completely eliminate the operation of one or more differentials. A locker on the center differential switches between full-time and part-time 4WD. Lockers on the front or rear differentials ensure that power remains equally applied to each set of wheels regardless of whether both have traction. Lockers may be controlled manually by a switch or lever in the vehicle, or they may be automatic.

Some brands provide the option of having manual lockers on all three differentials, while other brands offer manual locks on the center and rear differential. Manual lockers are the most controllable and effective devices for ensuring that power is provided to the wheels with traction. However, because they allow absolutely no slippage, they must be used only on slippery surfaces.

An alternative method for getting power to the wheels that have traction is to allow limited wheel slippage. Systems that work this way may be called limited-slip differentials, posi-traction systems, or in the center differential, viscous couplings. The advantage of these systems is that the limited difference they allow in rotational speed between wheels enables such systems to be used when driving on a dry surface. All full-time 4WD systems allow limited slippage in the center differential.

For off-highway use, a manually locking differential is the best of the above systems, but it is the most expensive. Limited-slip differentials are the cheapest but also the least satisfactory, as they require one wheel to be slipping at two to three mph before power is transferred to the other wheel. For the center differential, the best system combines a locking differential and, to enable full-time use, a viscous coupling.

Tires

The tires that came with your 4WD vehicle may be satisfactory, but many 4WDs are fitted with passenger-car tires. These are unlikely to be the best choice because they are less rugged and more likely to puncture on rocky trails. They are particularly prone to sidewall damage. Passenger vehicle tires also have a less aggressive tread pattern than specialized 4WD tires, providing less traction in mud.

For information on purchasing tires better suited to off-highway conditions, see Special 4WD Equipment on page 20.

Clearance

Road clearances vary considerably among different 4WD vehicles—from less than 7 inches to more than 10 inches. Special vehicles may have far greater clearance. For instance, the Hummer has 16-inch ground clearance. High ground clearance is particularly advantageous on the rockier or more rutted 4WD trails in this book.

When evaluating the ground clearance of your vehicle, you need to take into account the clearance of the body work between the wheels on each side of the vehicle. This is particularly relevant for crawling over larger rocks. Vehicles with sidesteps have significantly lower clearance than those without.

Another factor affecting clearance is the approach and departure angles of your vehicle—that is, the maximum angle the ground can slope without the front of the vehicle hitting the ridge on approach or the rear of the vehicle hitting on departure. Mounting a winch or tow hitch to your vehicle is likely to reduce your approach or departure angle.

If you do a lot of driving on rocky trails, you will inevitably hit the bottom of the vehicle sooner or later. When this happens, you will be far less likely to damage vulnerable areas such as the oil pan and gas tank if your vehicle is fitted with skid plates. Most manufacturers offer skid plates as an option. They are worth every penny.

Maneuverability

When you tackle tight switchbacks, you will quickly appreciate that maneuverability is an important criterion when assessing 4WD vehicles. Where a full-size vehicle may be forced to go back and forth a number of times to get around a sharp turn, a small 4WD might go straight around. This is not only easier, it's safer.

If you have a full-size vehicle, all is not lost. We have traveled many of the trails in this book in a Suburban. That is not to say that some of these trails wouldn't have been easier to negotiate in a smaller vehicle! We have noted in the route descriptions if a trail is not suitable for larger vehicles.

In Summary

Using the criteria above, you can evaluate how well your 4WD will handle off-road touring, and if you haven't yet purchased your vehicle, you can use these criteria to help select one. Choosing the best 4WD system is, at least partly, subjective. It is also a matter of your budget. However, for the type of off-highway driving covered in this book, we make the following recommendations:

- Select a 4WD system that offers low range and, at a minimum, has some form of limited slip differential on the rear axle.
- Use light truck, all-terrain tires as the standard tires on your vehicle. For sand and slickrock, these will be the ideal choice. If conditions are likely to be muddy, or traction will be improved by a tread pattern that will give more bite, consider an additional set of mud tires.
- For maximum clearance, select a vehicle with 16-inch wheels, or at least choose the tallest tires that your vehicle can accommodate. Note that if you install tires with a diameter greater than standard, the odometer will undercalculate the distance you have traveled. Your engine braking and gear ratios will also be affected.
- If you are going to try the rockier 4WD trails, don't install a sidestep or low hanging front bar. If you have the option, have underbody skid plates mounted.
- Remember that many of the obstacles you encounter on backcountry trails are more difficult to navigate in a full-size vehicle than in a compact 4WD.

Four-Wheel Driving Techniques

Safe four-wheel driving requires that you observe certain golden rules:

- Size up the situation in advance.
- Be careful and take your time.
- Maintain smooth, steady power and momentum.
- Engage 4WD and low-range gears before you get into a tight situation.
- Steer toward high spots, trying to put the wheel over large rocks.
- Straddle ruts.
- Use gears and not just the brakes to

hold the vehicle when driving downhill. On very steep slopes, chock the wheels if you park your vehicle.

- Watch for logging and mining trucks and smaller recreational vehicles, such as all-terrain vehicles (ATVs).
- Wear your seat belt and secure all luggage, especially heavy items such as tool boxes or coolers. Heavy items should be secured by ratchet tie-down straps rather than elastic-type straps, which are not strong enough to hold heavy items if the vehicle rolls.

Utah's 4WD trails have a number of common obstacles, and the following section provides an introduction to the techniques required to surmount them.

Rocks. Tire selection is important in negotiating rocks. Select a multiple-ply, tough sidewall, light-truck tire with a large-lug tread.

As you approach a rocky stretch, get into 4WD low range to give you maximum slow-speed control. Speed is rarely necessary, since traction on a rocky surface is usually good. Plan ahead and select the line you wish to take. If a rock appears to be larger than the clearance of your vehicle, don't try to straddle it. Check to see that it is not higher than the frame of your vehicle once you get a wheel over it. Put a wheel up on the rock and slowly climb it, then gently drop over the other side using the brake to ensure a smooth landing. Bouncing the car over rocks increases the likelihood of damage, as the body's clearance is reduced by the suspension compressing. Running boards also significantly reduce your clearance in this respect.

It is often helpful to use a "spotter" outside the vehicle to assist you with the best wheel placement.

Slickrock. When you encounter slickrock, first assess the correct direction of the trail. It is easy to lose sight of the trail on slickrock, as there are seldom any developed edges. Often the way is marked with small rock cairns, which are simply rocks stacked high enough to make a landmark.

All-terrain tires with tighter tread are more suited to slickrock than the more open, luggier type tires. As with rocks, a multiple-ply sidewall is important. In dry conditions, slickrock offers pavement-type grip. In rain or snow, you will soon learn how it got its name, and even the best tires may not get an adequate grip. Walk steep sections first; if you are slipping on foot, chances are your vehicle will slip too.

Slickrock is characterized by ledges and long sections of "pavement." Follow the guidelines for travel over rocks. Refrain from speeding over flat-looking sections, as you may hit an unexpected crevice or water pocket, and vehicles bend easier than slickrock! Turns and ledges can be tight, and vehicles with smaller overhangs and better maneuverability are at a distinct advantage—hence the popularity of the compacts in the slickrock mecca of Moab.

On the steepest sections, engage low range and pick a straight line up or down the slope. Do not attempt to traverse a steep slope sideways.

Steep Uphill Grades. Consider walking the trail to ensure that the steep hill before you is passable, especially if it is clear that backtracking is going to be a problem.

Select 4WD low range to ensure that you have adequate power to pull up the hill. If the wheels begin to lose traction, turn the steering wheel gently from side to side to give the wheels a chance to regain traction.

If you lose momentum, but the car is not in danger of sliding, use the foot brake, switch off the ignition, leave the vehicle in gear (if manual transmission) or park (if automatic), engage the parking brake, and get out to examine the situation. See if you can remove any obstacles, and figure out the line you need to take. Reversing a couple of yards and starting again may allow you to get better traction and momentum.

If, halfway up, you decide a stretch of road is impassably steep, back down the trail. Trying to turn the vehicle around on a steep hill is extremely dangerous; you will very likely cause it to roll over.

Steep Downhill Grades. Again, consider walking the trail to ensure that a steep hill is passable, especially if it is clear that backtracking uphill is going to be a problem.

Select 4WD low range and use first gear to maximize braking assistance from the engine. If the surface is loose and you are losing traction, change up to second or third gear. Do not use the brakes if you can avoid it, but don't let the vehicle's speed get out of control. Feather (lightly pump) the brakes if you slip under braking. For vehicles fitted with ABS, apply even pressure if you start to slip; the ABS helps keep vehicles on line.

Travel very slowly over rock ledges or ruts. Attempt to tackle these diagonally, letting one wheel down at a time.

If the back of the vehicle begins to slide around, gently apply the throttle and correct the steering. If the rear of the vehicle starts to slide sideways, do not apply the brakes.

Mud. Muddy trails are easily damaged, so they should be avoided if possible. But if you must traverse a section of mud, your success will depend heavily on whether you have open-lugged mud tires or chains. Thick mud fills the tighter tread on normal tires, leaving the tire with no more grip than if it were bald. If the muddy stretch is only a few yards long, the momentum of your vehicle may allow you to get through regardless.

If the muddy track is very steep, uphill or downhill, or off camber, do not attempt it. Your vehicle is very likely to skid in such conditions, and you may roll or slip off the edge of the road. Also, check to see that the mud has a reasonably firm base. Tackling deep mud is definitely not recommended unless you have a vehicle-mounted winch—and even then, be cautious, because the winch may not get you out. Finally, check to see that no ruts are too deep for the ground clearance of your vehicle.

When you decide you can get through and have selected the best route, use the following techniques to cross through the mud:

- Avoid making detours off existing tracks to minimize environmental damage.
- Select 4WD low range and a suitable gear; momentum is the key to success, so use a high enough gear to build up sufficient speed.
- Avoid accelerating heavily, so as to minimize wheel spinning and to provide maximum traction.
- Follow existing wheel ruts, unless they are too deep for the clearance of your vehicle.
- To correct slides, turn the steering wheel in the direction that the rear wheels are skidding, but don't be too aggressive or you'll overcorrect and lose control again.
- If the vehicle comes to a stop, don't continue to accelerate, as you will only spin your wheels and dig yourself into a rut. Try backing out and having another go.
- Be prepared to turn back before reaching the point of no return.

Stream Crossings. By crossing a stream that is too deep, drivers risk far more than water flowing in and ruining the interior of their vehicles. Water sucked into the engine's air intake will seriously damage the engine. Likewise, water that seeps into the air vent on the transmission or differential will mix with the lubricant and may lead to serious problems in due course.

Even worse, if the water is deep or fast flowing, it could easily carry your vehicle downstream, endangering the lives of everyone in the vehicle.

Some 4WD manuals tell you what fording depth the vehicle can negotiate safely. If your vehicle's owner's manual doesn't include this information, your local dealer may be able to assist. If you don't know, then avoid crossing through water that is more than a foot or so deep.

The first rule for crossing a stream is to know what you are getting into. You need to ascertain how deep the water is, whether there are any large rocks or holes, if the bottom is solid enough to avoid bogging down the vehicle, and whether the entry and exit points are negotiable. This may take some time and involve getting wet, but you take a great risk by crossing a stream without first properly assessing the situation.

The secret to water crossings is to keep moving, but not too fast. If you go too fast, you may drown the electrics, causing the vehicle to stall midstream. In shallow water (where the surface of the water is below the bumper), your primary concern is to safely negotiate the bottom of the stream, avoiding any rock damage and maintaining momentum if there is a danger of getting stuck or of slipping on the exit.

In deeper water (between 18 and 30 inches), the objective is to create a small bow wave in front of the moving vehicle. This requires a speed that is approximately walking pace. The bow wave reduces the depth of the water around the engine compartment. If the water's surface reaches your tailpipe, select a gear that will maintain moderate engine revs to avoid water backing up into the exhaust; and do not change gears midstream.

Crossing water deeper than 25 to 30 inches requires more extensive preparation of the vehicle and should be attempted only by experienced drivers.

Snow. The trails in this book that receive heavy snowfall are closed in winter. Therefore, the snow conditions that you are most likely to encounter are an occasional snowdrift that has not yet melted or fresh snow from an unexpected storm. Getting through such conditions depends on the depth of the snow, its consistency, the stability of the underlying surface, and your vehicle.

If the snow is no deeper than about nine inches and there is solid ground beneath it, crossing the snow should not be a problem. In deeper snow that seems solid enough to support your vehicle, be extremely cautious: If you break through a drift, you are likely to be stuck, and if conditions are bad, you may have a long wait.

The tires you use for off-highway driving, with a wide tread pattern, are probably suitable for these snow conditions. Nonetheless, it is wise to carry chains (preferably for all four wheels), and if you have a vehicle-mounted winch, even better.

Sand. As with most off-highway situations, your tires are the key to your ability to cross sand. It is difficult to tell how well a particular tire will handle in sand just by looking at it, so be guided by the manufacturer and your dealer.

The key to driving in soft sand is floatation, which is achieved by a combination of low tire pressure and momentum. Before crossing a stretch of sand, reduce your tire pressure to between 15 and 20 pounds. If necessary, you can safely go to as low as 12 pounds. As you cross, maintain momentum so that your vehicle rides on top of the soft sand without digging in or stalling. This may require plenty of engine power. Avoid using the brakes if possible; removing your foot from the accelerator alone is normally enough to slow or stop. Using the brakes digs the vehicle deep in the sand.

Air the tires back up as soon as you are out of the sand to avoid damage to the tires and the rims. Airing back up requires a high-quality air compressor. Even then, it is a slow process.

In the backcountry of Utah, sandy conditions are commonplace. You will therefore find a good compressor most useful.

Vehicle Recovery Methods

If you do enough four-wheel driving, you are sure to get stuck sooner or later. The following techniques will help you get back on the go. The most suitable method will depend on the equipment available and the situation you are in—whether you are stuck in sand, mud, or snow, or are high-centered or unable to negotiate a hill.

Towing. Use a nylon yank strap of the type discussed in the "Special 4WD Equipment" section on page 21. This type of strap will stretch 15 to 25 percent, and the elasticity will assist in extracting the vehicle.

Attach the strap only to a frame-mounted tow point. Ensure that the driver of the stuck vehicle is ready, take up all but about six feet of slack, then move the towing vehicle away at a moderate speed (in most circumstances this means using 4WD low range in second gear) so that the elasticity of the strap is employed in the way it is meant to be. Don't take off like a bat out of hell or you risk breaking the strap or damaging a vehicle.

Never join two yank straps together with a shackle. If one strap breaks, the shackle will become a lethal missile aimed at one of the vehicles (and anyone inside). For the same reason, never attach a yank strap to the tow ball on either vehicle.

Jacking. Jacking the vehicle allows you to pack under the wheel (with rocks, dirt, or logs) or use your shovel to remove an obstacle. However, the standard vehicle jack is unlikely to be of as much assistance as a high-lift jack. We highly recommend purchasing a good high-lift jack as a basic accessory if you decide that you are going to do a lot of serious, off-highway four-wheel driving. Remember a high-lift jack is of limited use if your vehicle does not have an appropriate jacking point. Some brush bars have two built-in forward jacking points.

Tire Chains. Tire chains can be of assistance in both mud and snow. Cable-type chains provide much less grip than link-type chains. There are also dedicated mud chains with larger, heavier links than on normal snow chains. It is best to have chains fitted to all four wheels.

Once you are bogged down is not the best time to try to fit the chains; if at all possible, try to predict their need and have them on the tires before trouble arises. An easy way to affix chains is to place two small cubes of wood under the center of the stretched-out chain. When you drive your tires up on the blocks of wood, it is easier to stretch the chains over the tires because the pressure is off.

Winching. Most recreational four-wheel drivers do not have a winch. But if you get serious about four-wheel driving, this is probably the first major accessory you should consider buying.

Under normal circumstances, a winch would be warranted only for the more difficult 4WD trails in this book. Having a winch is certainly comforting when you see a difficult section of road ahead and have to decide whether to risk it or turn back. Also, major obstacles can appear when you least expect them, even on trails that are otherwise easy.

Owning a winch is not a panacea to all your recovery problems. Winching depends on the availability of a good anchor point, and electric winches may not work if they are submerged in a stream. Despite these constraints, no accessory is more useful than a high-quality, powerful winch when you get into a difficult situation.

If you acquire a winch, learn to use it properly; take the time to study your owner's manual. Incorrect operation can be extremely dangerous and may cause damage to the winch or to your anchor points, which are usually trees.

Special 4WD Equipment

Tires

When 4WD touring, you will likely encounter a wide variety of terrain: rocks, mud, talus, slickrock, sand, gravel, dirt, and bitumen. The immense variety of tires on the market includes many specifically targeted at one or another of these types of terrain, as well as tires designed to handle a range of terrain adequately.

Every four-wheel driver seems to have his or her own preference when it comes to tire selection, but most people undertaking the 4WD trails in this book will need tires that can handle all of the above types of terrain adequately.

The first requirement is to select rugged, light-truck tires rather than passenger-vehicle tires. Check the size data on the sidewall: it should have "LT" rather than "P" before the number.

Among light-truck tires, you must choose between tires that are designated "all-terrain" and more-aggressive, wider-tread mud tires. Either type will be adequate, especially on rocks, gravel, talus, or dirt. Although mud tires have an advantage in muddy conditions and soft snow, all-terrain tires perform better on slickrock, in sand, and particularly on ice and paved roads.

When selecting tires, remember that they affect not just traction but also cornering ability, braking distances, fuel consumption, and noise levels. It pays to get good advice before making your decision.

Yank Straps

Yank straps are industrial-strength versions of the flimsy tow straps carried by the local discount store. They are made of heavy nylon, are 20 to 30 feet long and 2 to 3 inches wide, are rated to at least 20,000 pounds, and have looped ends.

Do not use tow straps with metal hooks in the ends (the hooks can become missiles in the event the strap breaks free). Likewise, never join two yank straps together using a shackle.

Winches

There are three main options when it comes to winches: manual winches, removable electric winches, and vehicle-mounted electric winches.

If you have a full-size 4WD vehicle—which can weigh in excess of 7,000 pounds when loaded—a manual winch is of limited use without a lot of effort and considerable time. However, a manual winch is a very handy and inexpensive accessory if you have a small 4WD. Typically, manual winches are rated to pull about 5,500 pounds.

Electric winches can be mounted to your vehicle's trailer hitch to enable them to be removed, relocated to the front of your vehicle (if you have a hitch installed), or moved to another vehicle. Although this is a very useful feature, a winch is heavy, so relocating one can be a two-person job. Consider that 5,000-pound-rated winches weigh only about 55 pounds, while 12,000-pound-rated models weigh around 140 pounds. Therefore, the larger models are best permanently front-mounted. Unfortunately, this position limits their ability to winch the vehicle backward.

When choosing between electric winches, be aware that they are rated for their maximum capacity on the first wind of the cable around the drum. As layers of cable wind onto the drum, they increase its diameter and thus decrease the maximum load the winch can handle. This decrease is significant: a winch rated to pull 8,000 pounds on a bare drum may only handle 6,500 pounds on the second layer, 5,750 pounds on the third layer, and 5,000 pounds on the fourth. Electric winches also draw a high level of current and may necessitate upgrading the battery in your 4WD or adding a second battery.

There is a wide range of mounting options—from a simple, body-mounted frame that holds the winch to heavy-duty winch bars that replace the original bumper and incorporate brush bars and mounts for auxiliary lights.

If you buy a winch, either electric or manual, you will also need quite a range of additional equipment so that you can operate it correctly:

- at least one choker chain with hooks on each end,
- winch extension straps or cables,
- shackles,
- a receiver shackle,
- a snatch block,
- a tree protector,
- gloves.

Grill/Brush Bars and Winch Bars

Brush bars protect the front of the vehicle from scratches and minor bumps; they also provide a solid mount for auxiliary lights and often high-lift jacking points. The level of protection they provide depends on how solid they are and on whether they are securely mounted onto the frame of the vehicle. Lighter models attach in front of the standard bumper, but the more substantial units replace the bumper. Prices range from about $150 to $450.

Winch bars replace the bumper and usually integrate a solid brush bar with a heavy-duty winch mount. Some have the brush bar as an optional extra to the winch bar component. Manufacturers such as Warn, ARB, and TJM offer a wide range of integrated winch bars. These are significantly more expensive, starting at about $650.

Remember that installing heavy equipment on the front of the vehicle may necessitate increasing the front suspension rating to cope with the additional weight.

Portable Air Compressors

Most portable air compressors on the market are flimsy models that plug into the cigarette lighter and are sold at the local discount store. These are of very limited use for four-wheel driving. They are very slow to inflate the large tires of a 4WD vehicle; for instance, to reinflate from 15 to 35 pounds typically takes about 10 minutes for each tire. They are also unlikely to be rated for continuous use, which means that they will overheat and cut off before completing the job. If you're lucky, they will start up again when they have cooled down, but this means that you are unlikely to reinflate your tires in less than an hour.

The easiest way to identify a useful air compressor is by the price—good ones cost $200 and over. Many of the quality units feature a Thomas-brand pump and are built to last. Another good unit is sold by ARB. All these pumps draw between 15 and 20 amps and thus should not be plugged into the cigarette lighter socket but attached to the vehicle's battery with clips. The ARB unit can be permanently mounted under the hood. Quick-Air makes a 10-amp compressor that can be plugged into the cigarette lighter socket and performs well.

Auxiliary Driving Lights

There is a vast array of auxiliary lights on the market today, and selecting the best lights for your purpose can be a confusing process.

Auxiliary lights greatly improve visibility in adverse weather conditions. Driving lights provide a strong, moderately wide beam to supplement headlamp high beams, giving improved lighting in the distance and to the sides of the main beam. Fog lamps throw a wide-dispersion, flat beam; and spots provide a high-power, narrow beam to improve lighting range directly in front of the vehicle. Rear-mounted auxiliary lights provide greatly improved visibility for backing up.

For off-highway use, you will need quality lights with strong mounting brackets. Some high-powered off-highway lights are not approved by the Department of Transportation.

Packing Checklist

Before embarking on any 4WD adventure, whether a lazy Sunday drive on an easy trail or a challenging climb over rugged terrain, be prepared. The following checklist will help you gather the items you need.

Essential

- ❒ Rain gear
- ❒ Small shovel or multipurpose ax, pick, shovel, and sledgehammer
- ❒ Heavy-duty yank strap
- ❒ Spare tire that matches the other tires on the vehicle
- ❒ Working jack and base plate for soft ground
- ❒ Maps
- ❒ Emergency medical kit, including sun protection and insect repellent
- ❒ Bottled water
- ❒ Blankets or space blankets
- ❒ Parka, gloves, and boots
- ❒ Spare vehicle key
- ❒ Jumper leads
- ❒ Heavy-duty flashlight
- ❒ Multipurpose tool, such as a Leatherman™
- ❒ Emergency food—high-energy bars or similar

Worth Considering

- ❒ Global Positioning System (GPS) receiver
- ❒ Cell phone
- ❒ A set of light-truck, off-highway tires and matching spare
- ❒ High-lift jack
- ❒ Additional tool kit
- ❒ Satellite phone
- ❒ Portable air compressor
- ❒ Tire gauge
- ❒ Tire-sealing kit
- ❒ Tire chains
- ❒ Handsaw and ax
- ❒ Binoculars
- ❒ Firearms
- ❒ Whistle
- ❒ Flares
- ❒ Vehicle fire extinguisher
- ❒ Gasoline, engine oil, and other vehicle fluids
- ❒ Portable hand winch
- ❒ Electric cooler

If Your Credit Cards Aren't Maxed Out

- ❒ Electric, vehicle-mounted winch and associated recovery straps, shackles, and snatch blocks
- ❒ Auxiliary lights
- ❒ Locking differential(s)

Trails in the Northern Region

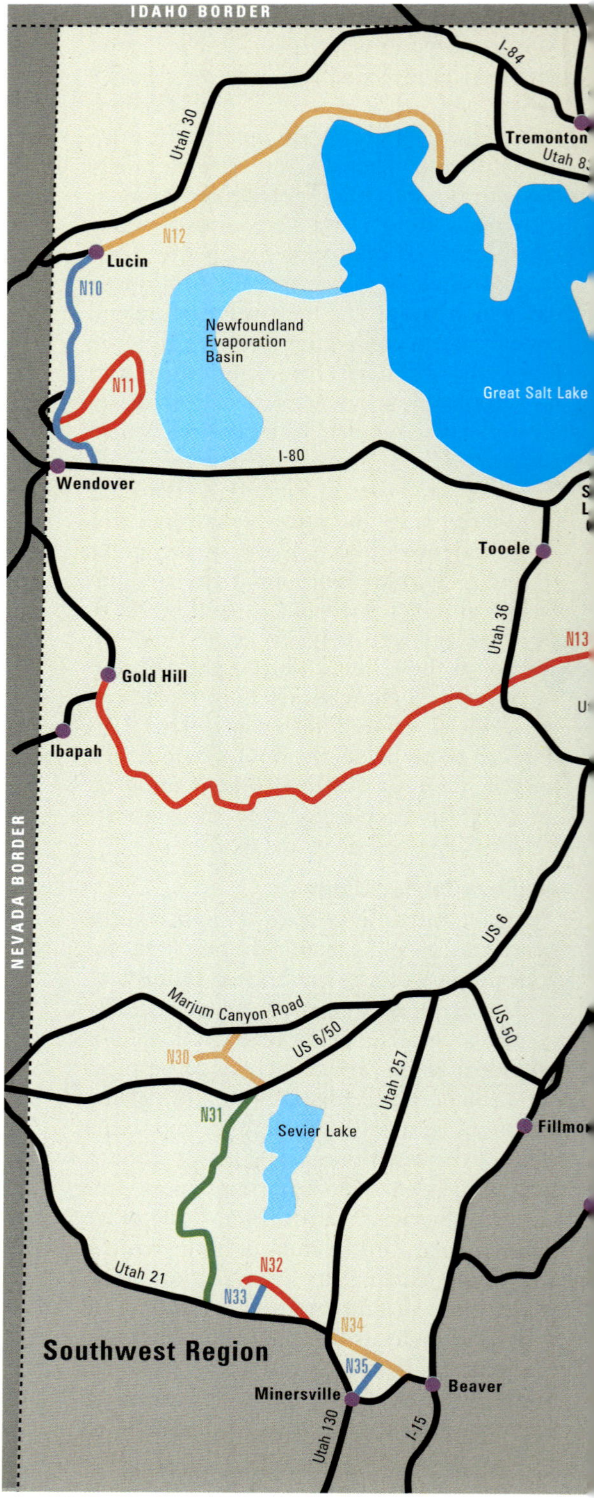

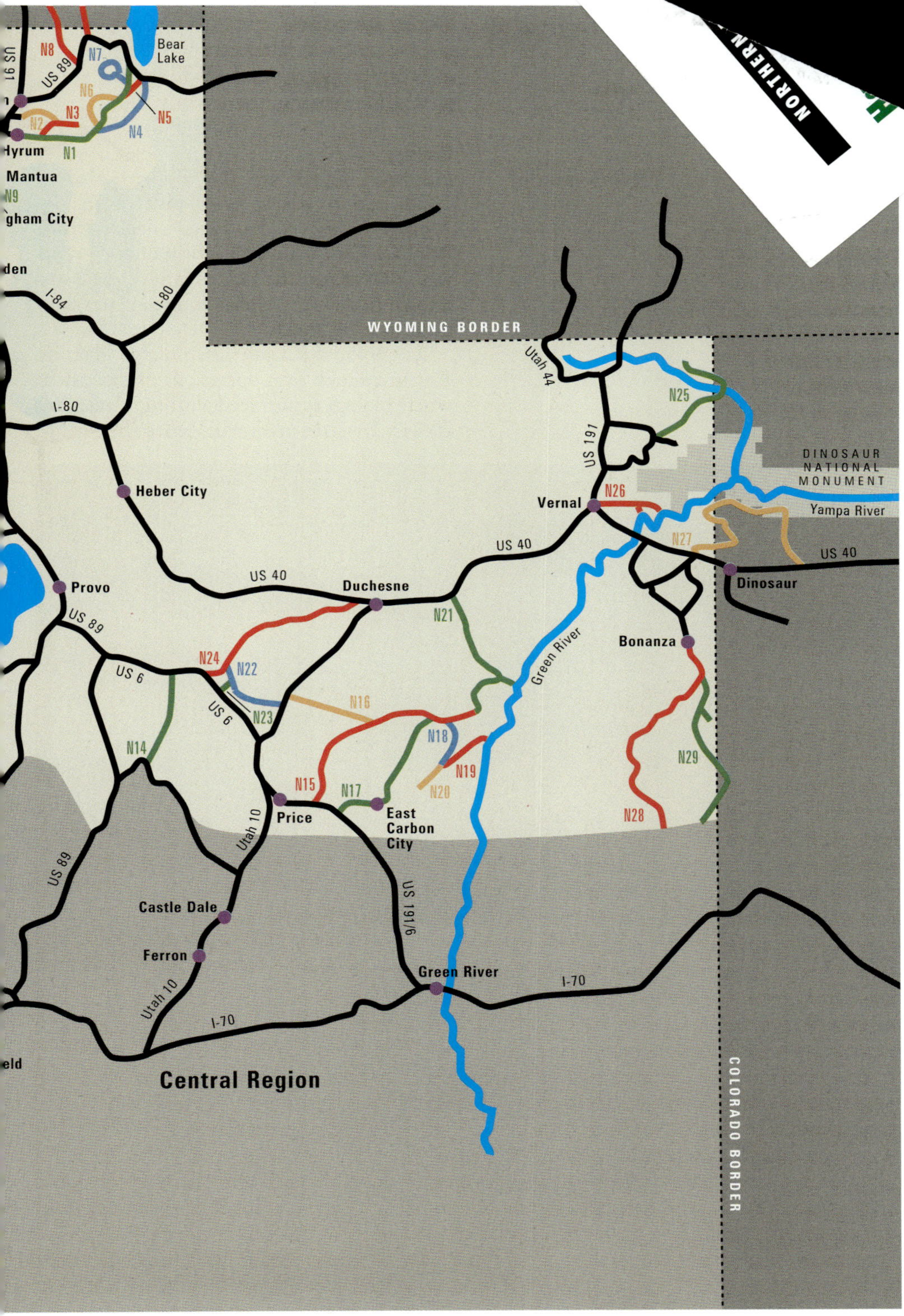

Bear Lake
US 91
US 89
N8
N7
N6
N5
N4
N3
N2
N1
Hyrum
Mantua
N9
gham City
den
I-84
I-80
WYOMING BORDER
Utah 44
N25
US 191
DINOSAUR NATIONAL MONUMENT
Yampa River
N26
Vernal
N27
US 40
Dinosaur
I-80
Heber City
Provo
US 89
US 40
Duchesne
N21
Green River
Bonanza
N24
N22
US 6
N16
N23
US 6
N18
N14
N19
N29
N15
N17
N20
N28
Price
East Carbon City
Utah 10
US 89
US 191/6
Castle Dale
Ferron
Green River
Utah 10
I-70
I-70
eld
Central Region
COLORADO BORDER

REGION TRAIL #1

Hardware Ranch Road

STARTING POINT Hyrum
FINISHING POINT US 89 and FR 055, west of Bear Lake
TOTAL MILEAGE 44 miles
UNPAVED MILEAGE 28.6 miles
DRIVING TIME 2 hours
ELEVATION RANGE 4,800–8,700 feet
USUALLY OPEN May to October
DIFFICULTY RATING 2
SCENIC RATING 7
REMOTENESS RATING +0

Special Attractions

- Easy trail with varied scenery.
- Access to many other 4WD trails.
- Wildlife viewing, particularly elk.

History

Hardware Ranch was first homesteaded in 1868, and it was at one point owned by Alonzo Snow, a hardware dealer from Brigham City. Though his base of operations was at his store, Box Elder Hardware, he was known to deliver supplies to the loggers who lived near his ranch.

In 1945, the Utah Division of Wildlife Resources took over operations of the ranch, where biologists now feed and study over 700 elk (Utah's state mammal). Since then it has

A view of the trail entering Saddle Creek Canyon

become one of the most popular winter wildlife viewing areas in the state. Sleigh rides to the ranch are currently offered in the winter if you want to see the animals up close. For more information and reservations, call Hardware Ranch at (435) 753-6168.

Description

To get to Hardware Ranch Road from Logan, head south along Main Street, then turn onto Utah 165 south, following signs to Providence and Hyrum. Hardware Ranch Road begins in Hyrum and heads east from town as a paved road.

After 7 miles, you reach Northern #3: Left Hand Fork Canyon Trail, and after 15.4 miles you reach the Hardware Ranch Visitors Center. From here to Danish Dugway, the road travels over imbedded rock along a rutted, bumpy surface; this section is by far the roughest part of Hardware Ranch Road. The trail here passes through grassland dotted with sagebrush, pinyons, and junipers and rolling hillsides with numerous stands of aspens and conifers.

After 21.6 miles, you come to Northern #4: Strawberry Valley Trail and Danish Dugway, where the road narrows and steeply descends for 1.1 miles. The surface is still corrugated and rocky, but should not cause any clearance problems.

The road levels out a bit after Danish Dugway, and half a mile later, you reach Northern #6: Old Ephraim Trail, a loop trail that returns you to Hardware Ranch Road 9.6 miles later. There are still a number of ruts and substantial mud holes along this section of the trail, and when wet, these otherwise benign road hazards can turn into formidable obstacles and make a high-clearance 4WD a must. It is the existence of the mud holes that warrants the 2 rating for this trail.

The road follows the course of Saddle Creek through a canyon, and as you continue along Hardware Ranch Road past the intersection with FR 211, the trail loops around a handful of beaver ponds and connects with Northern #5: Temple Canyon Trail.

The route progresses through Hells Hollow and Log Cabin Hollow, and then it passes the connection with the loop trail Northern #7: Peter Sinks Trail. The trail ends at US 89 near Bear Lake Summit. You must cross a number of dry washes in this last stretch of road, but they usually do not pose any great difficulty.

Current Road Information

Uinta-Wasatch-Cache National Forest
Logan Ranger District
1500 East Highway 89
Logan, UT 84321
(435) 755-3620

Map References

BLM Logan
USFS Uinta-Wasatch-Cache: Logan Ranger District
USGS 1:24,000 Logan, Paradise, Porcupine Reservoir, Logan Peak, Hardware Ranch, Boulder Mtn., Red Spur Mtn., Meadowville, Garden City
1:100,000 Logan
Trails Illustrated, #713
Utah Atlas & Gazetteer, pp. 12, 13
Utah Road & Recreation Atlas, pp. 37, 38

Route Directions

▼ 0.0		In Hyrum, at intersection of 800E (Utah 165) and Main Street (Utah 101), zero trip meter and turn east onto Utah 101.
7.0 ▲		Trail ends at intersection of 800E (Utah 165) and Main Street in Hyrum. Turn right for Logan and US 89/91.
		GPS: N 41°38.03 W 111°49.90'
▼ 7.0	SO	Northern #3: Left Hand Fork Canyon Trail is on left. Zero trip meter.
0.0 ▲		Continue west.
		GPS: N 41°37.91' W 111°42.41'
▼ 0.0		Continue east.
8.4 ▲	SO	Northern #3: Left Hand Fork Canyon Trail is on right. Zero trip meter.
▼ 8.1	SO	Hardware Ranch buildings. Marker on left and public toilets.
0.3 ▲	SO	Hardware Ranch buildings. Marker on right and public toilets.
		GPS: N 41°36.12' W 111°33.95'

Northern Trail #1: Hardware Ranch Road

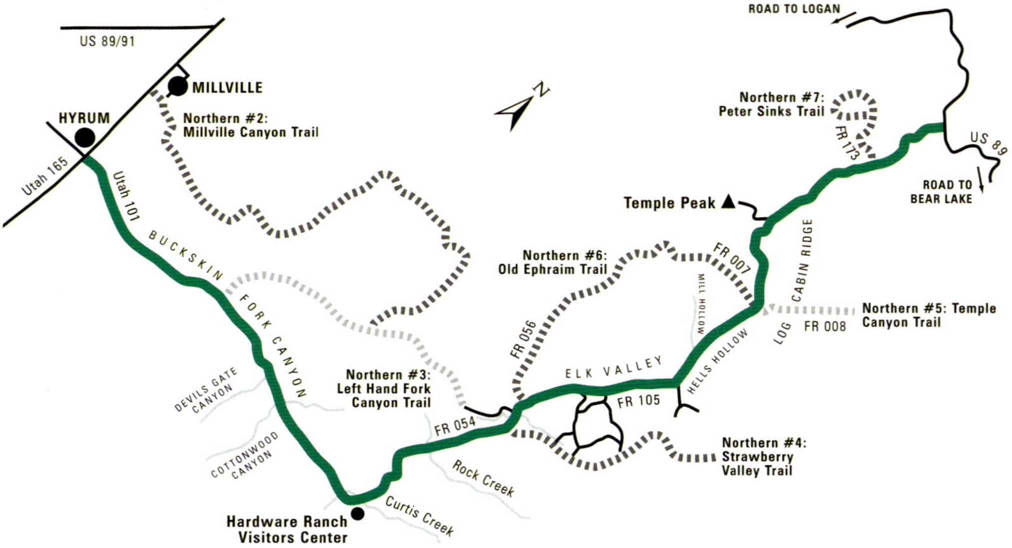

▼ 8.4 SO Hardware Ranch Visitors Center driveway on right. Zero trip meter. End of Utah 101; begin FR 054.

0.0 ▲ Continue west along paved road.

GPS: N 41°36.22' W 111°33.56'

▼ 0.0 Continue east along unpaved road.

6.2 ▲ SO Hardware Ranch Visitors Center driveway on left. Zero trip meter. Road becomes Utah 101.

▼ 2.3 SO Cattle guard.

3.9 ▲ SO Cattle guard.

▼ 3.3 BL Road on right. Cross over Rock Creek.

2.9 ▲ BR Cross over Rock Creek. Then road on left.

GPS: N 41°38.68' W 111°32.96'

▼ 5.4 SO Cattle guard.

0.7 ▲ SO Cattle guard.

▼ 6.2 BL Danish Dugway; switchback down into valley. Track on right is Northern #4: Strawberry Valley Trail. Zero trip meter.

0.0 ▲ Continue along Hardware Ranch Road.

GPS: N 41°40.71' W 111°31.21'

▼ 0.0 Continue down switchback.

1.1 ▲ BR End of Danish Dugway. Track on left is Northern #4: Strawberry Valley Trail. Zero trip meter.

▼ 0.4 SO Cross over creek.

0.7 ▲ SO Cross over creek.

▼ 1.1 SO/BR Cross through Saddle Creek; end of Danish Dugway. Then trail on left leads into Left Hand Fork Canyon. Zero trip meter.

0.0 ▲ Continue along Hardware Ranch Road.

GPS: N 41°41.20' W 111°31.38'

▼ 0.0 Continue along Hardware Ranch Road.

0.5 ▲ BL/SO Intersection; trail on right leads into Left Hand Fork Canyon. Cross through Saddle Creek. Start of Danish Dugway; switchback out of valley. Zero trip meter.

▼ 0.5 SO Track on left is Northern #6: Old Ephraim Trail (FR 056). Zero trip meter. Main trail becomes FR 105.

0.0 ▲ Continue along Hardware Ranch Road.

GPS: N 41°41.54' W 111°31.26'

▼ 0.0 Continue along Hardware Ranch Road.

2.9 ▲ SO Track on right is Northern #6: Old Ephraim Trail (FR 056). Zero trip meter.

Saddle Creek Crossing

Main trail becomes FR 054.

▼ 0.1 SO Left is part of delta also leading to Northern #6: Old Ephraim Trail.
2.8 ▲ SO Right is part of delta leading to Northern #6: Old Ephraim Trail.
GPS: N 41°41.57′ W 111°31.24′

▼ 0.6 SO Cattle guard.
2.3 ▲ SO Cattle guard.

▼ 2.6 SO Cattle guard.
0.2 ▲ SO Cattle guard.

▼ 2.9 SO Road on right is an attractive connecting spur to Northern #4: Strawberry Valley Trail. Zero trip meter.
0.0 ▲ Continue along Hardware Ranch Road.
GPS: N 41°43.42′ W 111°29.51′

▼ 0.0 Continue along Hardware Ranch Road.
6.5 ▲ SO Road on left is an attractive connecting spur to Northern #4: Strawberry Valley Trail. Zero trip meter.

▼ 0.4 SO Cattle guard.
6.1 ▲ SO Cattle guard.

▼ 1.1 BR Track on left to Elk Valley.
5.4 ▲ BL Track on right to Elk Valley.
GPS: N 41°44.32′ W 111°28.97′

▼ 1.6 SO Cattle guard.
4.9 ▲ SO Cattle guard.

▼ 2.1 SO Cross through wash.
4.4 ▲ SO Cross through wash.

▼ 2.4 BL Cross through wash. Then FR 182 on right.
4.1 ▲ BR FR 182 on left. Then cross through wash.
GPS: N 41°45.02′ W 111°28.05′

▼ 2.6 SO Cross through creek.
3.9 ▲ SO Cross through creek.

▼ 3.4 SO Cattle guard.
3.1 ▲ SO Cattle guard.

▼ 3.8 TR FR 211 to Nebeker Spring and Mill Hollow on left. Then cross creek.
2.7 ▲ TL Cross creek. Then FR 211 to Nebeker Spring and Mill Hollow on right.
GPS: N 41°46.09′ W 111°28.76′

▼ 5.6 SO Government Spring on left.
0.9 ▲ SO Government Spring on right.

▼ 6.4 SO Cattle guard.
0.1 ▲ SO Cattle guard.

▼ 6.5 TL T-intersection. Northern #5: Temple Canyon Trail (FR 008) on right. Zero trip meter. Hardware Ranch Road becomes FR 055.
0.0 ▲ Continue south.
GPS: N 41°48.17′ W 111°28.07′

▼ 0.0 Continue north.
0.2 ▲ TR Northern #5: Temple Canyon Trail (FR 008) is straight. Turn right to follow Hardware Ranch Road, which becomes FR 105. Zero trip meter.

▼ 0.2 SO Northern #6: Old Ephraim Trail (FR 007) on left. Zero trip meter.
0.0 ▲ Continue along Hardware Ranch Road.
GPS: N 41°48.24′ W 111°28.24′

▼ 0.0 Continue along Hardware Ranch Road.
8.4 ▲ SO Northern #6: Old Ephraim Trail (FR 007) on right. Zero trip meter.

▼ 0.4 BL Track on right.
8.0 ▲ BR Track on left.

▼ 1.3 SO Pond on left.
7.1 ▲ SO Pond on right.

▼ 3.7 SO Track on left is FR 251 to Temple Peak.
4.7 ▲ SO Track on right is FR 251 to Temple Peak.
GPS: N 41°50.29′ W 111°30.23′

▼ 4.3 SO FR 253 (labeled FR 252 on forest map) on left.
4.1 ▲ SO FR 253 (labeled FR 252 on forest map) on right.

▼ 5.1 SO Cattle guard. Then enter T. W. Daniel Experimental Forest.
3.3 ▲ SO Leave T. W. Daniel Experimental Forest. Cattle guard.

▼ 5.7 SO Road on right.
2.7 ▲ SO Road on left.

▼ 5.9 SO FR 175 on right.
2.5 ▲ SO FR 175 on left.
GPS: N 41°51.86' W 111°29.95'

▼ 7.0 SO FR 238 on left.
1.4 ▲ SO FR 238 on right.

▼ 7.5 SO FR 239 on right toward Cheny Creek Trail.
0.9 ▲ SO FR 239 on left toward Cheny Creek Trail.

▼ 7.8 SO Leave T. W. Daniel Experimental Forest.
0.6 ▲ SO Enter T. W. Daniel Experimental Forest.

▼ 8.4 SO Northern #7: Peter Sinks Trail (FR 173) on left. Zero trip meter.
0.0 ▲ Continue along Hardware Ranch Road.
GPS: N 41°53.41' W 111°29.09'

▼ 0.0 Continue along Hardware Ranch Road.
2.7 ▲ SO Northern #7: Peter Sinks Trail (FR 173) on right. Zero trip meter.

▼ 0.3 SO FR 240 on right.
2.3 ▲ SO FR 240 on left.

▼ 2.5 SO Cattle guard.
0.2 ▲ SO Cattle guard.

▼ 2.7 Trail ends at stop sign at US 89. Turn right for Garden City and Bear Lake, left for Logan.
0.0 ▲ On US 89, west of Bear Lake, zero trip meter and turn south on FR 055. This is also near the Limber Pine Nature Trail at the Cache County and Rich County lines.
GPS: N 41°55.55' W 111°28.39'

NORTHERN REGION TRAIL #2

Millville Canyon Trail

STARTING POINT Utah 165 in Millville, south of Logan
FINISHING POINT Northern #3: Left Hand Fork Canyon Trail
TOTAL MILEAGE 23.2 miles
UNPAVED MILEAGE 21.6 miles
DRIVING TIME 3 hours
ELEVATION RANGE 4,600–9,000 feet
USUALLY OPEN June to October
DIFFICULTY RATING 4
SCENIC RATING 9
REMOTENESS RATING +1

Special Attractions

- Remote crossing of the Bear River Range through the dense Uinta-Wasatch-Cache National Forest.
- Natural overlooks providing broad panoramic views.
- Numerous backcountry campsites.

History

In the 1850s, Brigham Young concentrated heavily on expanding Mormon settlements throughout Utah. Due to its proximity to Salt Lake City and abundance of natural resources, the Cache Valley quickly became a focal point in Young's plan of expansion.

In 1855, under the leadership of Bryant Stringham, a cattle company established Elkhorn Ranch about 3 miles southeast of present-day Logan. In the winter of 1856, Mormon settlers from the Elkhorn Ranch put cattle out to graze in Cache Valley. The cattle were soon overgrazing the land, which caused starvation among the local Shoshone. The Indians retaliated by killing the disruptive cows. These conflicts with the Indians, coupled with a particularly harsh winter, drove the Mormons off the land and back to Salt Lake City.

Elkhorn Ranch was eventually resettled in 1859, when the first sawmill in Cache Valley was built by Esias Edwards. Over the next 25 years, others followed suit—building a grist-

A rutted section of the trail

mill, broom mill, molasses mill, and distillery. The town's name was soon changed, appropriately enough, to Millville.

Description

From Utah 165, Millville Canyon Trail heads through the settlement of Millville toward the Millville Wildlife Management Area and the much larger Uinta-Wasatch-Cache National Forest. From the game control fence at the 1.9-mile mark to the first cattle guard about a mile later, the road becomes quite rough with a large amount of imbedded rock. In some places, rocks up to eight inches in diameter make choosing the right line very important for the welfare of your vehicle's undercarriage. In the early stages, numerous side roads make navigation tricky, but the correct route tends to be straight ahead. Although it remains bumpy throughout, the road surface smooths out considerably after you pass the gate at the 2.8-mile point.

The narrow, slow-going trail continues through the canyon along the creek and passes by cottonwoods and tall scrub. The trees close in on the road in many places and make passing difficult for the first 3.5 miles.

After about 5.5 miles, the road begins to level off at the top of Millville Canyon. Besides aspens and conifers, low brush now lines the trail and can scratch the lower portion of your vehicle. The road along this portion of the trail is rutted in spots and impassable during the wet, early spring months. As you travel along the ridgeline, panoramic views of the surrounding countryside open up across the north.

At about the 10-mile point a short track takes you to an overlook at the edge of the Bear River Range. The ledge stands about 2,000 feet above a series of hollows and offers excellent views to the east.

After 18.3 miles, FR 147 leads east to Northern #6: Old Ephraim Trail, and then the road switchbacks through a large stand of aspens as it descends into Herd Hollow. The large, mature trees close in on the road and make for a spectacular autumn drive. In Herd Hollow, the aspens are replaced by cottonwoods. Millville Canyon Trail eventually ends at Northern #3: Left Hand Fork Canyon Trail.

The stock troughs at Ferry Spring

Current Road Information
Uinta-Wasatch-Cache National Forest
Logan Ranger District
1500 East Highway 89
Logan, UT 84321
(435) 755-3620

Map References
BLM Logan
USFS Uinta-Wasatch-Cache: Logan Ranger District
USGS 1:24,000 Logan, Logan Peak, Boulder Mtn.
1:100,000 Logan
Trails Illustrated, #713
Utah Atlas & Gazetteer, p. 12
Utah Road & Recreation Atlas, p. 37

Route Directions

▼ 0.0 On Utah 165 in Millville, about 2.7 miles south of US 89/91, zero trip meter and turn onto Mill Road, signed for 238N.
7.5 ▲ Trail ends at Utah 165. Turn right for Logan and US 89/91.
GPS: N 41°40.60′ W 111°49.92′

▼ 0.4 TR Turn right onto Main Street.
7.1 ▲ TL Turn left onto Mill Road.

▼ 0.5 TL Turn left onto 300S.
7.0 ▲ TR Turn right onto Main Street.

▼ 1.3 TR Turn right onto 500E.
6.2 ▲ TL Turn left onto 300S.

▼ 1.6 BR Road forks and becomes gravel.
5.9 ▲ SO Continue toward Millville.

▼ 1.9 SO Pass through big game control fence of Millville Wildlife Management Area. Tracks on left and right but proceed straight. Road becomes FR 168.
5.6 ▲ SO Pass through big game control fence of Millville Wildlife Management Area. Tracks on left and right but proceed straight. Road becomes 500E.
GPS: N 41°40.07′ W 111°48.34′

▼ 2.8 SO Cattle guard and gate.
4.7 ▲ SO Gate and cattle guard.

▼ 3.8 BL Cross through creek. Then bear left.
3.7 ▲ BR Track on left. Then cross through creek.
GPS: N 41°39.53′ W 111°46.32′

▼ 4.3 BL Track on right is FR 023.
3.2 ▲ BR Track on left is FR 023.
GPS: N 41°39.44′ W 111°45.83′

▼ 5.0 BR Track on left rejoins main trail.
2.5 ▲ SO Track on right.

▼ 5.1 BL Bear left at top of hill. Tracks on left and right but stay on main road, continuing to climb.
2.4 ▲ SO Tracks left and right. Follow main track downhill.

▼ 5.6 SO/BL Small track on right, then bear left at fork in road; sign "Leatham Hollow Trail" on right.
1.9 ▲ SO/BR Track to Leatham Hollow enters on left; then small track on left.
GPS: N 41°39.50′ W 111°44.69′

▼ 7.0 SO Track on right and campsite.
0.5 ▲ SO Track on left and campsite.

▼ 7.3 BR Fork in road.
0.2 ▲ BL Track enters on right.

▼ 7.5 BR Water troughs. Zero trip meter.
0.0 ▲ Continue downhill.
GPS: N 41°40.14′ W 111°43.50′

▼ 0.0 Continue to climb.
2.8 ▲ BL Water troughs. Zero trip meter.

▼ 1.1 SO Track on right. Then track on left.
1.6 ▲ SO Track on right. Then track on left.
GPS: N 41°40.39′ W 111°42.41′

▼ 1.3 SO Track on right.
1.5 ▲ SO Track on left.

▼ 2.6 BL Track on right to overlook.
0.2 ▲ BR Track on left to overlook.

Northern Trail #2: Millville Canyon Trail

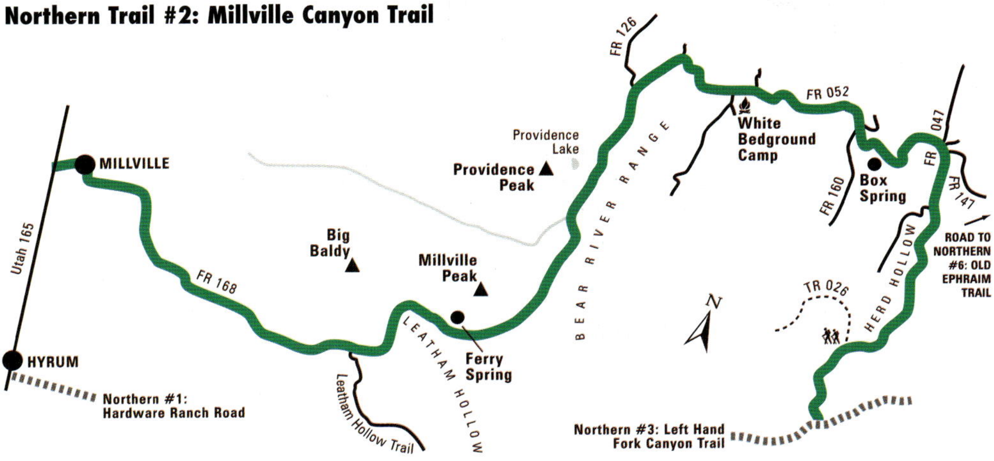

▼ 2.8 TR T-intersection; turn right. Zero trip meter.
0.0 ▲ Continue south.
GPS: N 41°41.73' W 111°42.10'

▼ 0.0 Continue north.
8.0 ▲ TL Turn left at intersection. Zero trip meter.

▼ 0.1 BR Road forks.
7.9 ▲ BL Road on right.

▼ 0.4 BR Road on left.
7.5 ▲ BL Road forks.
GPS: N 41°42.03' W 111°42.02'

▼ 1.1 BR Road forks.
6.9 ▲ TL Road on left.
GPS: N 41°42.65' W 111°41.86'

▼ 2.0 BR Road forks. FR 126 on left.
5.9 ▲ BL Road on right is FR 126.
GPS: N 41°43.34' W 111°41.65'

▼ 2.7 SO Track on left and right and campsite on right.
5.3 ▲ SO Campsite on left. Track on left and right.

▼ 2.8 SO Steep downhill. Track on right rejoins main trail in 0.2 miles.
5.2 ▲ SO Track on left rejoins.

▼ 3.0 SO Track on right rejoins.
5.0 ▲ SO Track on left rejoins main trail in 0.2 miles.

▼ 4.0 BL Track on right and campsite. Road becomes FR 052.
4.0 ▲ BR Track on left and campsite. Road becomes FR 168.
GPS: N 41°43.57' W 111°40.19'

▼ 4.0 SO Track enters on right.
3.9 ▲ BR Road forks.

▼ 4.2 SO Track on left.
3.8 ▲ SO Track on right.

▼ 4.9 BR Track forks off on left.
3.0 ▲ SO Track enters on right.
GPS: N 41°43.66' W 111°39.25'

▼ 6.1 SO FR 160 on right.
1.8 ▲ SO FR 160 on left.
GPS: N 41°43.56' W 111°38.22'

▼ 7.5 BR Road forks and rejoins main trail.
0.4 ▲ SO Road rejoins.

▼ 7.6 SO Road rejoins.
0.3 ▲ BL Road forks and rejoins main trail.

▼ 7.7 SO Stock troughs and pond on left.
0.3 ▲ SO Stock troughs and pond on right.

▼ 8.0 TR Intersection with FR 047. Zero trip meter.
0.0 ▲ Continue west on FR 052.
GPS: N 41°43.58′ W 111°36.98′

▼ 0.0 Continue south on FR 047.
4.8 ▲ TL Intersection with FR 052. Zero trip meter.

▼ 0.1 SO FR 147 on left leads east to Northern #6: Old Ephraim Trail.
4.7 ▲ SO FR 147 on right leads east to Northern #6: Old Ephraim Trail.

▼ 0.3 SO Cattle guard.
4.5 ▲ SO Cattle guard.

▼ 0.4 SO Track on left.
4.4 ▲ BL Track on right.

▼ 0.7 SO Track on right.
4.1 ▲ SO Track on left.

▼ 1.0 SO Track on right.
3.8 ▲ SO Track on left.

▼ 3.6 SO/BL Cattle guard, then bear left. Sheep Hollow Trail (TR 026) on right.
1.2 ▲ BR/SO Bear right; Sheep Hollow Trail (TR 026) on left. Then cross cattle guard.
GPS: N 41°41.05′ W 111°37.44′

▼ 3.9 SO Cattle guard.
0.9 ▲ SO Cattle guard.

▼ 4.8 Seasonal gate and trail ends at Northern #3: Left Hand Fork Canyon Trail. Turn right for Northern #1: Hardware Ranch Road, left for end of Left Hand Fork Canyon Trail.
0.0 ▲ On Northern #3: Left Hand Fork Canyon Trail, 5.7 miles from Northern #1: Hardware Ranch Road, zero trip meter and turn north onto FR 047.
GPS: N 41°40.04′ W 111°37.58′

NORTHERN REGION TRAIL #3

Left Hand Fork Canyon Trail

STARTING POINT Northern #1: Hardware Ranch Road
FINISHING POINT Rock slide, 3.6 miles past Gray Cliff Spring
TOTAL MILEAGE 10.1 miles
UNPAVED MILEAGE 9.6 miles
DRIVING TIME 45 minutes (one-way)
ELEVATION RANGE 5,200–6,200 feet
USUALLY OPEN Year-round
DIFFICULTY RATING 2
SCENIC RATING 8
REMOTENESS RATING +0

Special Attractions

- Gray Cliff Spring.
- Spectacular fall scenery.
- Numerous backcountry camping sites along the stream that provide easy access to the area's many 4WD trails.

Description

The trail starts out on the paved FR 245 and then becomes an easy, 1-rated maintained road. Left Hand Fork Canyon has gently sloping walls dotted with pinyon and juniper as well as an unusually pretty floor. The trail follows along the stream past many cottonwoods and several scenic camping spots.

After you pass Northern #2: Millville Canyon Trail at the 5.7-mile mark, the canyon becomes narrower and the road deteriorates, becoming very bumpy as it passes over sections of low, imbedded rock. Passing may present a slight problem in some areas as the brush leaves only a single lane. Navigation remains easy throughout, since there are few side roads.

Less than a mile later, Left Hand Fork Canyon Trail passes the very pretty Gray Cliff Spring, which cascades down the canyon wall on the left. The substantial flow of water feeds streams on either side of the trail, creating the unusual situation where the road becomes little more than a ribbon of dry land slicing between the two.

About 3.6 miles past Gray Cliff Spring there has been a substantial rock slide. Although this slide can be crossed by an expert in a suitable vehicle, we have ended the route at this point, since the difficulty of this section goes beyond the scope of this book. If you cross the rock slide, you'll find the road is extremely narrow as it forces its way through dense scrub. After 2 miles, the route rejoins Northern #1: Hardware Ranch Road.

Current Road Information

Uinta-Wasatch-Cache National Forest
Logan Ranger District
1500 East Highway 89
Logan, UT 84321
(435) 755-3620

Map References

BLM Logan
USFS Uinta-Wasatch-Cache: Logan Ranger District
USGS 1:24,000 Logan Peak, Boulder Mtn.
1:100,000 Logan
Trails Illustrated, #713
Utah Atlas & Gazetteer, p. 12
Utah Road & Recreation Atlas, p. 37

Route Directions

▼ 0.0	On Northern #1: Hardware Ranch Road, 7.0 miles from Hyrum, zero trip meter and turn northeast on FR 245.
5.7 ▲	Trail ends at Northern #1: Hardware Ranch Road. Turn right for Hyrum, left for US 89.
	GPS: N 41°37.91' W 111°42.41'

A view of one of the rock slides across the trail

A view of the trail

Northern Trail #3: Left Hand Fork Canyon Trail

▼ 0.2 SO Cross bridge.
5.4 ▲ SO Cross bridge.

▼ 0.5 SO Cattle guard.
5.1 ▲ SO Cattle guard.

▼ 0.7 SO Seasonal gate.
5.0 ▲ SO Seasonal gate.

▼ 3.0 SO Blacksmith Fork Guard Station on right.
2.7 ▲ SO Blacksmith Fork Guard Station on left.
GPS: N 41°39.57' W 111°40.41'

▼ 3.5 SO Cache USFS Friendship Campground on right.
2.2 ▲ SO Cache USFS Friendship Campground on left.

▼ 4.1 SO Cache USFS Spring Campground on right.
1.6 ▲ SO Cache USFS Spring Campground on left.

▼ 4.6 SO Cattle guard.
1.0 ▲ SO Cattle guard.

▼ 5.7 SO Left is Northern #2: Millville Canyon Trail (FR 047). Road becomes FR 231. Zero trip meter.
0.0 ▲ Road becomes FR 245.
GPS: N 41°40.04' W 111°37.58'

▼ 0.0 Continue along FR 231.
▼ 0.8 SO Gray Cliff Spring waterfall on left directly beside road.
GPS: N 41°40.44' W 111°36.89'

▼ 1.5 SO Cross through wash.
▼ 4.4 Trail ends at rock slide, 3.6 miles past Gray Cliff Spring.
GPS: N 41°40.28' W 111°33.06'

A waterfall flows down the walls of Left Hand Fork Canyon

NORTHERN REGION TRAIL #4

Strawberry Valley Trail

STARTING POINT Northern #1: Hardware Ranch Road
FINISHING POINT Bear Lake and junction with Northern #5: Temple Canyon Trail
TOTAL MILEAGE 17.6 miles
UNPAVED MILEAGE 12.7 miles
DRIVING TIME 1 hour
ELEVATION RANGE 6,000–7,200 feet
USUALLY OPEN May to October
DIFFICULTY RATING 1
SCENIC RATING 7
REMOTENESS RATING +0

Special Attractions

- Bear Lake.
- The town site of Round Valley.
- A gentle, easy, and scenic canyon road.

History

When the Mormons arrived in Utah, the fertile area south of Bear Lake was a natural place to settle. Full of lush meadows and big game, Round Valley was not only a practical spot but a beautiful one. The only problem for the newly arrived settlers was that the region was already inhabited by local Indians. Competition for land and resources escalated and soon led to the brink of war. However, a settlement was reached in 1870, which brought about 30 years of peace and prosperity for the Mormons.

In the 1910s, drought and locusts crippled Round Valley's crops and signaled the slow demise of the town. By the 1930s, Round Valley was almost completely deserted.

The old Round Valley cemetery is located off the main road on private property. A sign currently marks a walking path leading to the site.

Description

On Northern #1: Hardware Ranch Road, 21.6 miles from Hyrum, Strawberry Valley Trail heads northeast into a fairly shallow canyon. This relatively easy road follows beside a creek and travels through the scenic ranchland of Strawberry Valley. The trail enters Lodgepole Canyon and then crosses into Cottonwood Canyon before finally exiting onto the paved road to Laketown. Shortly after joining the paved road, the trail passes to the left of the old town site of Round Valley (and the walking track out to the old cemetery) as it travels through attractive, rolling ranchland.

The Strawberry Valley Trail comes to an end at the intersection of Main Street and Utah 30 in Laketown, on the southern shore of Bear Lake. To the left is the start of Northern #5: Temple Canyon Trail.

Current Road Information

Uinta-Wasatch-Cache National Forest
Logan Ranger District
1500 East Highway 89
Logan, UT 84321
(435) 755-3620

Map References

BLM Logan
USFS Uinta-Wasatch-Cache: Logan Ranger District
USGS 1:24,000 Boulder Mtn., Red Spur Mtn., Meadowville, Laketown
1:100,000 Logan
Trails Illustrated, #713
Utah Atlas & Gazetteer, pp. 13, 12
Utah Road & Recreation Atlas, p. 38

Route Directions

▼ 0.0		On Northern #1: Hardware Ranch Road, 21.6 miles from Hyrum, proceed northeast and zero trip meter.
4.8 ▲		Trail ends at Northern #1: Hardware Ranch Road. Turn left for Hyrum, right for US 89.
		GPS: N 41°40.71' W 111°31.21'
▼ 0.9	SO	Track on right.
3.9 ▲	SO	Track on left.
▼ 1.4	SO	Cross bridge.
3.4 ▲	SO	Cross bridge.

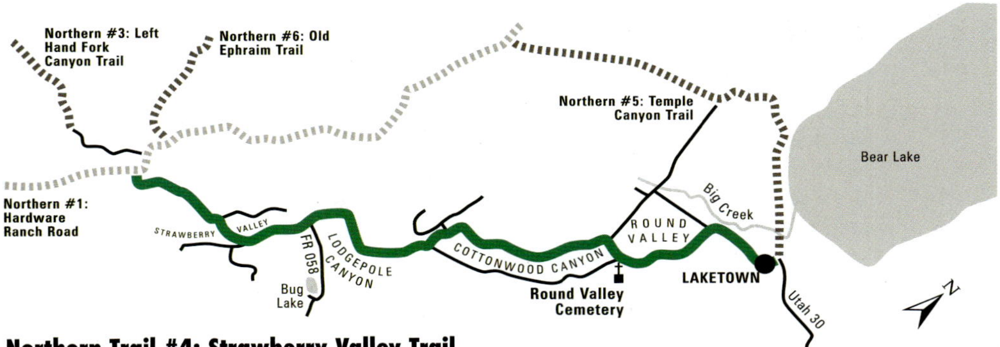

Northern Trail #4: Strawberry Valley Trail

▼ 4.1 BR Road forks.
0.7 ▲ SO Track enters on right.
GPS: N 41°42.36' W 111°27.68'

▼ 4.2 SO Cross over creek.
0.6 ▲ SO Cross over creek.

▼ 4.7 SO Track to corral on right.
0.1 ▲ SO Track to corral on left.

▼ 4.8 SO Intersection. FR 058 to Bug Lake and Randolph on right. Zero trip meter. Pass corral and travel through Lodgepole Canyon.
0.0 ▲ Continue along main road.
GPS: N 41°42.93' W 111°27.33'

▼ 0.0 Continue along main road.
7.8 ▲ SO Pass corral, then intersection. FR 058 to Bug Lake and Randolph on left. Zero trip meter.

▼ 0.6 SO Cattle guard.
7.2 ▲ SO Cattle guard.

▼ 0.8 SO Track on left.
7.0 ▲ SO Track on right.

▼ 2.1 SO Track on right.
5.7 ▲ SO Track on left.

▼ 2.3 SO Track on left and right.
5.5 ▲ SO Track on right and left.
GPS: N 41°43.61' W 111°25.70'

▼ 2.4 SO Cattle guard. Leave Uinta-Wasatch-Cache National Forest.
5.4 ▲ SO Enter Uinta-Wasatch-Cache National Forest. Cattle guard.

▼ 4.4 SO Cattle guard.
3.4 ▲ SO Cattle guard.

▼ 7.3 SO Cattle guard.
0.5 ▲ SO Cattle guard.

▼ 7.8 TR Cattle guard, then intersection with paved road. Zero trip meter.
0.0 ▲ Proceed south through Cottonwood Canyon.
GPS: N 41°47.39' W 111°22.44'

▼ 0.0 Proceed toward Laketown.
4.9 ▲ TL Intersection. Turn onto unpaved road, zero trip meter, then pass cattle guard.

▼ 0.6 SO Round Valley cemetery on right.
4.3 ▲ SO Round Valley cemetery on left.
GPS: N 41°47.36' W 111°21.80'

▼ 3.0 TR Intersection.
1.9 ▲ TL Intersection.

▼ 4.5 TL Laketown post office, then intersection at Old Rock Store. Turn left onto Main Street.
0.4 ▲ TR Intersection at Old Rock Store, then Laketown post office.

▼ 4.9 Trail ends at Bear Lake Boulevard

(Utah 30) in Laketown. Turn left on Utah 30 for Northern #5: Temple Canyon Trail.

0.0 ▲ At the intersection of Main Street and Bear Lake Boulevard (Utah 30) in Laketown, zero trip meter and proceed along Main Street.

GPS: N 41°49.85' W 111°19.33'

NORTHERN REGION TRAIL #5

Temple Canyon Trail

STARTING POINT Laketown, end of Northern #4: Strawberry Valley Trail
FINISHING POINT Northern #1: Hardware Ranch Road
TOTAL MILEAGE 10.9 miles
UNPAVED MILEAGE 8 miles
DRIVING TIME 1 hour
ELEVATION RANGE 5,900–7,600 feet
USUALLY OPEN May to October
DIFFICULTY RATING 1
SCENIC RATING 8
REMOTENESS RATING +0

Special Attractions

- Bear Lake.
- Forms loop trail with Northern #4: Strawberry Valley Trail off Northern #1: Hardware Ranch Road.

Description

In Laketown, at the northern endpoint of Northern #4: Strawberry Valley Trail, Temple Canyon Trail heads northwest on Bear Lake Boulevard, which runs along the shore of Bear Lake. After the trail enters Temple Canyon, it runs along a wide shelf road with plenty of places to pass oncoming vehicles. Although the trail is only about 50 feet above the canyon floor, views over the aspen- and conifer-laden valley are quite pretty. After crossing a cattle guard at the 8.4-mile mark, the road enters a forest. From here, the road is bumpier as it proceeds over sections of imbedded rock. The trail comes to an end at Northern #1: Hardware Ranch Road.

Current Road Information

Uinta-Wasatch-Cache National Forest
Logan Ranger District
1500 East Highway 89
Logan, UT 84321
(435) 755-3620

Map References

BLM Logan
USFS Uinta-Wasatch-Cache: Logan Ranger District
USGS 1:24,000 Laketown, Meadowville
1:100,000 Logan
Trails Illustrated, #713
Utah Atlas & Gazetteer, p. 13
Utah Road & Recreation Atlas, p. 38

Route Directions

▼ 0.0 At end of Northern #4: Strawberry Valley Trail, at intersection of Main Street and Bear Lake Boulevard (Utah 30) in Laketown, zero trip meter and proceed northwest along Bear Lake Boulevard.

2.9 ▲ Trail ends at Main Street in Laketown. Turn right on Main Street for Northern #4: Strawberry Valley Trail.

GPS: N 41°49.85' W 111°19.33'

▼ 2.7 SO Rest stop and picnic area on right.

0.1 ▲ SO Rest stop and picnic area on left.

▼ 2.9 TL Turn left onto unpaved Meadowville Road, cross cattle guard, and zero trip meter.

0.0 ▲ Continue toward Laketown.

GPS: N 41°51.56' W 111°21.87'

▼ 0.0 Follow unpaved road.

8.0 ▲ TR Turn right onto paved Bear Lake Boulevard (Utah 30). Zero trip meter.

▼ 1.1 SO Track on right.

6.9 ▲ SO Track on left.

▼ 1.6 SO Cattle guard.

A view of Bear Lake from the trail

Northern Trail #5: Temple Canyon Trail

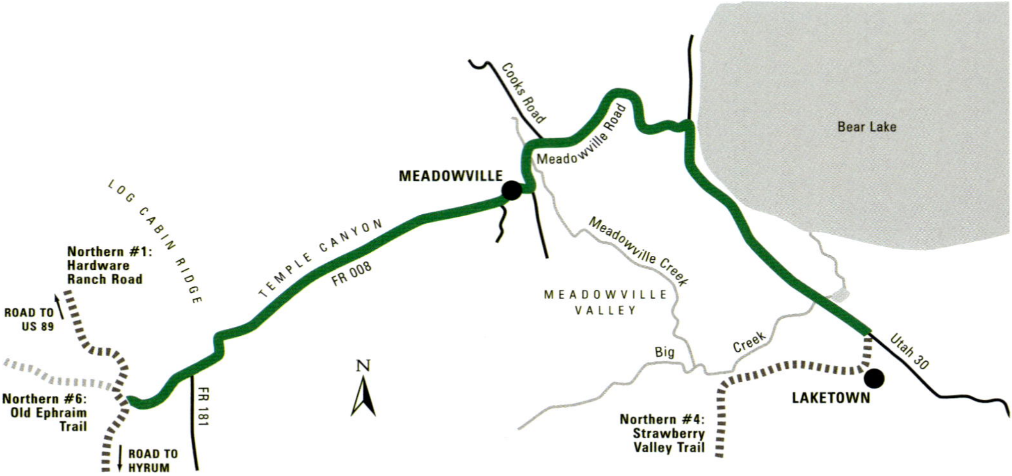

6.4 ▲ SO Cattle guard.

▼ 2.0 BL Cooks Road on right to Cooks Reservoir.
6.0 ▲ BL Cooks Road on left to Cooks Reservoir.
GPS: N 41°51.20' W 111°23.54'

▼ 2.6 TR Turn right onto dirt road.
5.3 ▲ TL Turn left at intersection.

▼ 2.8 TL Follow dirt road through Meadowville.
5.1 ▲ TR Pass through Meadowville and turn right at intersection.

▼ 2.9 TR Turn right onto road to Temple Canyon.
5.0 ▲ TL Turn left toward Meadowville.

▼ 3.5 SO Cattle guard.
4.5 ▲ SO Cattle guard.

▼ 5.5 SO Cattle guard and sign for Temple Canyon (FR 008).
2.5 ▲ SO Cattle guard.

▼ 6.4 SO Track on right.
1.6 ▲ SO Track on left.
GPS: N 41°49.02' W 111°27.03'

▼ 6.6 BL Track on right.
1.4 ▲ BR Track on left.

▼ 6.7 SO Track on left.
1.3 ▲ SO Track on right and sign for Temple Canyon.
GPS: N 41°48.82' W 111°27.10'

▼ 7.1 SO Follow sign for "Temple Flat, Blacksmith Fork, Sinks Road and Temple Fork" straight ahead. Then road on right.
0.9 ▲ SO Road on left.

▼ 7.2 SO Track on left is FR 181.
0.8 ▲ SO Track on right is FR 181.
GPS: N 41°48.50' W 111°27.51'

▼ 8.0 Trail ends at Northern #1: Hardware Ranch Road. Turn right for US 89, left for Hyrum.
0.0 ▲ On Northern #1: Hardware Ranch Road, 11.3 miles from US 89, zero trip meter and turn east onto FR 008 toward Temple Flat.
GPS: N 41°48.17' W 111°28.07'

NORTHERN REGION TRAIL #6

Old Ephraim Trail

STARTING POINT Northern #1: Hardware Ranch Road
FINISHING POINT Northern #1: Hardware Ranch Road
TOTAL MILEAGE 13.4 miles
UNPAVED MILEAGE 13.4 miles
DRIVING TIME 1.5 hours
ELEVATION RANGE 6,400–7,900 feet
USUALLY OPEN June to October
DIFFICULTY RATING 4
SCENIC RATING 8
REMOTENESS RATING +1

Special Attractions

- The story of, and monument to, Old Ephraim.
- Aspen viewing in the fall.
- Moderately challenging 4WD road.

History

The Old Ephraim Trail takes you to the gravesite of one of Cache Valley's most legendary figures. As far as anyone knows, Old Ephraim was the last grizzly bear to live in Utah. Before his death at the hands of Frank Clark on August 22, 1923, Old Ephraim was known to ranchers and sheepherders as an enormous, ghostlike predator who passed through the region snatching livestock without ever being seen by anyone. All the sheepherders like Clark knew about the bear were his hunting patterns and his distinctive footprint; Old Ephraim had a missing middle claw on his left hind foot.

Frank Clark lived in northern Utah for 12 years, and his sheep served as an occasional dinner for this clandestine grizzly

Memorial to Utah's last Grizzly bear

Close-up of the memorial to the legendary Grizzly bear

The monument erected by the local scouts to commemorate Old Ephraim

bear. Clark was determined to catch him even though he'd never even glimpsed Old Ephraim. Eventually, Ephraim was caught in one of Clark's traps. Since it was pitch dark, Clark climbed up the hillside and waited until morning to make his move. Then, at dawn, Clark approached the bear. Seeing the hunter, Ephraim raised up on his hind legs and charged. Clark shot off six rounds, but the bear kept coming. It was not until the seventh shot, which hit him in the head, that Old Ephraim fell back and died. Through the years, the story of the legendary meeting between the two in the late summer of 1923 has become a mix of fact and pioneer folklore. Ephraim's skull was later sent to the Smithsonian and can now be found at the Bridgerland Travel Region Office in Logan.

Description

The Old Ephraim Trail makes a loop off of Northern #1: Hardware Ranch Road, winding its way through a beautiful mountain forest. About 1.5 miles from the start, you come into a clearing with expansive views of the surrounding mountain landscape in all directions.

The trail runs in and out of the forest, which keeps a constant amount of moisture on the road's surface. This moisture has led to considerable erosion and rutting in the roads, making high clearance a must. In some of the more heavily rutted spots, choosing the right line often means brushing up against the bushes on the side of the road. The forest also closes in on the trail in spots, making the clearance between the trees tight.

Even though the road is quite often wet

A 4WD vehicle that slipped into a deep rut along one of the off-camber sections of the trail

Dog Spring

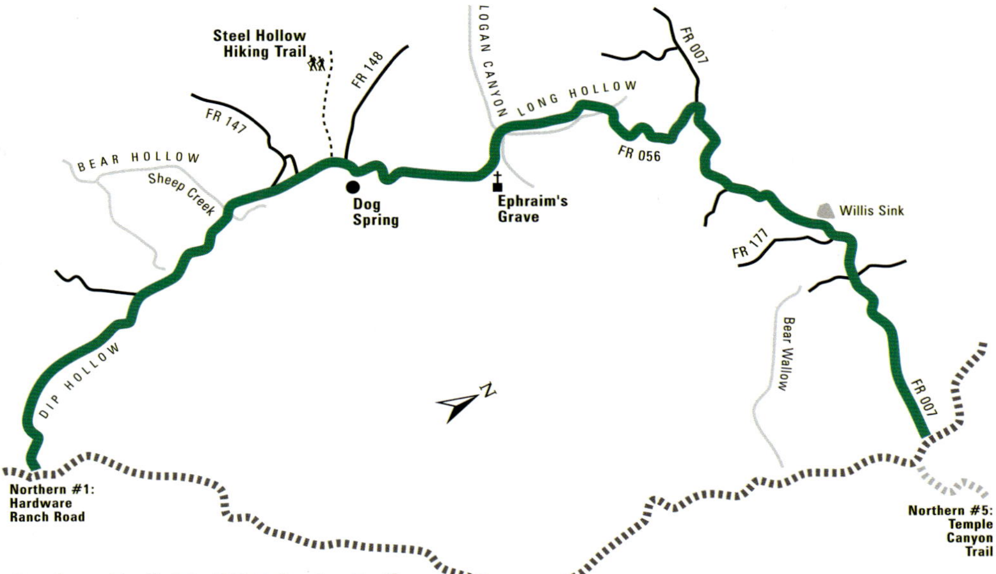

Northern Trail #6: Old Ephraim Trail

and boggy, imbedded rocks in the road's surface allow for good traction. This rough surface can be very helpful along some of the steeper sections of shelf road.

A little over halfway along the trail, at the 7.1-mile point, you come to the marker commemorating the death of Utah's last grizzly bear. The trail finishes through a few stands of aspen and returns you to Northern #1: Hardware Ranch Road.

Current Road Information

Uinta-Wasatch-Cache National Forest
Logan Ranger District
1500 East Highway 89
Logan, UT 84321
(435) 755-3620

Map References

BLM Logan
USFS Uinta-Wasatch-Cache: Logan Ranger District
USGS 1:24,000 Meadowville, Temple Peak, Boulder Mtn.
1:100,000 Logan
Trails Illustrated, #713
Utah Atlas & Gazetteer, pp. 13, 12
Utah Road & Recreation Atlas, pp. 38, 37

Route Directions

▼ 0.0		On Northern #1: Hardware Ranch Road, 11.1 miles south of US 89, zero trip meter and turn west onto FR 007.
4.4 ▲		Trail ends at Northern #1: Hardware Ranch Road. Turn left for US 89, right for Hyrum.
		GPS: N 41°48.24' W 111°28.24'
▼ 0.5	SO	Cattle guard.
3.8 ▲	SO	Cattle guard.
▼ 0.7	SO	Two tracks on left.
3.7 ▲	SO	Two tracks on right.
		GPS: N 41°48.27' W 111°29.08'
▼ 1.6	SO	Track on left.
2.7 ▲	SO	Track on right.
		GPS: N 41°48.19' W 111°30.01'
▼ 1.7	SO	Track on left (track on right seems deliberately blocked by rocks).
2.6 ▲	SO	Track on right (track on left seems deliberately blocked by rocks).
		GPS: N 41°48.21' W 111°30.17'

▼ 2.1 SO Cattle guard.
2.3 ▲ SO Cattle guard.

▼ 2.3 SO FR 177 on left.
2.1 ▲ SO FR 177 on right.
GPS: N 41°48.24' W 111°30.65'

▼ 4.4 TL Turn left onto FR 056 and zero trip meter. FR 007 continues straight ahead.
0.0 ▲ Continue along FR 007.
GPS: N 41°47.58' W 111°32.43'

▼ 0.0 Continue along FR 056.
2.7 ▲ TR Intersection. Turn right onto FR 007. Zero trip meter.

▼ 2.5 SO Cross over creek.
0.1 ▲ SO Cross over creek.

▼ 2.7 SO Old Ephraim's grave marker on left. Zero trip meter.
0.0 ▲ Continue along FR 056
GPS: N 41°45.84' W 111°32.59'

▼ 0.0 Continue along FR 056.
6.3 ▲ SO Old Ephraim's grave marker on right. Zero trip meter.

▼ 1.4 SO Dog Spring on left with trough.
4.8 ▲ SO Dog Spring on right with trough.

▼ 1.6 BL FR 148 on right.
4.7 ▲ BR FR 148 on left.
GPS: N 41°44.78' W 111°33.22'

▼ 1.7 SO Steel Hollow hiking trail on right.
4.6 ▲ SO Steel Hollow hiking trail on left.

▼ 2.4 SO FR 147 on right leads to Northern #2: Millville Canyon Trail.
3.8 ▲ SO FR 147 on left leads to Northern #2: Millville Canyon Trail.

▼ 5.4 SO Track on right.
0.9 ▲ SO Track on left.

▼ 5.8 SO Seasonal gate.
0.4 ▲ SO Seasonal gate.

▼ 6.2 BR Fork in road is part of an intersection delta: left also goes to Hardware Ranch Road.
0.1 ▲ SO Track on right.

▼ 6.3 Trail ends at Northern #1: Hardware Ranch Road. Turn right for Hyrum, left for US 89.
0.0 ▲ On Northern #1: Hardware Ranch Road, 23.2 miles from Hyrum, zero trip meter and turn northwest onto FR 056.
GPS: N 41°41.54' W 111°31.26'

NORTHERN REGION TRAIL #7

Peter Sinks Trail

STARTING POINT Northern #1: Hardware Ranch Road
FINISHING POINT Northern #1: Hardware Ranch Road
TOTAL MILEAGE 7.6 miles
UNPAVED MILEAGE 7.6 miles
DRIVING TIME 1 hour (one-way)
ELEVATION RANGE 8,000–8,600 feet
USUALLY OPEN June to October
DIFFICULTY RATING 3
SCENIC RATING 8
REMOTENESS RATING +1

Special Attractions

- Sinkholes in a remote alpine basin setting.
- Broad views across to Bear Lake.
- Fascinating side road from Northern #1: Hardware Ranch Road.

History

Peter Sinks Basin encompasses an area that is roughly 0.6 by 1.2 miles and about 600 to 700 feet lower than the surrounding terrain. The sinkholes in Peter Sinks were caused when underground water created caverns beneath the earth's surface. The caverns eventually collapsed and the ground caved in, leaving these deep holes. Do not try to explore the sinkholes; they are very deep and very dangerous.

A section of the trail that squeezes through the trees before reaching the sinks

A view of one of the sinks

Cold nighttime air also flows down into the lower elevations of Peter Sinks and collects in cold-air pools. Due to the high density of the cold air, the pools remain inside the basin and produce freezing cold temperatures. In the winter of 1985, Peter Sinks recorded the second lowest temperature in the continental United States—a frigid -56° Celsius (-69° Fahrenheit).

Currently, information gathered at the rural Peter Sinks is being used to study the nature of air pools in other more-urban basin environments such as Salt Lake City and Phoenix, Arizona.

Description

Peter Sinks Trail makes a loop that begins and ends at the same point on Northern #1: Hardware Ranch Road. It travels through the Engelmann spruce and Douglas firs of the Uinta-Wasatch-Cache National Forest. In areas where the landscape opens up, there are expansive views over Bear Lake. The trail also passes by the series of picturesque sinkholes that give the region its name.

The road itself is not very difficult, though you encounter the ruts, roots, and potholes that come hand in hand with forested trails. In spots, the trail becomes very narrow as it passes between the trees. There is little room to choose a line in these places because typically only one exists. The road is also usually damp and boggy, so high clearance and good tires are a big help in negotiating some of the more rock-rutted and slippery sections. After rains, the trail becomes very treacherous and is better left for another day.

The Great Western Hiking Trail crosses through the Peter Sinks Basin and offers an enjoyable walk through this unique region.

Over 1,600 miles of Great Western Trail exist in Utah

Northern Trail #7: Peter Sinks Trail

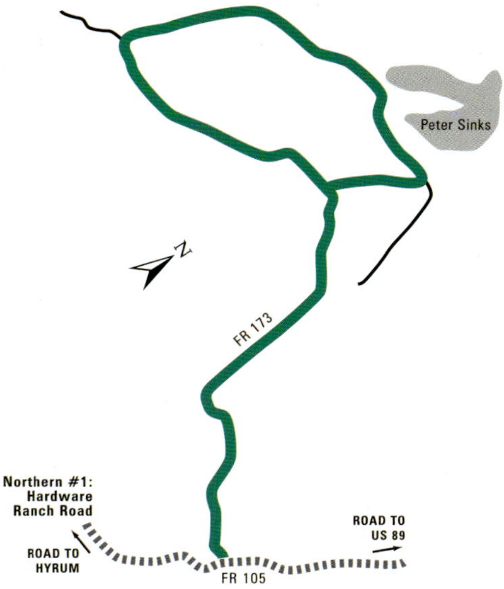

Current Road Information

Uinta-Wasatch-Cache National Forest
Logan Ranger District
1500 East Highway 89
Logan, UT 84327
(435) 755-3620

Map References

BLM Logan
USFS Uinta-Wasatch-Cache: Logan Ranger District
USGS 1:24,000 Garden City, Tony Grove Creek
1:100,000 Logan
Trails Illustrated, #713
Utah Atlas & Gazetteer, pp. 13, 12
Utah Road & Recreation Atlas, p. 38

Route Directions

▼ 0.0 On Northern #1: Hardware Ranch Road, 2.7 miles from US 89, zero trip meter and proceed west along FR 173. Follow sign to "West Hodges, Little Bear and Peter Sinks."

GPS: N 41°53.41' W 111°29.09'

▼ 2.0 TR Road on right is the beginning of loop trail.

GPS: N 41°54.32′ W 111°30.70′

▼ 2.5 TL Turn left.

GPS: N 41°54.71′ W 111°30.49′

▼ 3.7 SO Pass through gate.

GPS: N 41°54.31′ W 111°31.65′

▼ 4.1 SO Sinkhole beside the trail.

▼ 4.3 TL Intersection; turn left.

GPS: N 41°53.80′ W 111°31.76′

▼ 5.2 SO Track on right.

GPS: N 41°54.13′ W 111°30.99′

▼ 5.4 SO Pass through fence line.

▼ 5.6 SO Track on left completes the loop.

GPS: N 41°54.32′ W 111°30.70′

▼ 7.6 Trail ends at Northern #1: Hardware Ranch Road. Turn left for US 89, right for Hyrum.

GPS: N 41°53.41′ W 111°29.09′

NORTHERN REGION TRAIL #8

Idaho Loop

STARTING POINT US 89, at CR 243
FINISHING POINT US 89, at FR 006
TOTAL MILEAGE 23.7 miles
UNPAVED MILEAGE 23 miles
DRIVING TIME 1.5 hours
ELEVATION RANGE 6,600–8,500 feet
USUALLY OPEN June to October
DIFFICULTY RATING 2
SCENIC RATING 8
REMOTENESS RATING +1

Special Attractions

- Aspen viewing in the fall.
- Easy, pleasant 4WD trail with varied scenery.
- Numerous backcountry campsites with access to a network of 4WD roads to explore.

Description

The Idaho Loop trail, as its name implies, travels mainly through Idaho, making a loop off of US 89 in Utah. It begins beside Beaver Creek on a single-lane forest road. The road itself is only occasionally maintained and has been noticeably eroded in some spots. Stretches of imbedded rock can make this relatively easy road very rough in places.

For the first couple miles, the trail passes several camping spots as it winds through areas of aspen and conifer. Also, many beaver dams appear for mile after mile alongside the creek.

As you continue through Egan Basin toward Danish Pass, the trail can become slippery and muddy when wet. It is generally an easy road until the last couple miles, where it becomes rocky and considerably more rough.

As you come down from Danish Pass through the thick forest, turn onto FR 406 and head south back to Utah. On the return portion of the loop, the trail travels through large, open meadows dotted with conifers and thick stands of aspen that offer wonderful fall viewing. About a mile and a half before the trail's ending point, beaver dams once again become prominent along the creek. Campsites, too, are prevalent throughout this final portion of the trail before it ends at US 89.

Current Road Information

Uinta-Wasatch-Cache National Forest
Logan Ranger District
1500 East Highway 89
Logan, UT 84321
(435) 755-3620

Caribou-Targhee National Forest
Montpelier Ranger District
322 North Fourth Street
Montpelier, ID 83254
(208) 847-0375

The trail following beside Beaver Creek

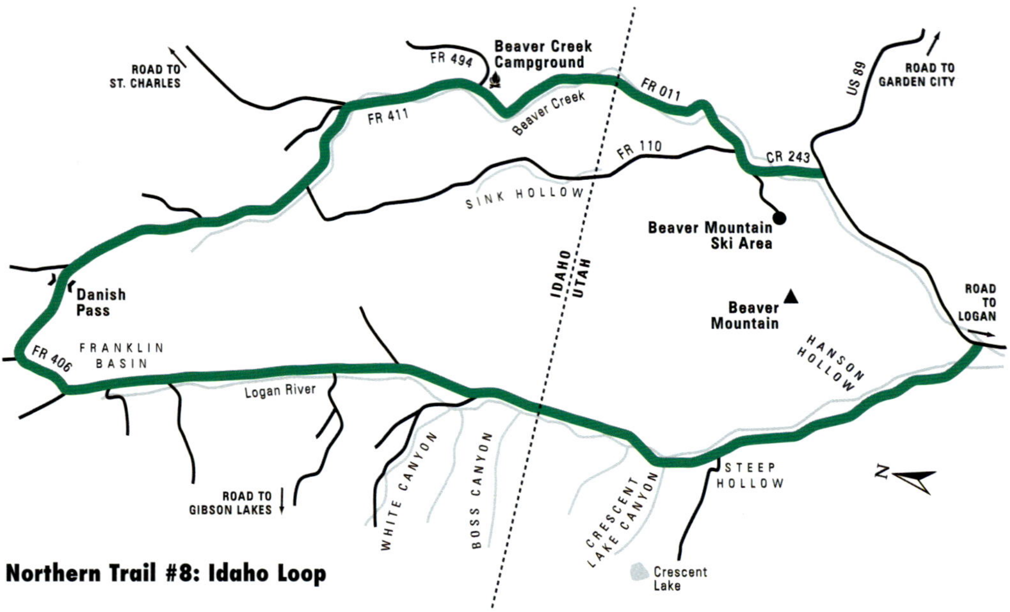

Northern Trail #8: Idaho Loop

Map References

BLM Logan (incomplete)
USFS Uinta-Wasatch-Cache: Logan Ranger District (incomplete)
USGS 1:24,000 Tony Grove Creek (incomplete)
1:100,000 Logan (incomplete)
Trails Illustrated, #713
Utah Atlas & Gazetteer, p. 12
Utah Road & Recreation Atlas, pp. 38, 37 (incomplete)
Idaho Atlas & Gazetteer, p. 78 (incomplete)
Idaho Road & Recreation Atlas, p. 88

Route Directions

▼ 0.0 On US 89, zero trip meter and proceed north along CR 243 toward Beaver Mountain ski area.
6.3 ▲ Trail ends at US 89. Turn right for Logan, left for Garden City and Bear Lake.
GPS: N 41°57.79' W 111°31.87'

▼ 0.7 BR Bear right onto unpaved track (FR 011). Public toilets on right and Travel Management Area sign.
5.6 ▲ BL Bear left onto CR 243.
GPS: N 41°58.41' W 111°31.85'

▼ 0.9 BR Track on left is FR 110 to Sink Hollow.
5.4 ▲ BL Track on right is FR 110 to Sink Hollow.

▼ 1.2 SO Tracks to camping area on left.
5.1 ▲ BL Tracks to camping area on right.

▼ 1.5 SO Cross over creek.
4.8 ▲ SO Cross over creek.

▼ 2.7 SO Bridge over creek.
3.6 ▲ SO Bridge over creek.

▼ 2.8 SO Idaho state line. Road is now FR 411.
3.5 ▲ SO Utah state line. Road is now FR 011.
GPS: N 41°59.94' W 111°31.09'

▼ 3.2 SO Cross bridge over creek, then cattle guard.
3.0 ▲ SO Cattle guard, then cross bridge over creek.

▼ 3.4 SO Track on right.
2.8 ▲ SO Track on left.

▼ 4.7 SO USFS Beaver Creek Campground on right.
1.6 ▲ SO USFS Beaver Creek Campground on left.

▼ 4.8 SO Track on right is FR 494.
1.5 ▲ SO Track on left is FR 494.

▼ 5.6 SO Cross over creek. Then track on left.
0.7 ▲ SO Track on right. Then cross over creek.
GPS: N 42°01.99' W 111°31.96'

▼ 6.2 SO Cross over creek.
0.1 ▲ SO Cross over creek.

▼ 6.3 BL Road forks. Bear left to Egan Basin and US 89. Right goes to St. Charles. Zero trip meter.
0.0 ▲ Continue along the trail.
GPS: N 42°02.57' W 111°32.20'

▼ 0.0 Continue along the trail.
4.2 ▲ BR Road to St. Charles enters on left. Zero trip meter.

▼0.5 SO/SO Road on right. Then road on right to Pat Hollow Crash site.
3.7 ▲ SO/BR Road to Pat Hollow Crash site on left. Then bear right at fork in road.

▼ 0.8 SO Corral on left.
3.4 ▲ SO Corral on right.

▼ 1.1 SO Track on left to Gibson Basin.
3.1 ▲ SO Track on right to Gibson Basin.
GPS: N 42°02.74' W 111°33.46'

▼ 1.4 SO Cattle guard.
2.8 ▲ SO Cattle guard.

▼ 2.1 SO Track on left.
2.1 ▲ SO Track on right.

▼ 2.5 SO Track on right.
1.7 ▲ SO Track on left.
GPS: N 42°03.74' W 111°34.23'

▼ 4.2 SO Highline Trail crosses road. Then cattle guard and Danish Pass. Zero trip meter.
0.0 ▲ Continue along the trail.
GPS: N 42°04.93' W 111°35.28'

▼ 0.0 Descend from pass.
2.4 ▲ SO Danish Pass. Then cattle guard and Highline Trail crosses road. Zero trip meter.

▼ 1.3 BL Intersection.
1.1 ▲ BR Intersection.
GPS: N 42°05.18' W 111°36.52'

▼ 2.3 BL Intersection; bear left onto FR 406 to Franklin Basin.
0.1 ▲ BR Intersection; bear right on road to Egan Basin.

▼ 2.4 SO Road forks; track on right. Zero trip meter.
0.0 ▲ Continue along trail.
GPS: N 42°04.57' W 111°36.82'

▼ 0.0 Continue along FR 406.
10.8 ▲ BR Track on left. Zero trip meter.

▼ 2.7 SO Track on left.
8.0 ▲ SO Track on right.

▼ 2.9 SO Track on right to Gibson Lakes.
7.9 ▲ SO Track on left to Gibson Lakes.
GPS: N 42°02.11' W 111°35.80'

▼ 3.5 SO Track on left.
7.2 ▲ SO Track on right.

▼ 4.5 SO Track on right to White Canyon.
6.3 ▲ SO Track on left to White Canyon.

▼ 5.2 SO Cross Utah state line.
5.6 ▲ SO Cross Idaho state line.
GPS: N 42°00.07' W 111°35.73'

▼ 6.6 SO Cross bridge.
4.2 ▲ SO Cross bridge.

▼ 7.4 SO Track on right.
3.4 ▲ SO Track on left.

▼ 7.5 SO Track on right.
3.3 ▲ SO Track on left.

▼ 7.6 SO Track on right.
3.2 ▲ SO Track on left.

▼ 7.9 SO Tracks on left and right.

CIVILIAN CONSERVATION CORPS

Designed to provide financial relief from the Great Depression and to aid in a variety of conservation and public works projects, the Civilian Conservation Corps (CCC) arrived in Utah during President Roosevelt's New Deal era. Young men between the ages of 18 and 23 and local experienced men who, during these difficult times, were out of work made up the CCC's labor force. These skilled workers directed the young men, who were by and large without any particular skills.

Upon enlisting in the CCC, each man received a week's training in basic fire fighting. The years of the Depression happened to be extremely dry, and so the CCC was often called in to fight out-of-control forest fires. However, the bulk of the work included laying phone lines, controlling rodent and insect populations, and building roads, bridges, damns, dikes, cabins, and so on. Some of their larger projects in Utah included the bird refuges on Ogden Bay and Bear River as well as many roads in the Wasatch Range canyons. The men of the CCC were often noted for exceeding the call of duty. During harsh winter storms they would take convoys of food and dry wood to small towns otherwise cut off by the snow. They also worked in more urban areas to improve parks and other public facilities.

With the onset of World War II, the United States found itself once more with a growing economy. Like many New Deal programs, the CCC had run its course. In July 1942, the Corps was disbanded, but its impact on Utah remains to this day in the form of many roads, bridges, and public works. In the nine years of its existence, the CCC had 116 camps in 27 of Utah's 29 counties. You can still find the scattered remnants of old CCC camps tucked away throughout the state.

2.9 ▲ SO Tracks on right and left.

▼ 9.0 SO Track on left.
1.8 ▲ SO Track on right.

▼ 9.3 SO Track on right.
1.5 ▲ SO Track on left.

▼ 9.5 SO Cross creek.
1.3 ▲ SO Cross creek.

▼ 10.4 SO Track on right.
0.4 ▲ SO Track on left.

▼ 10.5 SO Cross bridge.
0.3 ▲ SO Cross bridge.

GPS: N 41°56.02′ W 111°33.95′

▼ 10.7 SO Public toilets on right.
0.1 ▲ SO Public toilets on left.

▼ 10.8 Trail ends at US 89. Turn right for Logan, left for Garden City and Bear Lake.
0.0 ▲ On US 89, zero trip meter and turn north onto Franklin Basin Road (FR 006).

GPS: N 41°55.88′ W 111°33.67′

NORTHERN REGION TRAIL #9

Inspiration Point Trail

STARTING POINT North Main Street in Mantua
FINISHING POINT Inspiration Point
TOTAL MILEAGE 13.7 miles
UNPAVED MILEAGE 11.6 miles
DRIVING TIME 1.5 hours (one-way)
ELEVATION RANGE 5,200–9,422 feet
USUALLY OPEN May to October
DIFFICULTY RATING 3
SCENIC RATING 10
REMOTENESS RATING +0

Special Attractions

- Spectacular 360-degree view from the parking spot on the absolute summit.
- Scenic 4WD trail that offers a reasonable challenge for less-experienced four-wheelers.
- Easy access from Salt Lake City.
- Good backcountry camping.

History

In the mid-1800s Brigham Young's cousin, Willard Richards, served as one of his most trusted counselors. Although a medical man by trade, Richards also held many prominent positions in local government and in the Mormon Church. Before his death in 1854, he served as general church historian, postmaster of Salt Lake City, and editor of the *Deseret News,* the Mormon newspaper. He published its first issue.

The area east of Bear River Bay has since been named Willard Basin. In 1923, this area was the scene of one of Utah's worst floods. Over the years, overgrazing had stripped most of the vegetation in Willard Basin, and during the spring of 1923, runoff from melting snow began to cause serious erosion to the land. The Willard Basin was in a very precarious position, and many felt there was a catastrophe waiting to happen.

On the night of August 13, 1923, thunder struck and the rains poured down. Flood waters soon followed causing multiple injuries, one death, and wiping out over 300 acres of prime agricultural land. Extensive damage was caused to many homes and barns. It took a crew of 250 men several weeks to clear the mud and rubble that had been deposited on the main road through the town of Willard. It took months of hard work and over $75,000 in relief funds for the town to recover from the flood.

However, the town still stood at risk for another flood. In the 1930s the federal government addressed the issue by establishing a

Cresting the summit of Inspiration Point

View across Willard Basin

A view of the trail as it winds around Black Mountain

Civilian Conservation Corps (CCC) camp in Willard Basin. The young men of the CCC constructed a dike and natural spillway to prevent further flooding. They also terraced the mountainside to further reduce the risk of flood in Willard Basin.

Description

The entire Inspiration Point Trail is very scenic, and it has a truly spectacular viewpoint at the end. The trail starts in Mantua in front of the municipal buildings (including the library and city offices) on North Main Street. After a couple of miles, the trail leaves paved roads behind and continues along a substantial, two-lane dirt road that offers a number of backcountry campsites.

At the 3.3-mile point, the road narrows as you begin to climb out of the valley. As you drive through the thick shrubbery of the Wasatch Range, you come across a number of side roads. However, they are noticeably minor tracks and navigation remains easy.

The trail then enters a coniferous forest on a steep shelf road that is closed in on either side by trees. At times, the trail passes along areas of less dense foliage that offer some remarkably expansive views. About 8 miles into the trail, the road climbs once again and becomes much more rough and narrow with sections of loose gravel. This half-mile stretch of road is about as difficult as the trail gets.

The trail eventually evens out near the Willard Point Overlook sign and continues along an open shelf road. This one-lane road has a number of places to pull off to allow someone to pass. From here, you loop around Willard Basin. The road is well below the ridgeline, which can make you feel as if you are driving through some kind of natural enclosure. There is a nice USFS campsite at the top of the basin.

The trail ends at Inspiration Point, where the top of the 9,422-foot peak offers views in every direction. To the east is Willard Basin. To the west is the Great Salt Lake, whose waters rest over 5,000 feet below in Willard Bay State Park. To the southeast, the

Panorama from Inspiration Point

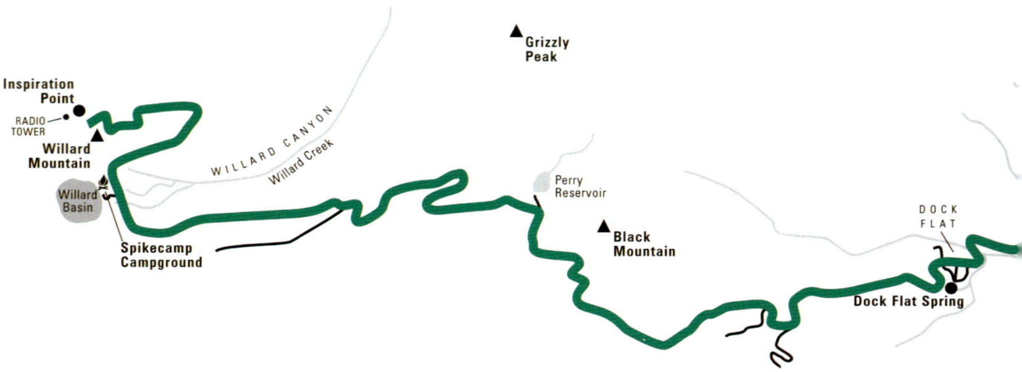

Northern Trail #9: Inspiration Point Trail

Wasatch Range continues, with Ogden Valley to the east. The view from Inspiration Point is truly magnificent and worth savoring before heading back down the trail.

Current Road Information

Uinta-Wasatch-Cache National Forest
Logan Ranger District
1500 East Highway 89
Logan, UT 84321
(435) 755-3620

Map References

BLM Ogden
USFS Uinta-Wasatch-Cache: Ogden Ranger District
USGS 1:24,000 Mantua
1:100,000 Ogden
Trails Illustrated, #700
Utah Atlas & Gazetteer, p. 12
Utah Road & Recreation Atlas, p. 37

Route Directions

▼ 0.0 On North Main Street in Mantua, between Fourth and Fifth Streets in front of the municipal buildings, zero trip meter and proceed south through town.

GPS: N 41°30.21′ W 111°56.55′

▼ 0.1 SO Stop sign and fork in road. Keep right

High above Willard Bay

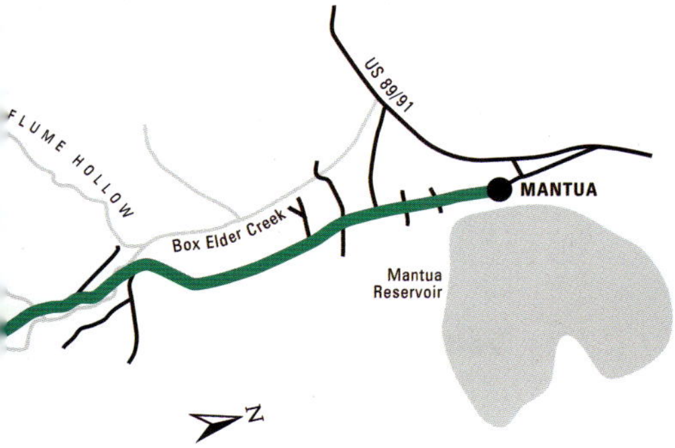

		of church. Road becomes Willard Peak Road.
▼ 2.1	SO	Road becomes graded gravel.
▼ 3.3	BL	Numerous tracks left and right. Road narrows.
▼ 4.8	BR	Tracks on left. **GPS: N 41°26.85' W 111°56.45'**
▼ 5.1	SO	Tracks on left and right across road.
▼ 6.5	BR	Road forks.
▼ 7.0	SO	Track on right.
▼ 7.7	BL	Track on right goes downhill to a pond. **GPS: N 41°25.65' W 111°57.71'**
▼ 8.5	TR	Road forks. Follow switchback.
▼ 9.9	SO	Track on left, then zero trip meter at sign for Willard Basin and overlook. Numerous tracks left and right. **GPS: N 41°24.67' W 111°58.13'**
▼ 0.0		Proceed downhill to the south. The correct road is left of the sign.
▼ 0.8	SO	Track on left rejoins later.
▼ 1.6	SO	USFS Spikecamp Campground and public toilets. **GPS: N 41°23.51' W 111°58.64'**
▼ 1.8	SO	Cross through wash.
▼ 3.5	SO	Track on left.
▼ 3.7	BL	Track on right. Continue on switchback to the left.
▼ 3.8		End at summit of Inspiration Point. An easy loop trail circles summit. **GPS: N 41°23.46' W 111°59.12'**

NORTHERN REGION TRAIL #10

Wendover to Lucin Trail

STARTING POINT I-80, exit 4, just east of Wendover
FINISHING POINT Lucin, Northern #12: Transcontinental Railroad Trail
TOTAL MILEAGE 55.3 miles
UNPAVED MILEAGE 54.2 miles
DRIVING TIME 3 hours
ELEVATION RANGE 4,200–5,200 feet
USUALLY OPEN Year-round
DIFFICULTY RATING 3
SCENIC RATING 8
REMOTENESS RATING +2

Special Attractions

- Remote trail through landscape of ancient Lake Bonneville.
- Provides access to two other historic trails.
- Access to Bonneville Speedway.

History

About 12,000 years ago, prehistoric Lake Bonneville began to shrink back to the current boundaries of the Great Salt Lake. As the lake's waters receded, they revealed the large, sprawling area known as the Bonneville Salt Flats. During most of the winter and spring months, the salt flats are submerged under shallow water. However, when dry, the salt flats that lie just northeast of Wendover are home to the Bonneville Speedway.

The speedway runs along natural terrain that remains consistently flat for many miles, and it has become the perfect area for both professional and amateur driving enthusiasts to attempt land speed records. Interest in the area as a natural speedway began in the early part of the 20th century when two drivers, W. D. Rishel and Ferg Johnson, promoted the area. In 1914, Terry Tetzlaff set the first unofficial land speed record at the Bonneville Speedway when he clocked in at 141 miles per hour. Then, in 1935, British racing pioneer Malcolm Campbell set an official record here of 301.13 miles per hour, and the speedway has been famous ever since.

Crossing the mud flats with the Pilot Range ahead

This area was also home to some of Utah's earliest inhabitants. Evidence of the Desert Archaic culture, which dates back over 10,000 years, was discovered in the 1940s and 1950s during an excavation of Danger Cave. The cave got its name in 1941 when a large slab of rock fell down and just missed one of the archaeologists who was working at the dig site. All of the artifacts have been removed from the cave, and today it remains much the same as it was when the excavations were finished. Even though it is located in a state park, there is no visitor center and no exhibits to mark Danger Cave.

Another historical attraction along the Wendover to Lucin Trail is the old cabin of Eugene Munsee. Built in 1880, the dovetail-notched cabin stands today as a brilliant example of a traditional western homestead. Munsee homesteaded the area about 50 years ago and today lives in Wendover. The roof was restored in 1990 by the Crossroads chapter of the Oregon-California Trails Association. Munsee's old cabin is now part of the McKeller Ranch.

The Wendover to Lucin Trail connects with two other historic routes: Northern #11: Silver Island Mountains Loop and Northern #12: Transcontinental Railroad Trail. The Silver Island trail follows part of the route taken by the ill-fated Donner-Reed Party. The other historic route follows a portion of the original transcontinental railroad. This branch of the railroad became obsolete after the 1904 Lucin Cutoff rerouted the railroad over the Great Salt Lake, thus making the line faster and more efficient. Not wanting to become obsolete, the citizens of Lucin moved the town about a mile west of its original location along the old line to a new spot beside the Lucin Cutoff. Today, a marker along the original transcontinental railroad indicates the spot of historic Lucin.

Description

Before setting out on the Wendover to Lucin Trail, make sure to check the weather and call ahead for information on road conditions, since the trail can easily become flooded and impassable after rains or as the winter snows melt. You should also bring extra water, especially during the hot summer months, as well as plenty of fuel and supplies, since the area is remote and unforgiving.

The trail starts just east of Wendover at I-80, exit 4. Take the paved road toward the Bonneville Speedway for about a mile; the trail then turns onto an unpaved gravel road that leads over Leppy Pass to a three-way intersection. From here, right is Northern #11: Silver Island Mountains Loop, left is the main road to Lucin, and straight is the 4WD route described here. The trail proceeds across a wide area of mud flats toward the Pilot Range before ultimately reconnecting with the main Lucin road. Be careful as you drive along this section because trucks still use the road despite its being rather narrow. Also, if you find that the mud flats are impassable, you can backtrack to the three-way intersection and take the main Lucin road until you reach the Pilot Range, where the trail diverges again from the main road to follow a higher 4WD trail along the eastern side of the mountains. This section is not only more interesting than the main road but has better views of the salt and mud flats.

As you traverse this area, the mountains jut out from this prehistoric lake bottom to surround you. As you approach the Pilot Range, the Leppy Hills rise up to the south and the Silver Island Mountains stand to the east. As you pass the northern limit of the Silver Island Mountains, the view widens across the remains of Lake Bonneville. Eventually, the trail traverses the Pilot Range's eastern foot, and you move from the barren flats to desert shrub country.

At Patterson Pass turnoff, you turn off the main Lucin road onto a single-lane track and head toward Governors Spring. The trail eventually rises about 1,000 feet above the salt flats as it proceeds along the lower part of the Pilot Range through a grassy area dotted with saltbush and juniper. From here you can look across the flats for miles and imagine the days when the entire region was submerged beneath Lake Bonneville.

Once you are back on the main road, the trail runs along a rough pebble-and-gravel surface that, though bumpy, is an easy 1-rated level of difficulty. The main challenge

Silver Island

along the earlier part of the trail is negotiating some potentially muddy areas, while the jagged rocks along this section can easily put a hole through your tires if you are not careful.

As you continue toward Coal Bank Springs, the single-lane trail narrows. Passing is difficult, but there is usually just enough room to pull over and allow another vehicle to get by. The character of the trail is quite different here, as you now must negotiate some deep and narrow washes. Depending on your vehicle's angles of entry and departure, crossing these washes can be tricky; take care when choosing the correct line to avoid getting hung up.

The trail eventually returns to the main road to Lucin; it continues past Lucin's railroad siding before coming to an end at the railroad tracks. This is the start of Northern #12: Transcontinental Railroad Trail. Head north for about 5 miles on the main road to get to Grouse Creek Junction and Utah 30.

If you are starting the trail from Lucin and driving south to Wendover, the intersection 5.8 miles from the railroad tracks at Lucin can be difficult to spot. It is sometimes marked with a white pole, but do not rely on the marker being there. Before you come to the turnoff, you pass a well-used track that leads to a radio tower.

Current Road Information

West Wendover Tourism & Convention Bureau
PO Box 2825
West Wendover, NV 89883
(775) 664-3138

BLM Salt Lake Field Office
2370 South Decker Lake Boulevard West Valley, UT 84119
(801) 977-4300

Map References

BLM Bonneville Salt Flats, Newfoundland Mtn.
USGS 1:24,000 Silsbee, Tetzlaff Peak, Leppy Peak, Silver Island Pass, Crater Island SW, Crater Island NW, Lucin
1:100,000 Bonneville Salt Flats, Newfoundland Mtn.
Utah Atlas & Gazetteer, p. 14
Utah Road & Recreation Atlas, p. 40

Looking across the ancient salt flats of Lake Bonneville to the Silver Island Mountains from Patterson Pass

LAKE BONNEVILLE

Lake Bonneville, the enormous Pleistocene lake that covered much of western Utah and even spread into Nevada and Idaho, was the distant ancestor of Utah's largest geological attraction, the Great Salt Lake. Twenty-five thousand years ago, Lake Bonneville was created from glacial activity and, at its peak, the lake spanned 19,800 miles and was 1,000-feet deep. Surprisingly, the water wasn't salty because the ancient lake drained into the Snake River in Idaho. But, as time went on the shores receded, the lake lost its point of drainage, and rivers draining into Lake Bonneville brought along their dissolved solids. Salt began to accumulate. Even today, as long as the Great Salt Lake has no drainage, its saltiness will gradually increase.

Signs of Lake Bonneville can still be seen. As the lake disappeared, it left behind large salt and mud flats; easily spotted rings that were cut into surrounding foothills by waves along its shoreline; and the smooth alluvial deltas and beaches that have provided the flat land for most of Utah's urban development.

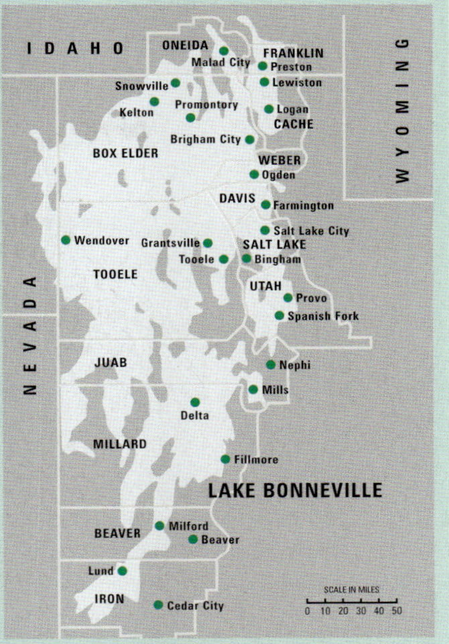

Map of Lake Bonneville, showing its relation to present cities, counties, and towns in Utah, Idaho, and Nevada

Route Directions

▼ 0.0 From I-80, exit 4, at the intersection of the exit/entry ramps and the overpass, zero trip meter and proceed north on paved road to Bonneville Speedway.

4.2 ▲ Trail ends at I-80, exit 4. Turn right for Wendover, left for Salt Lake City.

GPS: N 40°44.69' W 113°58.16'

▼ 0.3 SO Road on left to Danger Cave State Park.

3.9 ▲ SO Road on right to Danger Cave State Park.

▼ 1.1 TL Intersection. Turn left onto dirt road, following sign to Pilot Mountains and Silver Island Mountains. Straight goes to Bonneville Speedway.

3.1 ▲ TR T-intersection.

GPS: N 40°45.70' W 113°58.14'

▼ 1.7 SO Road on right.

2.5 ▲ SO Road on left.

▼ 1.9 BL Fork in road. Follow sign to Leppy Pass. Right is end of Northern #11: Silver Island Mountains Loop.

2.3 ▲ BR Track on left is end of Northern #11: Silver Island Mountains Loop.

GPS: N 40°46.17' W 113°58.76'

▼ 2.7 SO Track on left.

1.5 ▲ SO Track on right.

▼ 3.3 SO Track on left.

0.9 ▲ SO Track on right.

▼ 4.1 BR Track on left.

0.1 ▲ BL Track on right.

GPS: N 40°47.81' W 114°00.07'

▼ 4.2 SO Three-way intersection at Leppy Pass. Track on right is Northern #11: Silver Island Mountains Loop; track on left is

Northern Trail #10: Wendover to Lucin Trail

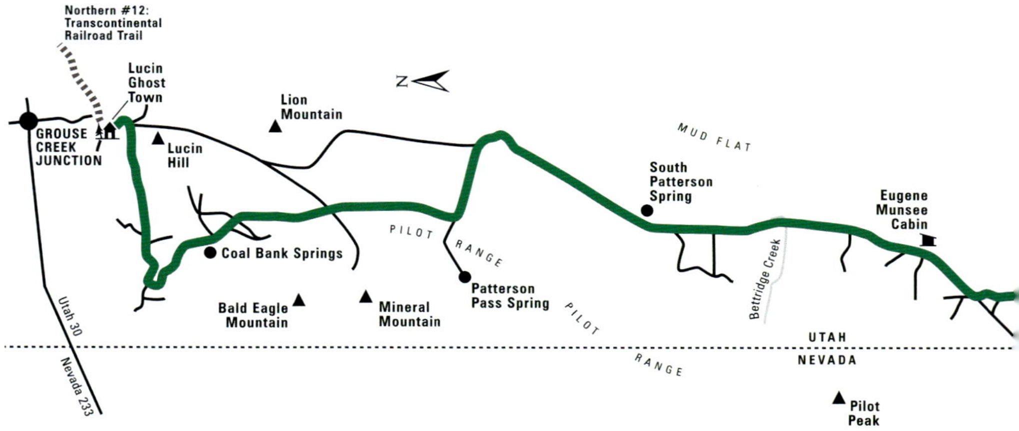

main road to Lucin. Zero trip meter and proceed north (straight) on unmarked road. (Return to this intersection and take main Lucin road if mud flats are impassable.)

0.0 ▲ Continue south.

GPS: N 40°47.89' W 114°00.03'

▼ 0.0 Continue north.

11.1 ▲ SO Leppy Pass. Track on left is Northern #11: Silver Island Mountains Loop. Zero trip meter.

▼ 0.3 SO Trail crosses.

10.7 ▲ SO Trail crosses.

▼ 2.4 SO Stock trough on left.

8.6 ▲ SO Stock trough on right.

▼ 11.1 TR Intersection with main Lucin road. Zero trip meter.

0.0 ▲ Continue toward mud flats.

GPS: N 40°57.71' W 114°00.75'

▼ 0.0 Continue toward Lucin.

16.5 ▲ TL Intersection. Zero trip meter and turn left. Main Lucin road continues straight. (Return to this intersection and take main Lucin road if mud flats are impassable.)

▼ 1.8 SO Track on right along fence line.

14.6 ▲ SO Track on left along fence line.

▼ 2.2 SO Information board about Eugene Munsee cabin on right.

14.3 ▲ SO Eugene Munsee cabin information board on left.

GPS: N 40°59.30' W 113°59.22'

▼ 16.5 TL Track on left to Patterson Pass. Zero trip meter.

0.0 ▲ Continue toward salt flats.

GPS: N 41°11.05' W 113°54.92'

▼ 0.0 Continue west.

2.6 ▲ TR Turn right onto larger, main Lucin road. Zero trip meter.

▼ 2.6 TR Intersection. Patterson Pass straight ahead. Zero trip meter.

0.0 ▲ Continue east.

GPS: N 41°11.75' W 113°57.75'

▼ 0.0 Continue toward Governors Spring.

4.3 ▲ TL Intersection. Zero trip meter.

▼ 0.2 SO Track on left.

4.1 ▲ BR Fork in road.

▼ 1.5 SO Track on left.

2.7 ▲ SO Track on right.

▼ 2.6 SO Track on left.

1.7 ▲ SO Track on right.

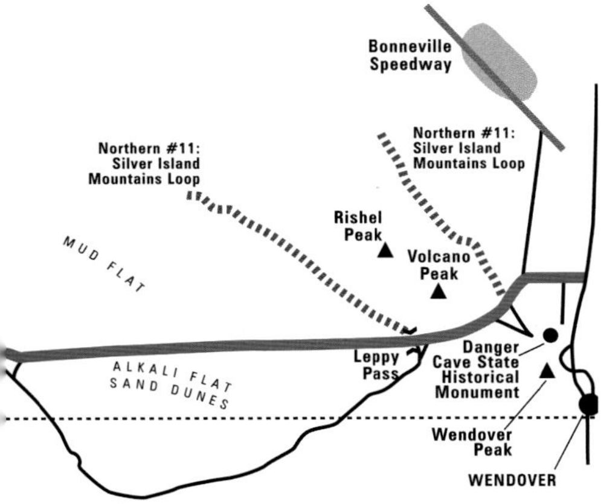

▼ 4.2 SO Track on left.
0.1 ▲ SO Track on right.

▼ 4.3 SO Intersection. Tracks on left and right. Follow sign to Coal Bank Springs. Zero trip meter.
0.0 ▲ Continue south.
GPS: N 41°15.33' W 113°57.51'

▼ 0.0 Continue north toward Coal Bank Springs.
6.5 ▲ SO Intersection. Track on right and left. Zero trip meter.

▼ 1.7 SO Track on left.
4.9 ▲ SO Track on right.
GPS: N 41°16.79' W 113°57.59'

▼ 2.9 BR Fork in road. Left travels through wash.
3.6 ▲ SO Road enters on right.

▼ 3.7 BL Track on right, then Coal Bank Springs and stock trough. Follow track behind trough.
2.8 ▲ BR Stock trough and Coal Bank Springs. Then track on left.
GPS: N 41°18.27' W 113°58.43'

▼ 5.0 SO Corral and stock trough on left and track on right.
1.5 ▲ SO Track on left. Corral and stock trough on right.
GPS: N 41°19.23' W 113°59.01'

▼ 5.7 BR Track on left.
0.8 ▲ SO Track on right.

▼ 6.3 BR Track on left.
0.2 ▲ SO Track on right.
GPS: N 41°19.89' W 114°00.14'

▼ 6.5 TR Intersection. Zero trip meter.
0.0 ▲ Continue south.
GPS: N 41°20.09' W 114°00.13'

▼ 0.0 Continue east on larger road.
5.8 ▲ TL Track on left. This can be hard to see. Zero trip meter.

▼ 1.1 SO Track on right.
4.7 ▲ SO Track on left.

▼ 1.2 SO Track on right.
4.6 ▲ SO Track on left.

▼ 1.3 SO Track on right.
4.5 ▲ SO Track on left.

▼ 2.1 SO Track on right.
3.7 ▲ SO Track on left.

▼ 5.1 TL T-intersection with main Lucin Road.
0.7 ▲ TR Road on right.
GPS: N 41°20.56' W 113°54.21'

▼ 5.3 SO Travel through Lucin.
0.5 ▲ SO Leave Lucin.

▼ 5.4 BL Cattle guard. Then track on right.
0.4 ▲ BR Track on left. Then cattle guard.

▼ 5.6 SO Lucin railroad siding building.
0.2 ▲ SO Lucin railroad siding building.

▼ 5.8 Trail ends at railroad tracks. This is start of Northern #12: Transcontinental Railroad Trail.
0.0 ▲ At railroad tracks near Lucin at the end of Northern #12: Transcontinental Railroad Trail, zero trip meter and proceed south. To get to the start of the trail from Utah 30, follow signs at Grouse Creek Junction south to Lucin.
GPS: N 41°21.05' W 113°54.50'

NORTHERN REGION TRAIL #11

Silver Island Mountains Loop

STARTING POINT Northern #10: Wendover to Lucin Trail
FINISHING POINT Northern #10: Wendover to Lucin Trail
TOTAL MILEAGE 49.4 miles
UNPAVED MILEAGE 49.4 miles
DRIVING TIME 3 hours
ELEVATION RANGE 4,200–4,800 feet
USUALLY OPEN Year-round
DIFFICULTY RATING 1
SCENIC RATING 8
REMOTENESS RATING +1

Special Attractions

- Easy but remote trail along the old shoreline of Lake Bonneville.
- Wonderful, unusual scenery, from the dead-flat desert and mud flats that were once the bottom of Lake Bonneville to the mountains that jut 6,000 feet skyward.
- Dozens of side trails to explore.
- Historic route of the Donner-Reed Party.

History

About 200 million years ago, the Silver Island Mountains began to push themselves up from the bottom of Lake Bonneville. As the mountains uplifted, the surrounding salt flats were kept smooth under the weight of the lake. Millions of years later, after the ever-changing Lake Bonneville had receded and returned once again to flood most of northern Utah, the Silver Island Mountains rose out of the water as an island. A crease that has been eroded into the mountain's lower slope provides geologists with evidence of this ancient shoreline.

Over the years, igneous rock intrusions have forced their way into the Paleozoic rocks of the Silver Island Mountains. These intrusions created the many valuable deposits of minerals in the mountains, which have been extensively mined. The most abundant mineral has been tungsten, while smaller amounts of copper, gold, silver, and lead have also been extracted from the mountains.

Looking across the salt and mud flats to Floating Island

Looking across to the Pilot Range from Donner-Reed Pass

There is little in the way of human history near the remote Silver Island Mountains. For the most part, people have just passed through on their way west. One infamous group of settlers to do so was the California-bound Donner-Reed Party in 1846. After experiencing many delays crossing the barren salt flats and Silver Island Mountains, the party was eventually caught in the early snowfall of the Sierra Nevadas near the California border. Most of the group died in the Sierras, and the survivors were forced to eat their dead or perish themselves.

Description

The Silver Island Mountains Loop begins and ends on Northern #10: Wendover to Lucin Trail. This 49.4-mile trail makes a clockwise loop around the Silver Island Mountains and through a desert environment. As you drive along the remote and barren trail, keep an eye out for the old shoreline of Lake Bonneville, which is marked by an eroded line along the side of the mountains where ancient waves once lapped.

The trail starts out along a wide, maintained gravel road that proceeds through saltbush and sparse grasses on the western side of the mountains with views across the mud flats. The flats are at an elevation of 4,200 feet and the distant Pilot Range rises up to 10,716 feet above sea level. After 8.6 miles, the road narrows but remains relatively flat and easy.

The trail is so flat, in fact, that you may be tempted to travel at speeds of 30 mph and up. However, appearances can be deceiving and very dangerous. A number of small wash crossings have dug narrow channels into the road. If you hit one of these dips too fast, it could do serious damage to the front end of your vehicle. Make sure to constantly scan the road ahead and keep your speed in check.

The Donner-Reed Pass marks the north end of the loop. Although it is not very high, the pass gives you a remarkably broad view of the Silver Island Mountains. As the trail winds around the east side of the mountains you can see Floating Island across the Great Salt Lake Desert. The appropriateness of the name will quickly become obvious as it seems to float above the shimmering desert flats.

Overall, the Silver Island Mountains Loop is rather easy, although after rains, some sections may become muddy and pres-

Silver Island Loop rock formations

ent some difficulty. There are also a number of side trails to explore along the way. The trail eventually makes its way back to Northern #10: Wendover to Lucin Trail, which provides access to Wendover and I-80.

Current Road Information

West Wendover Tourism & Convention Bureau
PO Box 2825
West Wendover, NV 89883
(775) 664-3138

BLM Salt Lake Field Office
2370 South Decker Lake Boulevard West Valley, UT 84119
(801) 977-4300

Map References

BLM Bonneville Salt Flats, Newfoundland Mtn.
USGS 1:24,000 Tetzlaff Peak, Silver Island Pass, Graham Peak, Crater Island, Floating Island, Bonneville Racetrack
1:100,000 Bonneville Salt Flats, Newfoundland Mtn.
Utah Atlas & Gazetteer, p. 14
Utah Road & Recreation Atlas, p. 40

Route Directions

▼ 0.0 On Northern #10: Wendover to Lucin Trail, 4.2 miles from I-80 at the three-way intersection, turn right on unmarked road and zero trip meter.
8.6 ▲ Trail ends at Northern #10: Wendover to Lucin Trail. Go straight for I-80.
GPS: N 40°47.89' W 114°00.03'

▼ 0.1 SO Track on right.
8.5 ▲ SO Track on left.

▼ 0.3 SO Track on right.
8.3 ▲ SO Track on left.

▼ 0.4 SO Tracks on right and left.
8.2 ▲ SO Tracks on left and right.

▼ 0.7 SO Track on right.

Northern Trail #11: Silver Island Mountains Loop

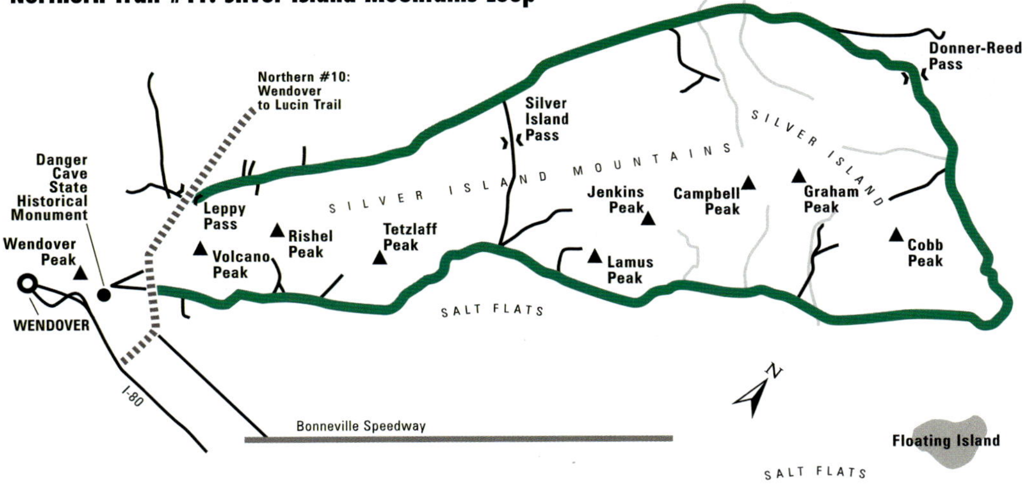

7.9 ▲ SO Track on left.

▼ 2.1 SO Track on left.
6.5 ▲ SO Track on right.

▼ 5.3 SO Track on right.
3.3 ▲ SO Track on left.

▼ 8.6 SO Track on right to Silver Island Pass. Connects with return loop of this trail. Zero trip meter.
0.0 ▲ Continue southwest.
GPS: N 40°54.38° W 113°55.23'

▼ 0.0 Continue northeast.
10.8 ▲ Track on left to Silver Island Pass. Zero trip meter.

▼ 0.9 SO Track on right.
9.8 ▲ SO Track on left.

▼ 2.7 SO Track on right.
8.1 ▲ SO Track on left.

▼ 4.2 SO Track on right.
6.6 ▲ SO Track on left.
GPS: N 40°57.78' W 113°53.12'

▼ 7.1 SO Sheep corral on left.
3.7 ▲ SO Sheep corral on right.

▼ 10.8 BR Fork in road. Zero trip meter.
0.0 ▲ Continue along main road.
GPS: N 41°00.65' W 113°46.92'

▼ 0.0 Continue along main road.
11.1 ▲ BL Road on right. Zero trip meter.

▼ 0.1 SO Roads on left and right.
11.0 ▲ SO Roads on right and left.

▼ 0.3 SO Donner-Reed Pass.
10.8 ▲ SO Donner-Reed Pass.
GPS: N 41°00.59' W 113°46.54'

▼ 0.8 BL Track on right.
10.3 ▲ BR Main road veers right. Track straight on.

▼ 2.3 SO Track on right.
8.8 ▲ SO Track on left.

▼ 2.7 BL Track on right.
8.4 ▲ SO Track on left.
GPS: N 40°59.60' W 113°44.25'

▼ 11.1 BR Track on left to Floating Island. Zero trip meter.
0.0 ▲ Continue straight ahead.
GPS: N 40°55.76' W 113°43.10'

▼ 0.0 Continue southwest.
9.8 ▲ BL Track on right to Floating Island. Zero trip meter.

▼ 3.0 SO Track on right.
6.7 ▲ SO Track on left.

▼ 9.8 SO Silver Island Pass road on right. Zero trip meter.
0.0 ▲ Continue northeast.
GPS: N 40°51.72' W 113°52.53'

▼ 0.0 Continue southwest.
9.1 ▲ SO Silver Island Pass road on left. Connects with return loop of this trail. Zero trip meter.

▼ 1.1 SO Track on right.
8.0 ▲ SO Track on left.

▼ 4.4 SO Track on right.
4.7 ▲ SO Track on left.

▼ 5.7 SO Track on right.
3.4 ▲ SO Track on left.

▼ 6.0 SO Track on right.
3.1 ▲ SO Track on left.

▼ 6.2 SO Track on right.
2.9 ▲ SO Track on left.

▼ 6.5 SO Track on right.
2.6 ▲ SO Track on left.

▼ 8.5 SO Track on right.
0.6 ▲ SO Track on left.

▼ 8.6 SO Track on right.
0.5 ▲ SO Track on left.

▼ 8.9 BL Track on right.
0.2 ▲ BR Track on left.

▼ 9.1 Trail ends at Northern #10: Wendover to Lucin Trail. Turn right for Lucin, left for Bonneville Speedway and I-80.
0.0 ▲ On Northern #10: Wendover to Lucin Trail, 1.9 miles from I-80, zero trip meter and proceed northeast.
GPS: N 40°46.17' W 113°58.76'

Transcontinental Railroad Trail

STARTING POINT Lucin, end of Northern #10: Wendover to Lucin Trail
FINISHING POINT Golden Spike National Historic Site at Promontory Point
TOTAL MILEAGE 87.1 miles
UNPAVED MILEAGE 87.1 miles
DRIVING TIME 5 hours
ELEVATION RANGE 4,200–4,800 feet
USUALLY OPEN Year-round
DIFFICULTY RATING 2
SCENIC RATING 8
REMOTENESS RATING +2

A typical straight-arrow section of the Transcontinental Railroad

Old trestle along the railroad grade

Special Attractions

- Traveling a portion of the original transcontinental railroad.
- Visiting the town sites and cemeteries along the old railroad grade.
- Golden Spike National Historic Site at Promontory Point.

History

Much like the Pony Express, the transcontinental railroad has gone down in history as a testament to 19th-century America's determination to link East and West over the treacherous mountain region. Completed on May 10, 1869, at Promontory Summit, the transcontinental railroad shortened the once expensive and arduous cross-country journey to four days at the relatively cheap cost of $100.

In 1902, officials of the Southern Pacific Railroad, which had taken over the Central Pacific, decided to shorten the route by crossing the Great Salt Lake, which meant laying an additional 102 miles of track between Ogden and Lucin, including 12 miles of trestle over the Great Salt Lake. The route was not only shortened by 44 miles, it made the railroad track more level, which saved in fuel costs.

The $8-million Lucin Cutoff took 3,000 men a year and a half to complete. When finished in 1904, it signaled the demise of the original line that ran around the northern rim of the lake, though this section was still used as an alternate route during bad weather. The original railroad tracks from Lucin to Corinne remained in place until 1942, when they were taken up and contributed as scrap metal to the war effort. A ceremonial pulling up of the "last spike" occurred in 1942 in much the same fashion as the ceremonies in May 1869.

Wheeler survey marker

Close-up of USGS medalion on survey maker

While the faster route across Utah was welcomed by railroad officials and passengers, it meant the end for many towns along the original line. Two of the more prominent towns were Terrace and Kelton. Both were home to many settlers and permanent facilities before the Lucin Cutoff dealt the local economies their deathblow. Many other railroad camps and smaller settlements, such as Watercress, also died because of the bypass. One such camp was Rozel, which was the site of the Central Pacific's most productive day. In a race to lay more track than the Union Pacific, the Central Pacific set a record by putting down over 10 miles of track in a single day. To fully appreciate this feat, bear in mind that each 28-foot section of track weighed approximately 522 pounds —a total of 88 tons of rail!

Seven acres of land near Promontory, the meeting point of the original transcontinental line, was set aside in 1957 as a National Historic Site. That site was enlarged in 1965 to 2,176 acres and a road was put in to prepare for centennial celebrations in 1969. Finally, a visitors center was added in 1980, which has an exhibit on the history of the transcontinental railroad.

Description

From Lucin, the trail runs dead straight along a single-lane, elevated railroad bed. In most places it's only a few feet higher than the surrounding terrain, but along some stretches it can be as high as six or seven feet, which makes passing impossible. However, the road typically breaks away from the railroad bed at old trestles every quarter mile or so, and these allow for passing. The trestles are typically no more than four or five feet high and were used by the railroad to cross small washes. Beside the old trestles, you can see many old railroad ties and spikes strewn along this early part of the trail. Although they are interesting artifacts, they can also be hazards to your vehicle, and tire punctures are not at all uncommon.

There are no trees in this area and hardly any shrubs. The landscape is mostly desert grassland with some dotted saltbush. The vast plains seem to roll on for miles and miles as the tops of mountain ranges rise up in the distance.

The road remains easy and rates a difficulty level of 2 only because of occasional ruts and eroded areas. Although it is not what you would typically refer to as scenic, the Transcontinental Railroad Trail remains interesting because of its incredible history. Today, it is almost inconceivable to imagine thousands of men building the railroad by hand in this vast and remote setting.

The road proceeds toward Kelton through grassland and sagebrush along gentle rolling hills. In some areas, such as around Kelton, potholes become prevalent along the railbed. Keep your eye out for a side road about 20 or 30 yards north of the trail if you want a smoother ride along the same route.

As you continue along the Central Pacific grade, you can look to the right to see some of the Union Pacific grade. Due to the fierce competition between the two railroad companies to complete more of the route than the other, they ended up overshooting each other for about 200 miles. The Union Pacific's track was deemed superfluous and was eventually abandoned.

The trail passes signs for the BLM Transcontinental Railroad Backcountry Byway on its way to the Golden Spike National Historic Site. After passing the sign for Rozel, the trail ends at the information board and the junction with the West Grade Auto Tour, which runs up behind the board on a small road marked "one way." This seasonal auto tour runs along the old Central Pacific grade before coming to an end at the Golden Spike National Historic Site.

Grave stone in Terrace Cemetery

Tread Lightly! in and around Terrace Cemetery

TRANSCONTINENTAL RAILROAD

Prior to May 10, 1869, there were only three options for individuals who wished to travel from one coast of the United States to the other: Travelers could journey six months via boat around the length of South America; they could walk the grueling cross-country trek that took five to seven months; or they could take a very bumpy and expensive 24-day stagecoach ride. However, after the fateful day when two trains met in Promontory, Utah, customers could buy a first-class ticket on the transcontinental railroad for $100 and make the journey in four comfortable days.

In 1862, Congress approved a venture to create the first coast-to-coast railroad in the United States. Two railroad companies were authorized for its construction: the Union Pacific in the East and the Central Pacific in the West. At this time the Civil War was still winding down and the California gold rush was still on. The railway companies were faced with a labor shortage, so they hired large numbers of immigrants to begin the work. Union Pacific hired over a thousand Irishmen and their beasts of burden, while Central Pacific shipped in 10,000 Chinese laborers, who worked for just $30 per month. Once the Civil War ended, German and Italian immigrants as well as war veterans and ex-slaves also became railroad employees. Construction in the east began in Omaha, Nebraska, with Union Pacific workers laying an average of one mile of rail per day over the flat Nebraska plains. Central Pacific employees experienced a much different and taxing job of laying rails over the treacherous Sierra Nevadas.

Joining of the rails ceremony at Promontory, 1869

Seven years after the railway's initial planning, a solid gold stake ceremoniously marked the completion of the first transcontinental railroad. Engraved upon that famous stake were the words, "May God continue the unity of our country as this Railroad unites the two great oceans of the world." Two trains, Central Pacific's *Jupiter* and Union Pacific's *119,* triumphantly came together, facing each other, joining two oceans and a world of individuals across what had previously been a vast and daunting expanse. A shorter route eventually closed the Promontory station, and the original rails were sold as scrap metal during World War II.

Golden Spike monument

Current Road Information

Golden Spike National Historic Site
PO Box 897
Brigham City, UT 84302
(435) 471-2209

BLM Salt Lake Field Office
2370 South Decker Lake Boulevard West
Valley, UT 84119
(801) 977-4300

Map References

BLM Newfoundland Mtn., Grouse Creek, Tremonton
USGS 1:24,000 Lucin, Lucin NE, Bovine, Terrace Mtn. West, Prohibition Spring, Red Dome, Matlin, Hogup Bar, Peplin Flats, Crocodile Mtn. NE, Kelton Pass SE, Locomotive Springs, Monument Point, Lake Ridge, Rozel
1:100,000 Newfoundland Mtn., Grouse Creek, Tremonton
Utah Atlas & Gazetteer, pp. 9, 10, 11
Utah Road & Recreation Atlas, pp. 34, 35, 36

Route Directions

▼ 0.0 At end of Northern #10: Wendover to Lucin Trail in Lucin, zero trip meter at railroad tracks and proceed north. Follow sign marked "Old Railroad Grade and Highway 30."
22.5 ▲ Trail ends at railroad tracks at Lucin. This is start of Northern #10: Wendover to Lucin Trail. To get to the start of the trail from Utah 30, follow signs at Grouse Creek Junction south to Lucin.
GPS: N 41°21.05' W 113°54.50'

▼ 0.8 TR Intersection. Two tracks on right; take the first one along the old railroad grade.
21.7 ▲ TL Turn left toward Lucin.
GPS: N 41°21.36' W 113°53.74'

▼ 1.3 SO Lucin information board on left.
21.2 ▲ SO Lucin information board on right.

▼ 2.8 SO Track crosses.
19.7 ▲ SO Track crosses.

▼ 6.9 SO Cattle guard.
15.6 ▲ SO Cattle guard.

▼ 8.5 SO Track crosses.
14.0 ▲ SO Track crosses.

▼ 12.1 SO Bovine railroad siding.
10.4 ▲ SO Bovine railroad siding.
GPS: N 41°26.01' W 113°41.81'

▼ 17.6 SO Walden railroad siding.
4.9 ▲ SO Walden railroad siding.
GPS: N 41°28.26' W 113°35.98'

▼ 20.0 BR Intersection with road on left. Then cattle guard and Watercress railroad siding.
2.5 ▲ BL Cattle guard and Watercress railroad siding. Road on right marked to Utah 30.

▼ 21.7 SO Cross over trestle.
0.8 ▲ SO Cross over trestle.
GPS: N 41°29.90' W 113°31.78'

▼ 22.0 SO Cross through wash.
0.5 ▲ SO Cross through wash.

▼ 22.5 SO Old town site of Terrace. Zero trip meter.
0.0 ▲ Continue northeast.
GPS: N 41°30.23' W 113°30.96'

▼ 0.0 Continue southwest.
29.2 ▲ SO Old town site of Terrace. Zero trip meter.

▼ 0.5 SO Terrace cemetery on right.
28.7 ▲ SO Terrace cemetery on left.
GPS: N 41°30.44' W 113°30.39'

▼ 1.4 SO Old Terrace railroad siding.
27.8 ▲ SO Old Terrace railroad siding.

▼ 2.7 SO Track on right.
26.5 ▲ SO Track on left.
GPS: N 41°31.81' W 113°29.11'

Northern Trail #12: Transcontinental Railroad Trail

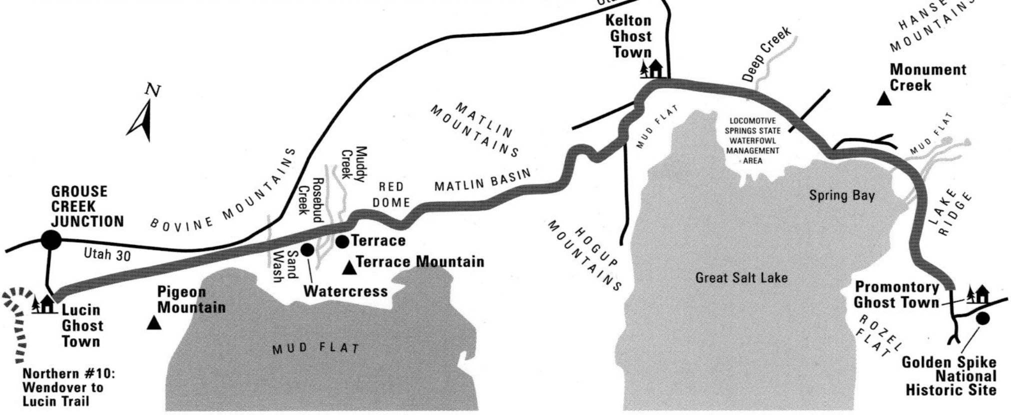

▼ 2.8 SO Track on left to Utah 30.
26.4 ▲ SO Track on right to Utah 30.

▼ 6.0 SO Red Dome railroad siding.
23.2 ▲ SO Red Dome railroad siding.

▼ 6.9 SO Track on left.
22.3 ▲ SO Track on right.

▼ 10.2 SO Matlin railroad siding.
19.0 ▲ SO Matlin railroad siding.
GPS: N 41°33.55' W 113°21.58'

▼ 12.9 SO Old corral on left.
16.3 ▲ SO Old corral on right.

▼ 15.1 SO Romola railroad siding.
14.1 ▲ SO Romola railroad siding.
GPS: N 41°35.44' W 113°16.54'

▼ 17.7 SO Intersection with CR 13. Right goes to Hogup Mountains.
11.5 ▲ SO Intersection with CR 13. Left goes to Hogup Mountains.
GPS: N 41°36.32' W 113°13.78'

▼ 18.2 SO Track on left.
11.0 ▲ SO Track on right.

▼ 19.8 SO Ombey railroad siding.
9.4 ▲ SO Ombey railroad siding.

▼ 21.5 BR Track on left.
7.7 ▲ BL Track on right.

▼ 22.7 BR Bear right onto side road to Kelton. Actual railroad grade continues straight.
6.5 ▲ BL Continue along railroad grade.
GPS: N 41°38.85' W 113°11.45'

▼ 25.9 TL T-intersection. Road on right.
3.3 ▲ TR Intersection.
GPS: N 41°40.65' W 113°09.16'

▼ 27.2 SO Track on left.
2.0 ▲ SO Track on right.

▼ 27.4 SO Old railroad grade crosses.
1.8 ▲ SO Old railroad grade crosses.
GPS: N 41°41.93' W 113°09.15'

▼ 28.4 SO Cattle guard.
0.8 ▲ SO Cattle guard.

▼ 29.2 TR T-intersection. Zero trip meter.
0.0 ▲ Continue southwest.
GPS: N 41°43.23' W 113°08.58'

▼ 0.0 Continue northeast.
2.8 ▲ TL Intersection. Road continues straight ahead. Turn left and zero trip meter.

▼ 2.4 TR Intersection.
0.4 ▲ TL Intersection. Follow sign to Terrace and Hogup Mountains.
GPS: N 41°44.84' W 113°06.68'

Crossing one of the many trestle bridges left over from the Transcontinental Railroad

▼ 2.5 SO Two tracks on left. Kelton Boot Hill Cemetery on right.
0.3 ▲ SO Kelton Boot Hill Cemetery on left. Two tracks on right.

▼ 2.6 BL Bear left onto railroad grade.
0.2 ▲ BR Old railroad grade continues straight (closed to vehicles).

▼ 2.7 SO Track on right and two tracks on left. Follow diversion around trestle bridge.
0.1 ▲ SO Two tracks on right and one track on left. Follow diversion around trestle bridge.

▼ 2.8 SO Track on left. Information board on right. Old town site of Kelton (Indian Creek) railroad siding. Zero trip meter and continue past road on left to Utah 30.
0.0 ▲ Continue southwest toward Kelton Cemetery.
GPS: N 41°44.78' W 113°06.39'

▼ 0.0 Continue toward Promontory.
10.1 ▲ SO Road on right to Utah 30, then old town site of Kelton (Indian Creek) railroad siding. Information board on left. Track on right. Zero trip meter.

▼ 0.1 SO Wheeler Survey marker on left.
10.0 ▲ SO Wheeler Survey marker on right.

▼ 2.6 SO Trestle/cattle guard.
7.5 ▲ SO Cattle guard/trestle.
GPS: N 41°45.04' W 113°03.31'

▼ 5.4 SO Cross trestle.
4.7 ▲ SO Cross trestle.

▼ 6.2 SO Track crosses.
3.9 ▲ SO Track crosses.

▼ 8.8 SO Seco railroad siding on left.
1.3 ▲ SO Seco railroad siding on right.

▼ 9.7 SO Nella railroad siding on left.
0.4 ▲ SO Nella railroad siding on right.

▼ 10.1 SO Road crosses. Right goes to Locomotive Springs. Left to Snowville. Zero trip meter.
0.0 ▲ Continue southeast.
GPS: N 41°44.07' W 112°54.68'

▼ 0.0 Continue northwest.
12.2 ▲ SO Road crosses. Right goes to Snowville. Left to Locomotive Springs. Zero trip meter.

▼ 1.3 SO Track crosses.
10.9 ▲ SO Track crosses.

▼ 2.1 SO Track crosses.
10.1 ▲ SO Track crosses.

▼ 3.4 SO Track crosses.
8.8 ▲ SO Track crosses.

▼ 3.5 BL Bear left around gate, across cattle guard, to return to railway grade.
8.7 ▲ BR Gate across railroad grade. Bear right across cattle guard, then return to railroad grade.

▼ 3.7 SO Track crosses.
8.5 ▲ SO Track crosses.

▼ 4.1 SO Track crosses.
8.1 ▲ SO Track crosses.
GPS: N 41°42.18' W 112°50.56'

▼ 6.9 TL Old concrete foundation. Railroad grade continues straight, but access closed to vehicles through Salt Wells Wildlife Habitat Area.
5.3 ▲ TR Turn right at old concrete foundation onto railroad grade.
GPS: N 41°42.95' W 112°47.44'

▼ 7.1 BR Fork in road.
5.1 ▲ BL Road enters on right.

▼ 7.2 SO Road enters on left.
5.0 ▲ BL Fork in road. Bear left to return to railroad grade.
GPS: N 41°43.17' W 112°47.36'

▼ 7.6 TR Road on right.
4.6 ▲ TL T-intersection.
GPS: N 41°43.37' W 112°46.95'

▼ 7.7 SO Cattle guard.
4.5 ▲ SO Cattle guard.

▼ 11.9 SO Cattle guard.
0.3 ▲ SO Cattle guard.

▼ 12.2 TR Road on right. Straight is alternative route to Golden Spike National Historic Site. Zero trip meter.
0.0 ▲ Continue toward Kelton.

GPS: N 41°42.08′ W 112°41.89′

▼ 0.0 Continue on railroad grade.
10.3 ▲ TL T-intersection. Right returns to Golden Spike National Historic Site. Follow sign to Kelton. Zero trip meter.

▼ 0.4 SO Track on right.
9.9 ▲ SO Track on left.

▼ 1.4 SO Track on left.
8.9 ▲ SO Track on right.

▼ 1.5 BL Road enters on right.
8.8 ▲ BR Road forks. Old railroad grade bears left; closed to vehicles through Salt Wells Wildlife Habitat Area.

GPS: N 41°40.84′ W 112°42.42′

▼ 4.9 SO Cattle guard.
5.4 ▲ SO Cattle guard.

▼ 5.5 SO Cattle guard.
4.8 ▲ SO Cattle guard.

▼ 6.0 SO Cattle guard.
4.3 ▲ SO Cattle guard.

▼ 6.7 SO Centre railroad siding.
3.6 ▲ SO Centre railroad siding.

▼ 7.7 SO Road on right. Then cattle guard.
2.6 ▲ SO Cattle guard. Then road on left.

GPS: N 41°35.87′ W 112°40.97′

▼ 8.8 SO Track on left.
1.5 ▲ SO Track on right.

▼ 9.6 SO Rozel railroad siding.
0.7 ▲ SO Rozel railroad siding.

▼ 9.8 SO Cattle guard.
0.5 ▲ SO Cattle guard.

▼ 10.1 BR Leave Central Pacific grade.
0.2 ▲ BL Join Central Pacific grade.

▼ 10.2 BL Join Union Pacific grade.
0.1 ▲ BR Fork in road. Union Pacific grade bears left.

▼ 10.3 Pass the transcontinental railroad information board on right. Then trail ends at information board on left, which is also start of West Grade Auto Tour.
0.0 ▲ Proceed west out of driveway of Golden Spike National Historic Site at Promontory Point. At start of West Grade Auto Tour (which turns off to the right), zero trip meter and continue west along county gravel road. Pass information boards for the transcontinental railroad on left.

GPS: N 41°34.92′ W 112°38.24′

NORTHERN REGION TRAIL #13

Pony Express Trail

STARTING POINT Gold Hill
FINISHING POINT Camp Floyd/Stagecoach Inn State Park
TOTAL MILEAGE 129.7 miles
UNPAVED MILEAGE 110.6 miles
DRIVING TIME 5 hours
ELEVATION RANGE 4,200–6,200 feet
USUALLY OPEN Year-round
DIFFICULTY RATING 1
SCENIC RATING 8
REMOTENESS RATING +2

Special Attractions

- Historic route used by the Pony Express and Overland Stage.
- Extremely remote but easy route through desert terrain that has scarcely changed from the days of the Pony Express.

- Desert scenery reflecting the impact of the ancient Great Salt Lake.
- Rockhounding for geodes.

History

During its brief life, the Pony Express delivered mail across 1,900 miles of America's frontier from St. Joseph, Missouri, to Sacramento, California. The original route entered Utah in the northeast from southwestern Wyoming and ran through Salt Lake City, across the western desert, and finally exited into Nevada near Ibapah. Although the Pony Express operated for only 19 months between 1860 and 1861, it has survived in American folklore as a testament to early pioneer ingenuity, fortitude, and determination. Even after the Pony Express went out of business, the trail was used as an Overland Stage route for cross-country travelers.

The portion of the trail that runs through western Utah crosses remote, desert terrain that looks much the same today as it did when the Pony Express was the fastest means of communication between East and West. Mark Twain once made the journey in 1861 and commented on the region's ruggedness in his book *Roughing It.* Upon reaching the way station at Callao, Twain wrote, "When we reached the station on the farther verge of the desert [Callao], we were glad, for the first time, that the dictionary was along, because we never could have found language to tell how glad we were, in any sort of dictionary but an unabridged one with pictures in it" (Twain, 95-98).

Northern #13: Pony Express Trail follows along most of the 133-mile-long Pony Express Trail National Backcountry Byway from Ibapah to Fairfield. The trail begins in the well-preserved mining town of Gold Hill, where gold, copper, arsenic, and tungsten were discovered in the region. During its life, the town suffered several boom-and-bust

The makeshift stone fort at the Canyon Pony Express Station

Simpson Springs Pony Express Station

mining cycles as different ores came to prominence. In the early days, when gold was the town's main attraction, a young Jack Dempsey came to Gold Hill to find his fortune. As history shows, Dempsey made the right decision to leave the mines and search out his real fortune in the boxing ring.

As the trail continues across the desert floor, it passes the remains of many other way stations along the old Pony Express Trail. Although some have been restored, others are little more than markers maintained by the BLM. One of these is Canyon Station, which was the site of an Indian attack in July 1863. Both Pony Express riders and Overland Stage passengers faced the constant danger of being attacked by Gosiute Indians, through whose land they were crossing. The attack at Canyon Station resulted in the deaths of a stage driver and four soldiers. Afterward, the Gosiutes burned the station to the ground.

Other way stations along the route—such as Willow Springs, Fish Springs, and Simpson Springs—were known for their availability of fresh water. In the harsh desert, water was perhaps the most valuable resource. The 10,000-acre marsh near Fish Springs was acquired by the U.S. Fish and Wildlife Service in 1959. The nine impoundment pools that make up Fish Springs were completed in 1964. Today, Fish Springs is home to a large bird refuge that is visited by many species, including blue herons, snowy egrets, and Canadian geese.

Simpson Springs was named after Captain J. H. Simpson, the man who discovered the spring. The station was originally used as a stop along the old mail route before being used by the Pony Express. From

1939 to 1942, Simpson Springs was home to a Civilian Conservation Corps (CCC) camp. The young men of the CCC are responsible for many of the signs and markers along the Pony Express Trail, as well as the general improvement of the road.

Near Simpson Springs, the trail passes the Dugway Proving Grounds. Since the 1940s, there have been many questionable chemical and biological weapons tests at this base. In 1968, nerve gas was released and drifted beyond the base's boundaries, killing 6,000 sheep that were grazing nearby.

The trail winds to a close near Fairfield at the site of the historic Camp Floyd. It was here that Colonel Johnston's army camped during the so-called Utah War. In 1857, President Buchanan sent some 3,000 men into Utah in order to replace Brigham Young as territorial governor and quash a rumored Mormon uprising. Camp Floyd quickly became one of the largest non-Mormon settlements in Utah and was home to the state's first non-Mormon newspaper. The restored Stagecoach Inn was originally built in 1858 by John Carson to house officers and other influential visitors. Once the bloodless "war" was over in the summer of 1858, the camp was soon deserted as troops were sent back East to fight in the Civil War.

Description

To get to the start of the Pony Express Trail, take I-80 to Wendover, then turn onto Alt US 93 south for about 24 miles (crossing into Nevada) until it intersects with a paved road to Ibapah. Turn left here and drive 15.2 miles until you come to the intersection with the unpaved Gold Hill Road. The trail starts at the abandoned general store in Gold Hill, 11.1 miles from the intersection of Gold Hill Road and the road to Ibapah. There are no

Expansive view form Digway Pass on the Pony Express Route

THE PONY EXPRESS

On April 3, 1860, the first riders of the Pony Express set out across the West. Opened and run by the firm of Russell, Majors, and Waddell, the Pony Express lasted only a brief 19 months. Yet for its short existence, it offered transcontinental mail delivery within 10 days, an exciting prospect since mail delivered by stagecoach usually took three weeks. Twenty of the 190 stations that ran from St. Joseph, Missouri, to Sacramento, California, were established in Utah.

Map of the Pony Express Route

The Pony Express only succeeded because of the extraordinary efforts of its riders, stationmasters, and work hands. Because the horses could efficiently carry only a relatively light load, riders had to keep to a weight of 120 pounds or less. They were equipped with a knife, revolver, horn, and some jerky. The land traversed by these men was some of the most desolate terrain in the country, and the riders would travel 100 to 125 miles daily (and nightly), braving Indian attacks and rough weather. It is said that Major Howard Egan, director of the Pony Express in Utah, once rode through a treacherous night of rain and sleet in which he and his horse fell off a bridge and carried on to cross the river before eventually making it to Salt Lake City. All this so the mail would go through on schedule.

Due to weight restrictions, the Pony Express was extremely expensive; one ounce of mail cost $5. As a result, much of the communication sent over the Pony Express was government or business related. Eventually, the expense of the operation outran income, and when no government subsidies came through, the Pony Express was forced to shut down with losses of about half a million dollars. Though its life was short, the Pony Express lives on in the national mindset, remembered as the first cross-country mail service.

The Pony Express route snaking out of Overland Canyon

facilities in Gold Hill, or at any point along the trail, so make sure you come prepared with plenty of gas, water, and food. The trail continues past a number of old Pony Express way stations and historical markers as it unfolds through miles of desert country and open range. Although the road has been well traveled and can be negotiated by a passenger car in good weather, the region is still no less remote than it was over a hundred years ago during the days of the Pony Express.

Leave the general store in Gold Hill on the road to Ibapah. After 5 miles the trail connects with the Pony Express Scenic Byway at the Overland Canyon turnoff. Turn left onto the byway and continue along the well-maintained county road.

As happens frequently along this route, the scenic byway only approximates the original route used by the Pony Express and Overland Stage, which runs a little southwest of the scenic byway. To travel along a short section of the old route, continue past the scenic byway along the road to Ibapah for three-quarters of a mile. From here, turn left onto a faint track. This is the actual route used by the Pony Express and Overland Stage and cuts the corner of the route now used by the main road. Almost immediately, the track splits in two, with the more defined track heading southwest toward the hill while the less-traveled Pony Express and Overland Stage route stays in the valley and heads southeast. After 2.2 miles along this faint trail, there is short dead-end track on the right that goes to a Pony Express commemorative pylon. The trail then reconnects with the scenic byway at the 2.1-mile mark. This 2.3-mile diversion trail along the unimproved stage road rates a 2 for difficulty because of a wash crossing and difficult navigation caused by the faintness of the trail.

Continuing along the scenic byway, you pass Canyon Station, Round Hill Station, and Willow Springs Station before reaching Callao. There are a number of original buildings from the Overland Stage era in Callao. Some are falling down, and others have remained in rather good shape and are still inhabited. However, note that all of Callao's buildings are on private property, so admire the structures from the trail, but do not go up to them.

The trail continues past Fish Springs, which is home to a large national bird sanctuary. Ornithologists and amateur bird watchers alike will find plenty to see in this unique desert oasis. After passing the Pony Express way station at Fish Springs, proceed past Black Rock Station to a road on the left signed to a geode field. At the field, you can hunt around for these bizarre rock formations. Although giving the appearance of plain rocks, geodes can be broken open to reveal hollowed-out centers that house fascinating crystal structures.

Because of the length of the trail, you may wish to take two days to drive it. If you need a place to camp overnight, there is fresh water and a campground at Simpson Springs Station. There are foundations of many old buildings at Simpson Springs as well as a restored Pony Express station and a historic marker. A few miles after the way station at Simpson Springs, you can look about 11 miles to the northwest to the Dugway Proving Grounds.

The trail ends at Camp Floyd/Stagecoach Inn State Park. Although not much is left of this military camp, you can still visit the cemetery, commissary, and the restored Stagecoach Inn.

Current Road Information

BLM Salt Lake Field Office
2370 South Decker Lake Boulevard West
Valley, UT 84119
(801) 977-4300

Map References

BLM Wildcat Mtn., Fish Springs, Lynndyl, Rush Valley
USGS 1:24,000 Gold Hill, Clifton, Goshute Canyon, Callao, Mud Lake Reservoir, Boyd Station, Fish Springs SW, Fish Springs NW, Fish Springs SE, Fish Springs NE, Dugway Range SW, Dugway Pass, Dugway Range NE, Table Mtn., Coyote Springs, Simpson Springs, Indian Peaks, Onaqui Mtn. South, Lookout Pass, Faust, Vernon NE, Fivemile Pass, Cedar Fort
1:100,000 Wildcat Mtn., Fish Springs, Lynndyl, Rush Valley
Utah Atlas & Gazetteer, pp. 22, 23, 24, 25
Utah Road & Recreation Atlas, pp. 48, 56, 57, 50, 51

Route Directions

▼ 0.0 From Alt US 93 in Nevada, take paved road to Ibapah to Gold Hill Road. Take Gold Hill Road to Gold Hill; in front of abandoned general store on corner, turn south on the road to Ibapah and zero trip meter.
5.0 ▲ Trail ends at intersection in Gold Hill. Left is Gold Hill Road, which leads to Alt US 93 and Wendover.

GPS: N 40°09.98' W 113°49.81'

▼ 1.0 SO Track on left.
4.0 ▲ SO Track on right.

▼ 1.2 SO Tracks on right.
3.8 ▲ SO Tracks on left.

▼ 2.4 SO Track on left.
2.5 ▲ SO Track on right.

▼ 3.9 SO Road on left, then track on right.
1.1 ▲ SO Track on left, then road on right.

▼ 4.1 SO Road on left.
0.8 ▲ SO Road on right.

▼ 5.0 TL Road on left and track on right. Straight goes 0.7 miles to a short section of original, unimproved Pony Express Trail (see description above). Zero trip meter and turn left.
0.0 ▲ Continue toward Gold Hill.

GPS: N 40°06.32' W 113°51.88'

Be prepared when traveling the old Pony Express route

▼ 0.0		Proceed southeast along Pony Express route.
5.6 ▲	TR	Intersecton. Zero trip meter and turn right.
▼ 1.3	SO	Road on left.
4.3 ▲	SO	Road on right.
▼ 2.1	SO	Track on right is a portion of actual, unimproved Pony Express route. 0.1 miles along that trail is a track on left that leads to an old, vandalized Pony Express marker.
3.5 ▲	SO	Track on left is portion of actual, unimproved Pony Express route. 0.1 miles along that trail is a track on left that leads to an old, vandalized Pony Express marker (see description above).
▼ 2.2	SO	Old Pony Express marker on right (100 yards from road).
3.4 ▲	SO	Old Pony Express marker on left (100 yards from road).
▼ 3.4	SO	Track on right.
2.2 ▲	SO	Track on left.
▼ 3.8	SO	Track on left.
1.8 ▲	SO	Track on right.
▼ 5.6	SO	Track on right to Pony Express Canyon Station and storyboards. Zero trip meter.
0.0 ▲		Continue along main road.
		GPS: N 40°02.69′ W 113°48.20′
▼ 0.0		Continue along main road.
8.0 ▲	SO	Track on left to Pony Express Canyon Station and storyboards. Zero trip meter.
▼ 4.8	SO	Track on right.
3.1 ▲	SO	Track on left.
▼ 6.8	SO	Six-mile Ranch on right. Springs behind ranch were used by the Pony Express.
1.1 ▲	SO	Six-mile Ranch on left. Springs behind ranch were used by the Pony Express.
▼ 6.9	BL	Road on right to ranch.
1.0 ▲	BR	Road forks.
▼ 8.0	TR	T-intersection. Zero trip meter.
0.0 ▲		Continue northwest.
		GPS: N 39°57.49′ W 113°43.87′
▼ 0.0		Continue toward Callao.
14.0 ▲	TL	Road on left. Zero trip meter.
▼ 3.7	SO	Cattle guard.
10.3 ▲	SO	Cattle guard.
▼ 4.0	TL	T-intersection. Then cross cattle guard.
10.0 ▲	TR	Cattle guard, then intersection.
		GPS: N 39°54.13′ W 113°43.45′

▼ 4.5 SO Willow Springs Station and historic marker on left.

9.5 ▲ SO Willow Springs Station and historic marker on right.

GPS: N 39°54.02' W 113°42.81'

▼ 4.8 SO Callao schoolhouse on left.

9.2 ▲ SO Callao schoolhouse on right.

▼ 6.4 SO Cattle guard.

7.6 ▲ SO Cattle guard.

▼ 11.2 SO Cattle guard.

2.7 ▲ SO Cattle guard.

▼ 13.0 SO Track on right.

1.0 ▲ SO Track on left.

▼ 14.0 SO Pull-off on left for Boyd Station. Road to Trout Creek and Partoun on right. Zero trip meter.

0.0 ▲ Continue toward Callao.

GPS: N 39°50.62' W 113°33.17'

▼ 0.0 Continue toward Fish Springs.

12.7 ▲ SO Pull-off on right for Boyd Station. Road to Trout Creek and Partoun on left. Zero trip meter.

▼ 0.1 SO Road on right.

12.6 ▲ BR Road forks.

▼ 3.2 SO Track on right.

9.4 ▲ SO Track on left.

▼ 4.4 SO Track on right.

8.3 ▲ SO Track on left.

▼ 4.7 SO Track on right.

7.9 ▲ SO Track on left.

▼ 9.5 SO Cattle guard. Entering Fish Springs National Wildlife Refuge.

3.1 ▲ SO Leaving Fish Springs National Wildlife Refuge. Cattle guard.

▼ 12.7 SO Historic marker for Fish Springs Pony Express Station on left. Track on right. Zero trip meter.

0.0 ▲ Continue on main road.

GPS: N 39°50.88' W 113°24.62'

▼ 0.0 Continue on main road.

10.1 ▲ SO Historic marker for Fish Springs Pony Express Station on right. Track on left. Zero trip meter.

▼ 0.7 SO Fish Springs National Wildlife Refuge headquarters on left.

9.4 ▲ SO Fish Springs National Wildlife Refuge headquarters on right.

▼ 1.7 SO Cattle guard.

8.4 ▲ SO Cattle guard.

▼ 2.0 SO Road to Sand Pass on right.

8.1 ▲ SO Road to Sand Pass on left.

▼ 6.2 SO Cattle guard. Leaving Fish Springs National Wildlife Refuge.

4.0 ▲ SO Entering Fish Springs National Wildlife Refuge. Cattle guard.

▼ 6.8 SO Road on right.

3.3 ▲ SO Road on left.

GPS: N 39°50.52' W 113°18.84'

▼ 10.1 SO Black Rock Pony Express Station monument on left. Zero trip meter.

0.0 ▲ Continue along main road.

GPS: N 39°52.68' W 113°16.24'

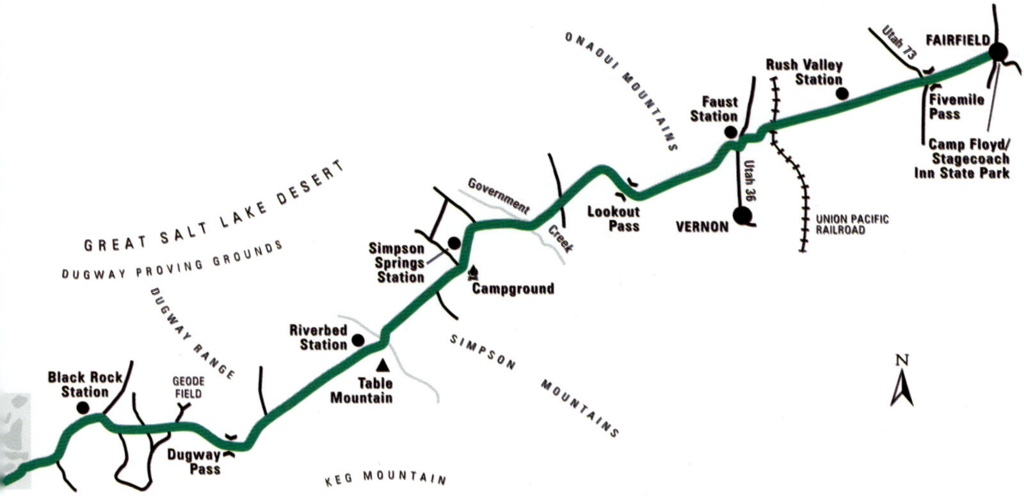

Northern Trail #13: Pony Express Trail

▼ 0.0 Continue along main road.
14.7 ▲ SO Black Rock Pony Express Station monument on right. Zero trip meter.

▼ 0.8 SO Road on left.
13.9 ▲ SO Road on right.

▼ 2.2 SO Track on right.
12.5 ▲ SO Track on left.

▼ 4.3 SO Tracks on right and left.
10.4 ▲ SO Tracks on left and right.

▼ 6.1 SO Track on right.
8.6 ▲ SO Track on left.

▼ 6.5 SO Track on right.
8.2 ▲ SO Track on left.

▼ 7.3 SO Road to geode field on left.
7.4 ▲ SO Road to geode field on right.
GPS: N 39°52.37' W 113°08.27'

▼ 12.3 SO Track on right.
2.4 ▲ SO Track on left.

▼ 14.3 SO Track on left.
0.4 ▲ SO Track on right.

▼ 14.7 SO Track on right. Zero trip meter.
0.0 ▲ Continue along main road.
GPS: N 39°53.08' W 113°01.74'

▼ 0.0 Continue along main road.
8.6 ▲ SO Track on left. Zero trip meter.

▼ 1.7 SO Track on left.
6.9 ▲ SO Track on right.

▼ 7.4 SO Track on right.
1.2 ▲ SO Track on left.

▼ 7.6 SO Track on right.
1.0 ▲ SO Track on left.

▼ 8.6 SO Track on left to Riverbed Pony Express Station historical marker. Zero trip meter.
0.0 ▲ Continue along main road.
GPS: N 39°57.58' W 112°53.67'

▼ 0.0 Continue along main road.
7.7 ▲ SO Track on right to Riverbed Pony Express Station historical marker. Zero trip meter.

▼ 0.2 SO Tracks on right and left.
7.4 ▲ SO Tracks on left and right.

▼ 5.4 SO Track on right.

2.2 ▲ SO Track on left.

▼ 7.7 SO Simpson Springs Pony Express Station marker on left. Public toilets, campground, and recreation area on right. Several old structures. Zero trip meter at historic marker.
0.0 ▲ Continue along main road.
GPS: N 40°02.34′ W 112°47.19′

▼ 0.0 Continue along main road.
15.4 ▲ SO Simpson Springs Pony Express Station marker on right. Public toilets, campground, and recreation area on left. Several old structures. Zero trip meter at historic marker.

▼ 3.2 SO Track on left to Dugway Proving Grounds.
12.2 ▲ SO Track on right to Dugway Proving Grounds.

▼ 9.3 SO Intersection. Right goes to Erickson Pass, left to Dugway.
6.1 ▲ SO Intersection. Left goes to Erickson Pass, right to Dugway.
GPS: N 40°06.17′ W 112°39.66′

▼ 12.6 BR Road on left to Dugway Proving Grounds.
2.8 ▲ BL Intersection. Bear left toward Callao and Fish Springs, following Pony Express route.
GPS: N 40°08.29′ W 112°37.03′

▼ 13.8 BR Road on left to Terra.
1.5 ▲ BL Road on right to Terra.

▼ 15.4 SO Lookout Pass Pony Express Station historical marker. Zero trip meter.
0.0 ▲ Continue along main road.
GPS: N 40°07.19′ W 112°34.56′

▼ 0.0 Continue toward Lookout Pass.
9.5 ▲ SO Lookout Pass Pony Express Station historical marker. Zero trip meter.

▼ 0.7 SO Lookout Pass.
8.8 ▲ SO Lookout Pass.

▼ 1.5 BL Fork in road. Right goes to Vernon.
8.0 ▲ SO Road enters on left.
GPS: N 40°06.74′ W 112°33.07′

▼ 7.1 SO Road on left to scenic view.
2.3 ▲ SO Road on right to scenic view.

▼ 8.8 TL T-intersection. Turn left onto Utah 36.
0.6 ▲ TR Turn onto gravel road.
GPS: N 40°09.92′ W 112°25.79′

▼ 9.5 TR Faust Pony Express Station historical marker on left. Zero trip meter.
0.0 ▲ Proceed south on Utah 36.
GPS: N 40°10.45′ W 112°25.58′

▼ 0.0 Proceed east on paved road opposite the historical marker.
7.4 ▲ TL Intersection with Utah 36. Cross road to Faust Pony Express Station historical marker. Zero trip meter.

▼ 2.0 SO Cross railroad tracks.
5.4 ▲ SO Cross railroad tracks.

▼ 7.4 SO Rush Valley Pony Express Station historical marker. Zero trip meter.
0.0 ▲ Continue along main road.
GPS: N 40°12.39′ W 112°17.55′

▼ 0.0 Continue along paved road.
11.0 ▲ SO Rush Valley Pony Express Station historical marker. Zero trip meter.

▼ 5.9 TR T-intersection with Utah 73.
5.1 ▲ TL Intersection.
GPS: N 40°13.85′ W 112°10.99′

▼ 10.9 TR Turn right onto 1500 North toward the Stagecoach Museum.
0.1 ▲ TL Turn left onto Utah 73.

▼ 11.0 Trail ends at Camp Floyd/Stagecoach Inn State Park and Museum.
0.0 ▲ In front of the Stagecoach Inn at Camp Floyd Pony Express Station marker, proceed west on paved road.
GPS: N 40°15.65′ W 112°05.54′

NORTHERN REGION TRAIL #14

Clear Creek Ridge Trail

STARTING POINT US 6, at the site of Tucker
FINISHING POINT Utah 31
TOTAL MILEAGE 27.6 miles
UNPAVED MILEAGE 27.6 miles
DRIVING TIME 1 hour
ELEVATION RANGE 6,200–9,200 feet
USUALLY OPEN May to November
DIFFICULTY RATING 1
SCENIC RATING 8
REMOTENESS RATING +0

Special Attractions

- Easy high-elevation scenic drive with good views.
- Wildflowers in spring and summer and wonderful fall colors.
- Many good backcountry campsites.

History

Although there is little evidence of the town now, the trail begins at Tucker, a once-important railroad town along the Denver & Rio Grande Western (D&RGW) Railroad. When the D&RGW decided to reroute the line in 1915 to avoid the steep grade up to Soldier Summit, Tucker was buried beneath large amounts of fillwork. All that remained of the once-booming town was a small station stop and a railroad siding. Over the years, Tucker cemetery, once located about a half mile from town along this trail, also vanished from the landscape.

Description

The Clear Creek Ridge Trail begins at the Tucker rest stop off US 6 and is one of the trails that makes up the popular route known as Skyline Drive. As you drive southwest from the Tucker rest stop, the trail climbs 3,000 feet along a 9-mile stretch of rough and bumpy road. Though some sections are rather narrow, the road is generally wide and easy to drive. The trail runs along an attractive, tree-lined forest road passing several stands of aspen around the 7-mile mark.

There are quite a few backcountry campsites along the way, especially in the first 10 miles. As the trail reaches the top of the plateau, the views open up over the countryside and extend into the distance. These expansive overlooks at the higher elevations of the Clear Creek Ridge Trail are well worth the trip.

For its entire length, the trail can be driven either by SUV or passenger car. To continue farther along Skyline Drive, take Utah 31 south for 4.8 miles and connect with the slightly more difficult, 3-rated Central #7:

A stand of aspens along Skyline Drive

Skyline Drive Trail. More information about this trail can be found in *Utah Trails: Central Region*.

Current Road Information

Manti-La Sal National Forest
Sanpete Ranger District
540 North Main Street
Ephraim, UT 84627
(435) 283-4151

Map References

BLM Nephi
USFS Manti-La Sal National Forest: Sanpete & Price Ranger Districts
USGS 1:24,000 Tucker, Mill Fork, C Canyon, Fairview Lakes
1:100,000 Nephi
Trails Illustrated, #701
Utah Atlas & Gazetteer, pp. 26, 36
Utah Road & Recreation Atlas, pp. 52, 60

Route Directions

▼ 0.0 On US 6, several miles north of Soldier Summit, turn into the Tucker rest stop. Bear right past the picnic area on Skyline Drive and zero trip meter on the bridge over Clear Creek. This is CR 150.
9.6 ▲ Trail ends at bridge near site of Tucker. US 6 is straight ahead; turn right for Soldier Summit, left for Spanish Fork.
GPS: N 39°56.13' W 111°11.97'

▼ 0.1 SO Cattle guard.
9.5 ▲ SO Cattle guard.

▼ 1.5 SO Track on right.
8.1 ▲ SO Track on left.

▼ 1.7 SO Track on right. Cross bridge over Clear Creek.
7.9 ▲ SO Cross bridge over Clear Creek. Track on left.

▼ 2.6 SO Entering Manti-La Sal National Forest; road becomes FR 150. Track on left.
7.0 ▲ SO Track on right. Leaving Manti-La Sal National Forest.

▼ 3.1 SO Track on left.
6.5 ▲ SO Track on right.

▼ 4.2 SO Track on left.
5.4 ▲ SO Track on right.

▼ 5.3 SO Track on left.
4.3 ▲ SO Track on right.

▼ 5.9 SO Track on right to backcountry campsites.
3.7 ▲ SO Track on left to backcountry campsites.

▼ 6.4–6.6 SO Tracks on right to several campsites.
3.0–3.2 ▲ SO Tracks on left to several campsites.

▼ 8.0 SO Track on left.
1.6 ▲ SO Track on right.

▼ 8.2 SO Track on right. Then track on left.
1.4 ▲ SO Track on left. Then track on right.

▼ 8.6 SO Track on right.
1.0 ▲ SO Track on left.

▼ 8.7 SO FR 157 on left.
0.9 ▲ BL FR 157 on right.

▼ 9.6 SO FR 008 on left to Bear Ridge and Scofield Reservoir. Zero trip meter.
0.0 ▲ Continue north.
GPS: N 39°51.35' W 111°18.06'

▼ 0.0 Continue south on Skyline Drive.
10.1 ▲ SO FR 008 on right to Bear Ridge and Scofield Reservoir. Zero trip meter.

▼ 0.3 SO FR 122 on left to Fish Creek Ridge and Scofield.
9.8 ▲ SO FR 122 on right to Fish Creek Ridge and Scofield.

▼ 0.6 SO Track on right.
9.5 ▲ SO Track on left.

▼ 1.2 SO FR 215 to Garret Ridge on right.
8.9 ▲ SO FR 215 to Garret Ridge on left.
GPS: N 39°51.34' W 111°19.45'

Northern Trail #14: Clear Creek Ridge Trail

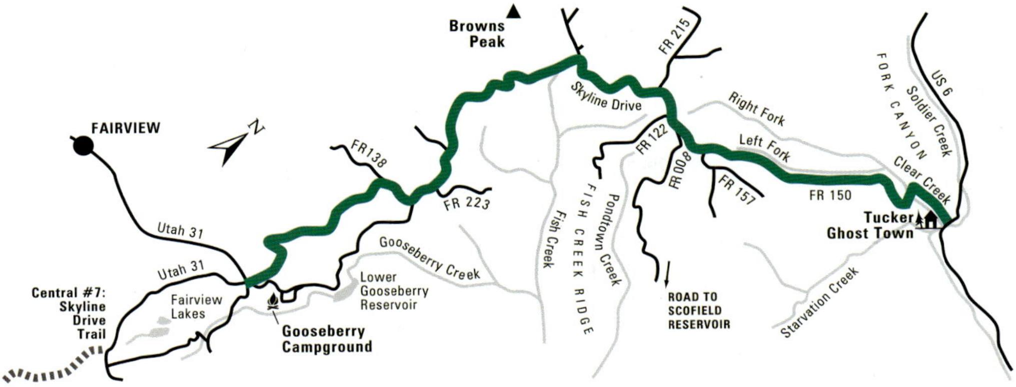

▼ 1.6 SO Track to microwave towers on right.
8.5 ▲ SO Track to microwave towers on left.

▼ 4.5 SO Fish Creek National Recreation Trailhead on left.
5.6 ▲ SO Fish Creek National Recreation Trailhead on right.

▼ 6.3 SO Track on right. Then Trail #040 on right.
3.8 ▲ SO Trail #040 on left. Then track on left.

▼ 10.1 SO FR 223 on left. Zero trip meter.
0.0 ▲ Continue along main road.
GPS: N 39°45.68' W 111°19.36'

▼ 0.0 Continue along main road.
7.8 ▲ SO FR 223 on right. Zero trip meter.

▼ 0.4 SO FR 177 on right.
7.4 ▲ SO FR 177 on left.

▼ 0.8 SO Track on left.
6.9 ▲ SO Track on right.

▼ 1.5 SO Cabin Hollow track on left.
6.3 ▲ SO Cabin Hollow track on right.

▼ 2.0 SO FR 138 on right—Dry Creek Stock Driveway.
5.8 ▲ SO FR 138 on left—Dry Creek Stock Driveway.

▼ 2.4 SO Cattle guard.
5.3 ▲ SO Cattle guard.

▼ 4.6 SO FR 055 on right.
3.1 ▲ SO FR 055 on left.

▼ 4.9 SO Cattle guard.
2.8 ▲ SO Cattle guard.

▼ 5.6-5.7 SO Tracks on right.
2.1-2.2 ▲ SO Tracks on left.

▼ 6.9 SO Cattle guard.
0.9 ▲ SO Cattle guard.

▼ 7.5 SO Track on left to Mammoth Guard Station, Gooseberry Campground, and Lower Gooseberry Reservoir.
0.3 ▲ SO Follow sign to US 6 and Skyline Drive. Track on right to Mammoth Guard Station, Gooseberry Campground, and Lower Gooseberry Reservoir.

▼ 7.6 SO Intersection. Paved road on left.
0.2 ▲ BL Bear left onto unpaved road.

▼ 7.8 Trail ends at Utah 31; turn right for Fairview, left for Huntington.
0.0 ▲ On Utah 31, 4.8 miles north of Central #7: Skyline Drive Trail and 9.5 miles northwest of Central #6: Upper Joe's Valley Trail, zero trip meter and turn north onto FR 150. Further information about both of these trails can be found in *Utah Trails: Central Region*.
GPS: N 39°40.58' W 111°18.82'

NORTHERN REGION TRAIL #15

Nine Mile Canyon Trail

STARTING POINT US 6/191, 1.9 miles east of Wellington
FINISHING POINT Northern #21: Franks Canyon and Sand Wash Trail
TOTAL MILEAGE 48.7 miles
UNPAVED MILEAGE 36.2 miles
DRIVING TIME 2 hours
ELEVATION RANGE 5,200–7,600 feet
USUALLY OPEN Year-round
DIFFICULTY RATING 1
SCENIC RATING 9
REMOTENESS RATING +0

Special Attractions

- Easy, scenic route that connects with numerous other 4WD trails.
- The greatest concentration of petroglyphs in the United States.
- Numerous granaries and cliff dwellings built by the Fremont Indians.

History

One of the first things you notice as you drive along Nine Mile Canyon is that it is much longer than 9 miles. Over the years, several stories have arisen to explain how this 40-mile-long canyon got its name. One says it was because of the nine-member Miles family that lived in the area in the late 1800s. However, the most believable story says that it was named by mapmaker Frank M. Bishop, on John Wesley Powell's 1869 survey expedition through the region. Some say Bishop used the name because he'd charted the canyon in a 9-mile triangulation drawing, while others say he found the creek that cuts through the canyon near his 9-mile marker. Whatever the case may be, Nine Mile Canyon is most assuredly about 30 miles longer than its name suggests.

Over a thousand years ago when the Fremont inhabited Nine Mile Canyon, they turned it into one of America's longest art galleries with a phenomenal amount of pictographs and petroglyphs. The Fremont were among the most prolific rock artists of Utah's early Indian inhabitants. The walls of Nine Mile Canyon reveal countless geometric patterns and images of humans and animals. As you drive by the images, remember to respect them as irreplaceable historic treasures.

Besides creating rock art, the Fremont also built a number of granaries into the canyon's cliffs. These storage shelters are typically camouflaged and located some distance up the cliffs, indicating that the Fremont felt they needed to go to great lengths to protect their food supply. It takes a keen eye to spot the remains of the small rock walls built into the horizontal indentations of the stratified cliffs.

In the 19th century, white men began traveling through the canyon. The first to blaze a footpath through the region were early explorers and trappers. In 1886, the path was upgraded to a federal highway by the U.S. Ninth Cavalry, which was composed of African Americans. A telegraph line was also run through the canyon to connect Fort Duchesne with Price and the rest of Utah.

Encouraged by the new road, the first permanent white settlers moved in and homesteaded this part of Duchesne County. A few scattered ranches and stopping points soon became the ranching community of Harper. In 1902, ranching tycoon Preston Nutter moved his headquarters into Nine Mile Canyon near Harper. Besides owning upward of 25,000 cattle all throughout the Southwest, this unique character had a flock of peacocks that could always be seen roaming about his headquarters.

In 1990, with the completion of US 40 and US 191, the road through Nine Mile Canyon became a National Backcountry Byway and can now be enjoyed at a slow, leisurely pace.

Description

On US 6/191, 1.9 miles east of Wellington, turn northeast onto paved Soldier Creek Road, which is signed to Nine Mile Canyon. The first 12.5 miles of the trail are paved, after which the road turns to gravel. The trail remains wide and maintained throughout

Old structures at Harper town site

and can be driven in a passenger car.

As you proceed, keep an eye out for the now idle telegraph poles. Some are made of wood, but many are metal, built to withstand Indian attempts to destroy them. These old telegraph poles are particularly abundant between Harper and the area near the turnoff to Argyle Canyon.

To see the Fremont petroglyphs, pictographs, and granaries along the way, a set of binoculars is highly recommended. Although a number of them are pointed out below in the route directions, there are many more to be found at all levels up and down the cliff walls. Pay particular attention to the places where smaller canyons intersect with Nine Mile Canyon; rock art often becomes more prevalent in these areas. Granaries are often much more difficult to spot. Look for an impressed horizontal line that extends about halfway up the side of the canyon. The Fremont constructed their granaries into the cliff along these indentations and built up a pile of rocks and mud to close off the protective structures. Over the years, these protective front walls have crumbled away, though the bases of the walls have remained in some instances. It may take some looking, but these slightly out-of-place rock bases are in fact an indication of old Fremont granaries.

After about 42 miles, you reach the old town site of Harper, and about a mile past that is the intersection with Northern #16: Argyle Canyon Trail. Half a mile past this intersection is a precariously balanced rock near a set of petroglyphs. Over the years, the general consensus seems to be that the balanced rock looks similar to Porky Pig, though it's also named, quite simply, Balanced Rock. Shortly thereafter, you come to a stone building that was once home to Nine Mile Canyon's longtime resident and telegraph operator Ed Harmon.

Marking from the Argyle Canyon Trail intersection, you reach Northern #17: Dry

The location of a granary (cirled)

Close-up of the granary (circled on left)

Northern Trail #15: Nine Mile Canyon Trail

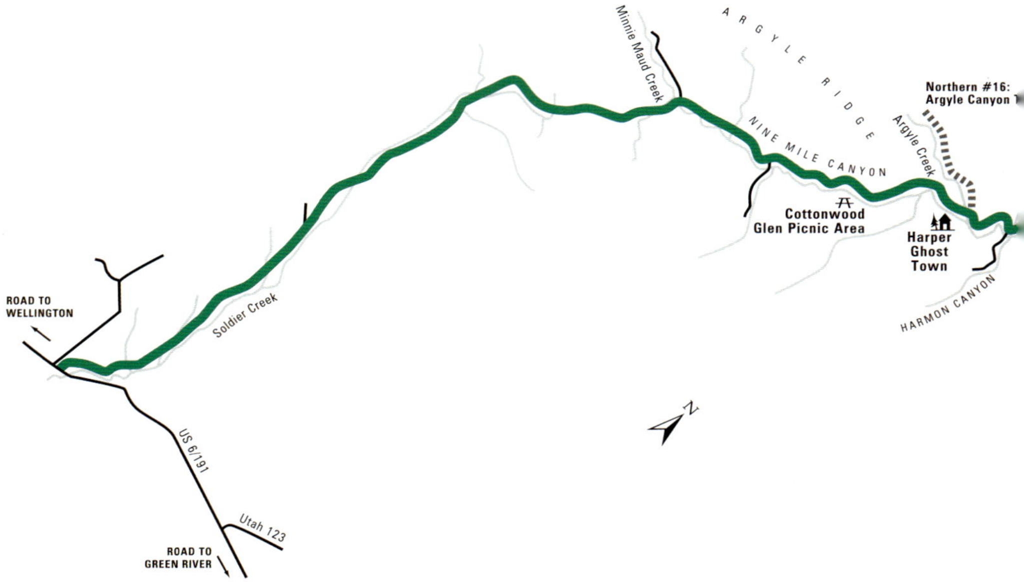

Canyon Trail in 11.7 miles and Northern #18: Cottonwood Canyon Trail in 13.1 miles. In between these two trail intersections is the interesting Rasmussen's Cave. Besides having some wonderful pictographs, the cave was the site of early excavations that unearthed a number of Indian artifacts and mummies.

The latter portion of Nine Mile Canyon Trail becomes noticeably more narrow. While it continues as a 1-rated trail, you will now have to pull over to allow an oncoming vehicle to pass. The scenery also becomes more striking and dramatic as the rock walls close in and tower above the road. It is not uncommon to see deer and elk roaming through the canyon. About 1.7 miles after passing Cottonwood Canyon Trail, you pass a stone building and log cabin by the cliff; these buildings served as a telegraph relay station at the midway point between Price and the Fort Duchesne garrison. Past this, all the ranches and buildings along the trail are private property.

The trail ends at the locked gates to the old Nutter Ranch, where the trail connects with Northern #21: Franks Canyon and Sand Wash Trail.

Current Road Information

BLM Price Field Office
125 South 600 West
Price, UT 84501
(435) 636-3600

Map References

BLM Price
USGS 1:24,000 Wellington, Deadman Canyon, Pine Canyon, Minnie Maud Creek East, Wood Canyon, Currant Canyon, Cowboy Bench
1:100,000 Price
Utah Atlas & Gazetteer, pp. 37, 38
Utah Road & Recreation Atlas, pp. 61, 62

Route Directions

▼ 0.0 On US 6/191, 1.9 miles east of the Wellington post office, turn northeast onto Soldier Creek Road and zero trip meter. The intersection is well marked and signed to Nine Mile Canyon.

12.5 ▲ Trail ends at US 6/191; turn right for Wellington, left for Green River.

GPS: N 39°32.59' W 110°41.22'

▼ 5.6 BL Road on right.
6.9 ▲ BR Road on left.

▼ 12.5 SO Start of gravel road. Zero trip meter.
0.0 ▲ Continue on main road.

GPS: N 39°42.18' W 110°36.64'

▼ 0.0 Continue on main road.
18.1 ▲ SO Pavement begins. Zero trip meter.

▼ 1.5 SO Cross cattle guard.
16.6 ▲ SO Cross cattle guard.

▼ 2.1 SO Dirt road on left.
16.0 ▲ SO Dirt road on right.

▼ 4.9 SO Cross cattle guard.
13.2 ▲ SO Cross cattle guard.

▼ 6.0 SO Old cabin on right.
12.1 ▲ SO Old cabin on left.

▼ 8.3 SO Cross bridge over Minnie Maud Creek.
9.8 ▲ SO Cross bridge over Minnie Maud Creek.

▼ 8.5 SO Old cabin on left.
9.6 ▲ SO Old cabin on right.

▼ 8.9 SO Nine Mile Canyon BLM information board.
9.2 ▲ SO Nine Mile Canyon BLM information board.

▼ 9.8 SO Old homestead on left. Cross cattle guard.
8.2 ▲ SO Cross cattle guard. Old homestead on right.

▼ 10.7 SO Nine Mile Ranch B&B and Campground on right.
7.4 ▲ SO Nine Mile Ranch B&B and Campground on left.

▼ 12.3 SO Cross cattle guard.
5.8 ▲ SO Cross cattle guard.

▼ 13.1 SO Pictographs on left, pull-over area on right. Walk through entry in log fence for best viewing.
4.9 ▲ SO Pictographs on right, pull-over area on left.

GPS: N 39°46.79' W 110°25.42'

▼ 14.1 SO Old cabin on right. Nine Mile Canyon Cottonwood Glen Picnic Area (day use only) on right.
3.9 ▲ SO Picnic area (day use only) on left. Old cabin on left.

▼ 14.7 SO Old log structures left and right.
3.3 ▲ SO Old log structures left and right.

▼ 15.4 SO Cross cattle guard.
2.7 ▲ SO Cross cattle guard.

▼ 17.2 SO Site of Harper.
0.9 ▲ SO Site of Harper.

GPS: N 39°48.03' W 110°22.08'

▼ 18.1 SO Cross creek. Northern #16: Argyle Canyon Trail on left. Zero trip meter at intersection.

FREMONT INDIANS AND ROCK ART

"Fremont" is a collective name given to the scattered groups of Indians who lived throughout the Great Basin. They arrived in Utah around A.D. 100 and were at first primarily nomadic hunter-gatherers. Although they were not quite as advanced as the Anasazi, their contemporaries in southern Utah, the Fremont developed a horticultural system and an elaborate culture evidenced today by excavated ceremonial clay figures and their famous rock art. By 750 the Fremont had mostly abandoned their nomadic ways and settled in more permanent dwellings. Evidence of pit houses has been discovered, as well as houses built precariously into the sides of cliffs. They also built camouflaged lookout towers high on the top of bluffs, presumably to keep guard over the surrounding land.

Fremont petroglyphs

Despite their widespread presence in the region and advanced agriculture, the Fremont faded from existence some time after 1250. Like the Anasazi, this culture's disappearance is shrouded in mystery. Most archaeologists believe a period of severe drought probably drove them away, and the survivors were likely absorbed into other, newer cultures. However, their enigmatic story lives on through the art that they left on Utah's canyon walls.

Anthropologists have studied the rock art of eastern Utah for years, and yet are still left wondering: what does it mean? The majority of the rock art throughout Utah has been attributed to the Fremont Indians, and it comes in two forms: petroglyphs, which are pictures etched into the rock, and pictographs, which are figures painted on the rock. Humans and animals are the typical subjects, and images of hunting parties are very common. A variety of animals such as bighorn sheep, grizzly bears, snakes, and coyotes are represented. Often, hunters of these animals are themselves dressed in the animals' skins. Other rock art includes shapes and designs as well as unexplained symbols that are thought to be a form of picture writing. Some of the figures may relate to the heavens above and act as some sort of calendar.

Nine Mile Canyon, located to the northeast of Price, has become known as America's longest art gallery. Though its name suggests otherwise, this canyon is actually 40 miles long and it contains a number of pictographs and petroglyphs. Excellent examples of Fremont rock art can be viewed in the canyon, featured in this book in Northern #15: Nine Mile Canyon Trail. Just remember, when you run across unprotected, unexpected rock art, it is a historic treasure and should be left undisturbed.

0.0 ▲ Continue west.

GPS: N 39°48.21′ W 110°21.11′

▼ 0.0 Continue east.

6.8 ▲ SO Northern #16: Argyle Canyon Trail on right. Zero trip meter and cross creek.

▼ 0.6 SO Balanced Rock and petroglyphs to right of rock, about 20 feet above ground.

6.1 ▲ SO Balanced Rock and petroglyphs to right of rock, about 20 feet above ground.

GPS: N 39°48.06′ W 110°20.49′

▼ 0.9 SO Wimer Ranch buildings.

5.9 ▲ SO Wimer Ranch buildings.

▼ 1.3 SO Stone building on right was old tele graph office.

5.5 ▲ SO Stone building on left was old telegraph office.

GPS: N 39°48.58′ W 110°20.38′

▼ 1.9 SO Track on left. Then track to Harmon Canyon on right. Numerous petroglyphs on left, 20 feet above ground on patina rocks.

4.9 ▲ SO Track to Harmon Canyon on left. Numerous petroglyphs on right, 20 feet above ground. Track on right.

GPS: N 39°48.46′ W 110°19.83′

▼ 3.5 SO Stone ranch building on left.

View of Nine Mile Canyon Trail

Two Fremont structures on a ledge (circled)

A close-up of the Fremont granary (circled on the left in the photo at left)

A close-up of the Fremont granary (circled on the right in the photo at left)

The petroglyphs at Balanced Rock

3.2 ▲ SO Stone ranch building on right.

▼ 4.1 SO Cross cattle guard.
2.7 ▲ SO Cross cattle guard.

▼ 6.3 SO Historic Nutter's Ranch buildings.
0.4 ▲ SO Historic Nutter's Ranch buildings.

▼ 6.8 SO Sign and intersection; zero trip meter. Straight for Prickly Pear Canyon, Dry Canyon, and Cottonwood Canyon. Myton via Gate Canyon to left.
0.0 ▲ Continue along Nine Mile Canyon Road.

GPS: N 39°48.71′ W 110°15.09′

▼ 0.0 Continue on Nine Mile Canyon Road.
4.9 ▲ SO Sign and intersection; zero trip meter. Straight for Wellington. Myton via Gate Canyon to right.

▼ 0.1 SO Cross cattle guard; 15 feet after cattle guard on left is petroglyph about 6 feet above ground.
4.8 ▲ SO About 15 feet before cattle guard on right is petroglyph about 6 feet above ground. Cross cattle guard.

GPS: N 39°48.63′ W 110°14.88′

▼ 0.4 SO Very old corral in sage bushes on left, partly obscured.
4.4 ▲ SO Very old corral in sage bushes on right, partly obscured.

▼ 2.4 SO Cross cattle guard. Granary on left (pictured).
2.5 ▲ SO Granary on right (pictured). Cross cattle guard.

GPS: N 39°47.76′ W 110°12.72′

▼ 3.0 SO Track to Prickly Pear Canyon on right.
1.9 ▲ SO Track to Prickly Pear Canyon on left.

▼ 4.8 SO Cross cattle guard. Rock formation called "The Mummy" is ahead in the distance on right.
0.1 ▲ SO Rock formation called "The Mummy" is behind in the distance on left. Cross cattle guard.

▼ 4.9 SO Track on right is Northern #17: Dry Canyon Trail. Zero trip meter.
0.0 ▲ Continue along main trail.
GPS: N 39°47.06' W 110°10.38'

▼ 0.0 Continue along main trail.
1.4 ▲ SO Track on left is Northern #17: Dry Canyon Trail. Zero trip meter.

▼ 0.4 SO Rasmussen's Cave on left with pictographs. Pull-over area a little farther opposite corral. More pictographs on canyon wall between cave and corral.
0.9 ▲ SO Pictographs on canyon wall between cave and corral on right. A little farther is Rasmussen's Cave on right with pictographs.
GPS: N 39°47.14' W 110°10.06'

▼ 1.4 BL Fork in the road. Right is Northern #18: Cottonwood Canyon Trail. Zero trip meter.
0.0 ▲ Continue along Nine Mile Canyon Road.
GPS: N 39°47.02' W 110°09.01'

▼ 0.0 Continue along Nine Mile Canyon Road.
5.0 ▲ BR Track on left is Northern #18: Cottonwood Canyon Trail. Zero trip meter.

▼ 0.3 SO Pass through gate.
4.7 ▲ SO Pass through gate.

▼ 0.7 SO Cross cattle guard.
4.3 ▲ SO Cross cattle guard.

▼ 1.7 SO Pass through gate and close behind you. Stone building and log cabin by cliff were telegraph relay station. Old corral on right. From this point, all buildings are private property.
3.3 ▲ SO Pass through gate and close behind you. Stone building and log cabin by cliff were telegraph relay station.
GPS: N 39°47.13' W 110°07.32'

▼ 2.2 SO Several good petroglyphs on left, about 20 feet above ground.
2.8 ▲ SO Several good petroglyphs on right, about 20 feet above ground.
GPS: N 39°47.28' W 110°06.91'

▼ 2.4 SO Track on left.
2.6 ▲ SO Track on right.

▼ 2.5 SO Pass through gate and close behind you. Corral on left.
2.5 ▲ SO Pass through gate and close behind you. Corral on right.

▼ 3.2 SO Pass through gate and close behind you.
1.8 ▲ SO Pass through gate and close behind you.

▼ 3.7 SO Old ranch buildings on left and right.
1.3 ▲ SO Old ranch buildings on left and right.

▼ 4.3 SO Eye-level petroglyphs on a large rock directly beside road on right.
0.7 ▲ SO Eye-level petroglyphs on a large rock directly beside road on left.

▼ 4.5 SO Track on left.
0.5 ▲ SO Track on right.

▼ 4.6 SO Old stone buildings on left and a corral on right.
0.4 ▲ SO Old stone buildings on right and a corral on left.
GPS: N 39°48.00' W 110°04.87'

▼ 5.0 Trail ends at padlocked gate to old Nutter Ranch. Track on left is Northern #21: Franks Canyon and Sand Wash Trail.
0.0 ▲ At end of Northern #21: Franks Canyon and Sand Wash Trail, zero trip meter and turn right toward Nine Mile Canyon.
GPS: N 39°48.33' W 110°04.62'

NORTHERN REGION TRAIL #16

Argyle Canyon Trail

STARTING POINT US 191, near Northern #22: Reservation Ridge Trail
FINISHING POINT Northern #15: Nine Mile Canyon Trail
TOTAL MILEAGE 23.9 miles
UNPAVED MILEAGE 23.9 miles
DRIVING TIME 45 minutes
ELEVATION RANGE 6,400–9,100 feet
USUALLY OPEN Year-round
DIFFICULTY RATING 1
SCENIC RATING 6
REMOTENESS RATING +0

Special Attractions

- Links Northern #15: Nine Mile Canyon Trail with Northern #22: Reservation Ridge Trail.

Description

According to the sign along US 191, the beginning of Argyle Canyon Trail is called Timber Lane. The maintained gravel road is used by logging trucks and is kept graded. The trail starts out through private forest land composed mainly of fir and aspen. Under normal circumstances, the road is not difficult; however, its clay-based surface can become slippery when wet.

As you drive farther into Argyle Canyon, fir and aspens give way to cottonwoods, pinyon, and sage. The canyon is generally broad and used as ranchland. Its walls are quite gentle and look more like hills than the cliff faces typical of most canyons in the region.

The Argyle Canyon trail eventually comes to an end at Northern #15: Nine Mile Canyon Trail less than a mile from the old ghost town of Harper.

Current Road Information

BLM Price Field Office
125 South 600 West
Price, UT 84501
(435) 636-3600

Map References

BLM Price
USFS Ashley National Forest
USGS 1:24,000 Jones Hollow, Lance Canyon, Minnie Maud Creek East, Wood Canyon
1:100,000 Price
Utah Atlas & Gazetteer, pp. 37, 27
Utah Road & Recreation Atlas, pp. 61, 53

Route Directions

▼ 0.0	On US 191 (0.9 miles from turnoff for Avintaquin Campground), turn northeast onto dirt road marked "Timberlane," and zero trip meter. Sign to Argyle Canyon and Nine Mile Canyon.
23.9 ▲	Trail ends at US 191; turn left for

Fall foliage in Argyle Canyon

Northern Trail #16: Argyle Canyon Trail

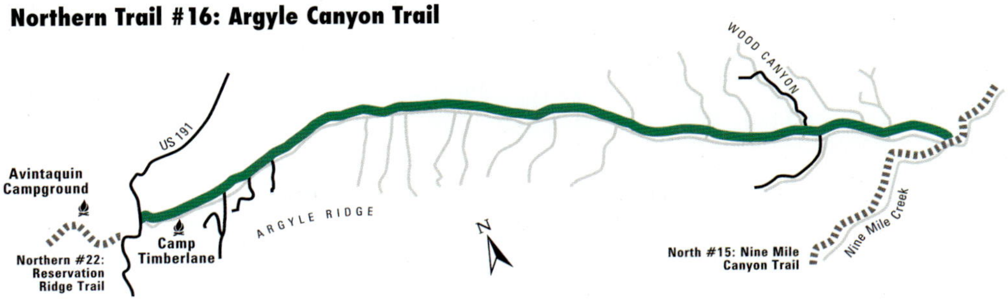

Northern #22: Reservation Ridge Trail, right for Duchesne.

GPS: N 39°53.02' W 110°44.82'

▼ 0.3 SO Tracks on left and right.
23.6 ▲ SO Tracks on left and right.

▼ 1.5 SO Camp Timberlane on right.
22.4 ▲ SO Camp Timberlane on left.

▼ 4.8 SO Pass through gate and close behind you. Private property along both sides of road.
19.1 ▲ SO Pass through gate and close behind you.

GPS: N 39°53.35 W 110°39.93'

▼ 7.3 SO Cattle guard.
16.6 ▲ SO Cattle guard.

▼ 7.8 SO Gate.
16.1 ▲ SO Gate.

▼ 8.9 SO Cattle guard.
15.0 ▲ SO Cattle guard.

Pictographs

Cottonwoods cloaked in fall foliage along the trail

▼ 12.8 SO Gate.
11.1 ▲ SO Gate.

▼ 14.9 SO Cattle guard.
9.0 ▲ SO Cattle guard.

▼ 16.7 SO Cattle guard.
7.2 ▲ SO Cattle guard.

▼ 17.6 SO Cattle guard.
6.3 ▲ SO Cattle guard.

▼ 18.6 SO Cattle guard.
5.3 ▲ SO Cattle guard.

▼ 19.3 SO Cattle guard.
4.6 ▲ SO Cattle guard.

▼ 19.8 SO Track to Wood Canyon on left.
4.0 ▲ SO Track to Wood Canyon on right.

▼ 19.9 SO Cattle guard.
4.0 ▲ SO Cattle guard.

▼ 20.3 SO Cattle guard.
3.6 ▲ SO Cattle guard.

▼ 21.2 SO Cattle guard.
2.6 ▲ SO Cattle guard.

▼ 22.0 SO Cattle guard.
1.9 ▲ SO Cattle guard.

▼ 23.2 SO Cattle guard.
0.7 ▲ SO Cattle guard.

▼ 23.7 SO Gate.
0.2 ▲ SO Gate.

▼ 23.9 Trail ends at Northern #15: Nine Mile Canyon Trail. Turn right for US 6/191, left for Northern #21: Franks Canyon and Sand Wash Trail.
0.0 ▲ On Northern #15: Nine Mile Canyon Trail, 30.6 miles from US 6/191, zero trip meter and turn toward Argyle Canyon.

GPS: N 39°48.21′ W 110°21.15′

NORTHERN REGION TRAIL #17

Dry Canyon Trail

STARTING POINT Northern #15: Nine Mile Canyon Trail
FINISHING POINT US 6/191
TOTAL MILEAGE 39 miles
UNPAVED MILEAGE 26.4 miles
DRIVING TIME 3 hours
ELEVATION RANGE 5,500–10,200 feet
USUALLY OPEN May to November
DIFFICULTY RATING 3
SCENIC RATING 9
REMOTENESS RATING +1

Special Attractions

- Moderate 4WD trail that crosses the high West Tavaputs Plateau with its high desert vegetation.
- Wonderful panoramic vistas from several viewpoints.
- Dry Canyon with its many cottonwoods, and Water Canyon with its stands of aspen.
- Fremont Indian petroglyphs and pictographs.

History

The histories of both East Carbon City and Sunnyside are inextricably intertwined with the history of coal mining in Carbon County. The coal-mining town of Sunnyside was officially settled in 1898, and within five years it had its own coke ovens. This enabled the town to begin on-site production of coke, a lighter fuel that burns at a higher temperature than coal; eventually the town had a total of 480 ovens. Sunnyside rode the highs and lows of the coal industry through the 20th century, which improved during World War II but then collapsed in the 1960s.

In 1973, East Carbon City incorporated the coal-producing towns of Dragerton and Columbia which, in 1899, had been the original eastern terminus for the Carbon County Railway. This railroad had one function only—to ship coal from the mines scat-

Creek through Dry Canyon

tered throughout the region. Eventually the line was extended farther south just west of the route followed by Utah 124.

Description

On Northern #15: Nine Mile Canyon Trail, toward the eastern end, head southwest along Dry Creek into the canyon. Dry Canyon has a lot in common with Cottonwood Canyon. Both are narrow and steep-walled and lined with cottonwoods and sagebrush. They are very attractive drives for viewing autumn colors. About 6 or 7 miles into the trail, aspens also become prevalent.

Like many other areas in this part of Utah, Dry Canyon can be extremely dusty (especially in the summer). Deep patches of powder-fine sand can slow down your vehicle at times and kick up thick clouds of dust.

The climb out of Dry Canyon follows a relatively gentle grade along a 3-mile stretch of broad, single-lane shelf road lined with trees. In some areas you may have to back up a short distance to allow someone to pass. There are many mature cottonwoods along this stretch of road and a good section of petroglyphs as well.

As you reach the top of the canyon, the scenery opens up and offers many good views from atop West Tavaputs Plateau. The trail continues to climb from here, ascending another 2,700 feet to the communication towers at Bruin Point.

On a clear day, you get a panoramic view from Bruin Point that stretches as far as 30 miles across the plains to the San Rafael Swell. Deer and elk are a common sight at the top of the plateau, as are golden eagles.

The descent south of Bruin Point runs along a much wider road than the northern approach. You will have no problem passing other vehicles along this graded, dirt road. About 3 miles from Bruin Point, the trail passes an old tramway with old cars still sitting on it.

Overall, the trail is not especially difficult. Navigation can become somewhat difficult on the plateau due to the number of side tracks. As you come down toward Sunnyside and East Carbon City, the gravel road is wide and maintained. As you reach Sunnyside, the trail passes a railroad spur and a mine entrance. A number of old, abandoned cottages remain in this once-thriving town.

The trail becomes paved 4.2 miles before the turnoff for Utah 124. Continue another 8.4 miles past this intersection along Utah 123 until the trail ends at US 6/191.

Current Road Information

BLM Price Field Office
125 South 600 West
Price, UT 84501
(435) 636-3600

Pictographs in Dry Canyon

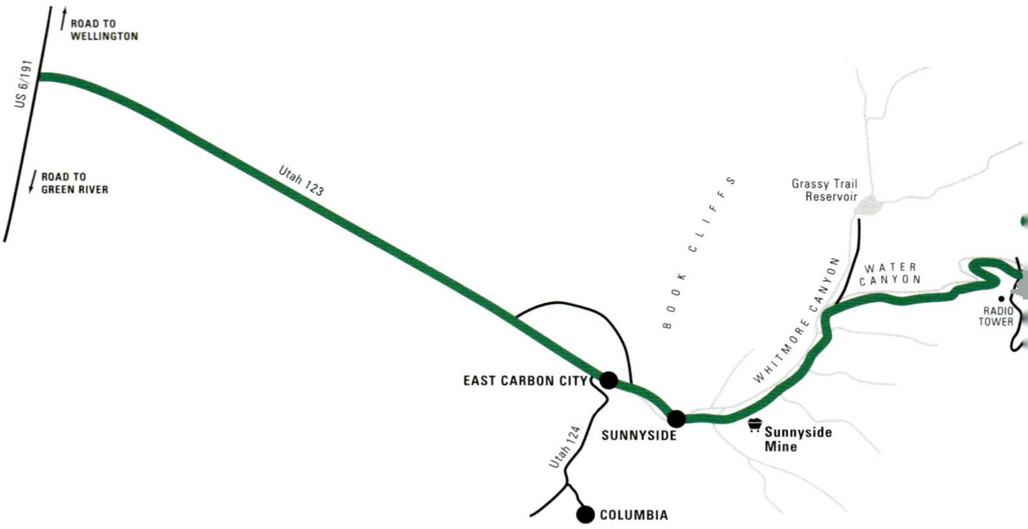

Northern Trail #17: Dry Canyon Trail

Map References

BLM Price
USGS 1:24,000 Cowboy Bench, Twin Hollow, Bruin Point, Patmos Head, Sunnyside, Sunnyside Junction
1:100,000 Price
Utah Atlas & Gazetteer, p. 37
Utah Road & Recreation Atlas, p. 61

Route Directions

▼ 0.0 On Northern #15: Nine Mile Canyon Trail, zero trip meter and turn south onto unmarked dirt track into Dry Canyon.
6.5 ▲ Trail ends at Northern #15: Nine Mile Canyon Trail. Turn left for US 6/191, right for Northern #21: Franks Canyon and Sand Wash Trail.
GPS: N 39°47.06′ W 110°10.38′

▼ 0.1 SO Cross through creek.
6.4 ▲ SO Cross through creek.

▼ 0.3 SO Cattle guard.
6.2 ▲ SO Cattle guard.

▼ 0.4 SO Track on left.
6.1 ▲ SO Track on right.

▼ 1.9 SO Various petroglyphs on large patina rock outcropping 6 to 20 feet above ground on right.
4.6 ▲ SO Various petroglyphs on large patina rock outcropping 6 to 20 feet above ground on left.
GPS: N 39°45.62′ W 110°10.25′

▼ 3.0 SO Petroglyphs to right of cave on right. Human figure with animal.
3.5 ▲ SO Petroglyphs to right of cave on left. Human figure with animal.

▼ 4.6 SO Gate.
1.9 ▲ SO Gate.

▼ 5.6 SO Oil tank on left.
0.9 ▲ SO Oil tank on right.

▼ 6.5 BL Fork in road. Bear left to Bruin Point. Stone Cabin Canyon to right. Zero trip meter.
0.0 ▲ Continue toward Nine Mile Canyon.
GPS: N 39°44.49′ W 110°14.37′

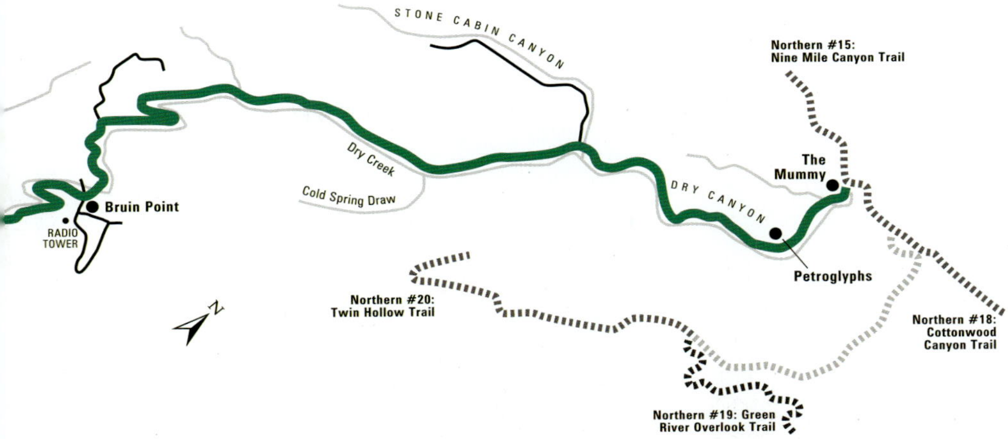

Northern Trail #17: Dry Canyon Trail

▼ 0.0 Continue southwest.
9.8 ▲ BR Track on left to Stone Cabin Canyon. Zero trip meter.

▼ 0.5 SO Cross through creek (usually dry).
9.3 ▲ SO Cross through creek (usually dry).

▼ 0.8 SO Cross through creek (usually dry).
9.0 ▲ SO Cross through creek (usually dry).

▼ 1.3 SO Cross through creek (usually dry).
8.4 ▲ SO Cross through creek (usually dry).

▼ 1.6 SO Cross through creek (usually dry).
8.2 ▲ SO Cross through creek (usually dry).

▼ 4.1 SO Cross through creek.
5.7 ▲ SO Cross through creek.

▼ 6.4 SO Track on left.
3.3 ▲ SO Track on right.

▼ 6.7 SO Cross over creek.
3.1 ▲ SO Cross over creek.

▼ 6.8 SO Ascend out of canyon.
3.0 ▲ SO Descend into canyon.

▼ 9.8 SO Track on left. Zero trip meter.
0.0 ▲ Continue along trail.

GPS: N 39°40.33′ W 110°20.41′

▼ 0.0 Continue along trail.
3.1 ▲ SO Track on right. Zero trip meter.

▼ 0.4 SO Track on right.
2.7 ▲ SO Track on left.

▼ 1.3 BL Track on right. Then fork in road.
1.7 ▲ BR Two tracks on left.

GPS: N 39°39.51′ W 110°21.25′

▼ 3.1 BR Track on left. Zero trip meter.
0.0 ▲ Continue along trail.

GPS: N 39°38.64′ W 110°20.40′

▼ 0.0 Continue toward East Carbon City.
11.2 ▲ BL Track on right. Zero trip meter.

▼ 0.1 SO Cattle guard.
11.1 ▲ SO Cattle guard.

▼ 0.2 SO Bruin Point. Track on right to radio tower.
10.9 ▲ SO Bruin Point. Track on left to radio tower.

▼ 0.4 SO Track on right. Then track on left to radio tower.

The view from Bruin Point

10.8 ▲ SO Track on right to radio tower. Then bear right at fork in road.

GPS: N 39°38.44′ W 110°20.74′

▼ 2.1 SO Track on left.

9.1 ▲ SO Track on right.

▼ 3.5 BR Track on left.

7.7 ▲ BL Track straight on.

▼ 5.0 SO Track on right to private property.

6.2 ▲ SO Track on left to private property.

▼ 5.6 SO Cattle guard.

5.5 ▲ SO Cattle guard.

▼ 5.7 SO Track on right heads north into Whitmore Canyon.

5.4 ▲ SO Track on left continues north in Whitmore Canyon.

GPS: N 39°35.98′ W 110°22.67′

▼ 5.9 SO Track on right.

5.3 ▲ SO Track on left.

▼ 6.3 SO Track on left.

4.9 ▲ SO Track on right.

▼ 7.0 SO Track on left.

4.2 ▲ SO Track on right.

▼ 8.5 SO Sunnyside Mine (closed) on left.

2.7 ▲ SO Sunnyside Mine (closed) on right.

▼ 11.2 SO Utah 124 on left to Columbia. Zero trip meter.

0.0 ▲ Continue toward Sunnyside.

GPS: N 39°32.62′ W 110°24.82′

▼ 0.0 Continue toward US 6/191.

8.4 ▲ SO Utah 124 on right to Columbia. Zero trip meter.

▼ 8.4 Trail ends at US 6/191. Turn right for Wellington, left for Green River.

0.0 ▲ On US 6/191, about 8 miles south of Wellington, zero trip meter and turn east on Utah 123 toward East Carbon City.

GPS: N 39°31.57′ W 110°34.38′

Expansive view from the trail near Burin Point

The location of the hunting scene petroglyph above the trail in Cottonwood Canyon

NORTHERN REGION TRAIL #18

Cottonwood Canyon Trail

STARTING POINT Northern #15: Nine Mile Canyon Trail
FINISHING POINT Intersection of Northern #20: Twin Hollow Trail and Northern #19: Green River Overlook Trail
TOTAL MILEAGE 6.5 miles
UNPAVED MILEAGE 6.5 miles
DRIVING TIME 30 minutes (one-way)
ELEVATION RANGE 5,400–7,200 feet
USUALLY OPEN Year-round
DIFFICULTY RATING 2
SCENIC RATING 8
REMOTENESS RATING +0

Special Attractions

- Fremont Indian pictographs.
- Good view of Fremont granaries.
- Scenic canyon with high walls and cottonwoods along wash.
- Access to two spur trails onto West Tavaputs Plateau.

Description

Cottonwood Canyon Trail turns off of Northern #15: Nine Mile Canyon Trail and heads south through a deep, narrow canyon. In many ways, this short spur trail—with its many cottonwoods and some of the best pictographs in the region—is even more interesting than Nine Mile Canyon. The pictographs include a detailed hunting scene from the days of the Fremont Indians.

Besides the pictographs, remnants of ancient granaries indicate that the area around Cottonwood Canyon has been inhabited for well over a thousand years. Located back along the face of Nine Mile Canyon, but best viewed from Cottonwood Canyon, these granaries can be very difficult to see. Binoculars are often a great help in locating the remains of these hidden cliff structures.

The road is suitable for a passenger car in good weather, and navigation is easy. The trail ends at an intersection with two other spur trails, Northern #19: Green River Overlook Trail and Northern #20: Twin Hollow Trail.

Current Road Information

BLM Price Field Office
125 South 600 West
Price, UT 84501
(435) 636-3600

Map References

BLM Price
USGS 1:24,000 Cowboy Bench, Twin Hollow
1:100,000 Price
Utah Atlas & Gazetteer, p. 38

A close-up of famous hunting scene petroglyph in Cottonwood Canyon

Beautiful fall foliage in Cottonwood Canyon

View from Cottonwood Canyon Overlook

Northern Trail #18: Cottonwood Canyon Trail

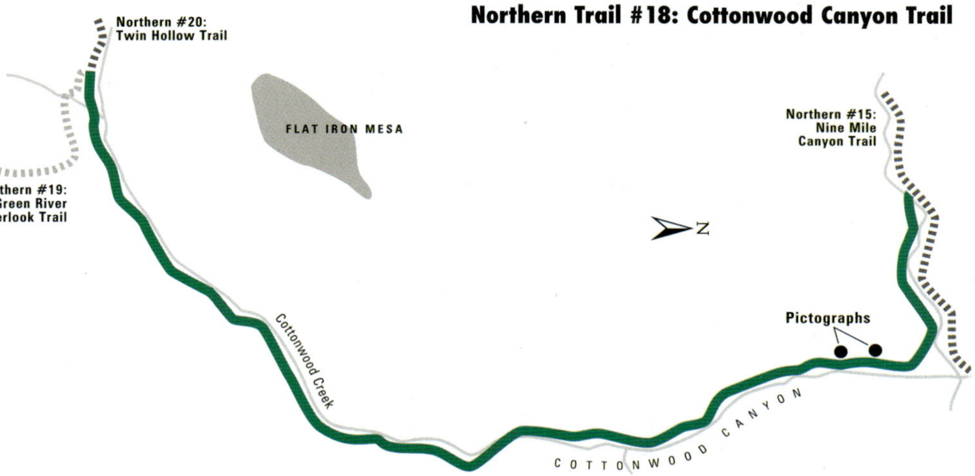

Route Directions

▼ 0.0 On Northern #15: Nine Mile Canyon Trail, 43.7 miles from US 6/191, zero trip meter and turn south into Cottonwood Canyon. Cross bridge over Nine Mile Creek.

GPS: N 39°47.02' W 110°09.01'

▼ 0.2 SO Cattle guard.

The trail winds through Cottonwood Canyon

▼ 0.7 SO Viewpoint for a Fremont granary looking back to the left to Nine Mile Canyon. Look on the green strata ledge between two large rocks.

▼ 1.2 SO Pictographs (including hunting scene) on right on a rock outcropping beside road.

GPS: N 39°46.83′ W 110°03.05′

▼ 1.3 SO Pictographs on right about 6 feet from ground.

▼ 1.7 SO Cattle guard.

▼ 4.9 SO Aqueduct across road overhead.

GPS: N 39°44.14′ W 110°08.67′

▼ 5.6 SO Cattle guard.

▼ 6.5 Trail ends at gate. Track on right is Northern #20: Twin Hollow Trail. Straight ahead is Northern #19: Green River Overlook Trail.

GPS: N 39°43.59′ W 110°10.18′

NORTHERN REGION TRAIL #19

Green River Overlook Trail

STARTING POINT End of Northern #18: Cottonwood Canyon Trail
FINISHING POINT Overlook of the Green River
TOTAL MILEAGE 15.9 miles
UNPAVED MILEAGE 15.9 miles
DRIVING TIME 2 hours (one-way)
ELEVATION RANGE 5,400–7,200 feet
USUALLY OPEN May to November
DIFFICULTY RATING 4
SCENIC RATING 10
REMOTENESS RATING +2

Special Attractions

- Extremely remote 4WD spur trail across the West Tavaputs Plateau.
- Spectacular Green River overlook.
- More challenging 4WD trail than most in the region.

Rocky shelf section of trail descends toward the ridge on Green River Overlook Trail

Overlook of Green River from the end of the trail

Cottonwood Canyon

A section of shelf road

Description

The Green River Overlook Trail is both extremely remote and wonderfully scenic. There are good views of Cottonwood Canyon as you ascend one of its walls, and the flat terrain of West Tavaputs Plateau leads you to a 1,000-foot cliff overlooking the Green River.

Beginning at the end of Northern #18: Cottonwood Canyon Trail, you immediately climb a steep stretch of fairly broad shelf road. Once out of Cottonwood Canyon, the trail crosses Sage Brush Flat past an old, graded airstrip before coming to another section of shelf road, which is narrow and off-camber. You then descend to a short, narrow ridgeline that extends across to Horse Bench. In spots, this section of the trail becomes narrow enough to make passing difficult without one vehicle reversing for a short distance. Erosion has collapsed the outside edge of the road in some places as well, thereby making the driving surface even more narrow and potentially intimidating.

The final portion of the trail runs across the perfectly flat landscape of West Tavaputs Plateau. Besides low open scrub, this area of flatland is dotted with pinyon and juniper. Although the last section of the trail is normally the easiest part, it becomes very boggy and impassable in wet weather.

The trail ends abruptly where the plateau falls away into the Green River. After enjoying this spectacular overlook, head back toward the trail's starting point in Cottonwood Canyon.

Trail along a narrow ridge

Northern Trail #19: Green River Overlook Trail

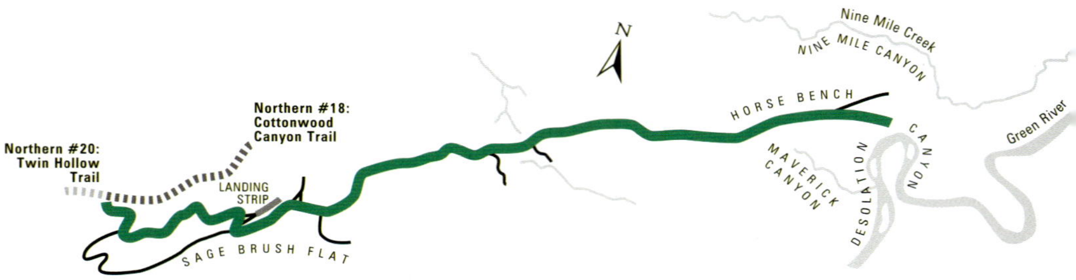

Current Road Information

BLM Price Field Office
125 South 600 West
Price, UT 84501
(435) 636-3600

Map References

BLM Price, Seep Ridge (incomplete)
USGS 1:24,000 Twin Hollow, Cedar Ridge Canyon, Pinnacle Canyon, Duches Hole
1:100,000 Price, Seep Ridge (incomplete)
Utah Atlas & Gazetteer, pp. 37, 38

Route Directions

▼ 0.0 At the end of Northern #18: Cottonwood Canyon Trail, where it meets Northern #20: Twin Hollow Trail, zero trip meter and bear left onto shelf road, climbing out of canyon.
GPS: N 39°43.59' W 110°10.18'

▼ 1.0 BL Fork in track at top of plateau.
GPS: N 39°43.18' W 110°09.61'

▼ 1.5 SO Cross through gate.
▼ 2.2 SO Mining operation on left.
▼ 2.6 SO Abandoned buildings on left.
▼ 3.7 TL Track on left. Zero trip meter.
GPS: N 39°43.81' W 110°07.45'

▼ 0.0 Continue along trail.
▼ 0.1 TL T-intersection.
▼ 0.8 SO Airstrip on left beside road.
▼ 1.1 SO Track enters on left.
▼ 1.5 SO Track on right.
▼ 2.9 SO Travel along spectacular ridgeline.
GPS: N 39°45.18' W 110°05.21'

▼ 4.4 SO Cross through gate.
▼ 4.8 BL Fork in road. The right trail dead-ends. Zero trip meter.
GPS: N 39°45.95' W 110°03.31'

▼ 0.0 Continue along route.
▼ 0.7 SO Road on right.
▼ 1.1 SO Various small tracks on left and right.
▼ 1.9 BR Fork in road.
GPS: N 39°46.75' W 110°01.52'

▼ 6.5 BR Fork in road.
GPS: N 39°48.11' W 109°56.60'

▼ 7.4 End at spectacular overlook of Green River.
GPS: N 39°48.23' W 109°55.62'

Twin Hollow Trail

STARTING POINT At end of Northern #18: Cottonwood Canyon Trail
FINISHING POINT Scenic overlook
TOTAL MILEAGE 7.4 miles
UNPAVED MILEAGE 7.4 miles
DRIVING TIME 45 minutes (one-way)
ELEVATION RANGE 6,400–8,300 feet
USUALLY OPEN May to November
DIFFICULTY RATING 4
SCENIC RATING 7
REMOTENESS RATING +1

Special Attractions

- The top end of Cottonwood Canyon, which is less traveled and very scenic.
- A network of remote 4WD trails, popular in hunting season.
- The high desert country of the Tavaputs Plateau.
- Endless remote backcountry campsites well away from the crowds.

Description

The Twin Hollow Trail begins at the end of Northern #18: Cottonwood Canyon Trail, at the same starting point as Northern #19: Green River Overlook Trail. After a couple of miles, the trail climbs about 600 feet out of Cottonwood Canyon.

The trail becomes more difficult on the plateau, as it is noticeably rutted, rocky, and off-camber in spots. Tire damage is possible along this section of narrow road, which proceeds through tall pinyon pine and the occasional juniper. At the same time, be sure not to miss the spectacular, panoramic views that go on for miles.

After 6.2 miles, a short spur trail leads to the remains of what used to be an old landing strip off to the left. Though it certainly has not been used for many years, it appears to have at one time been graded. A little over a mile later, the trail dead-ends, and a short walk takes you to an overlook at the edge of Flat Iron Mesa.

Ruts in Twin Hollow Trail

Creek crossing on Twin Hollow Trail

Twin Hollow Trail is scenic, moderately challenging, and provides a pleasant change from the canyon floors traversed by many of the trails in the region.

Current Road Information

BLM Price Field Office
125 South 600 West
Price, UT 84501
(435) 636-3600

Map References

BLM Price
USGS 1:24,000 Twin Hollow, Bruin Point
1:100,000 Price
Utah Atlas & Gazetteer, p. 38
Utah Road & Recreation Atlas, p. 62

Twin Hollow Trail

A rutted section of the trail

Route Directions

▼ 0.0 At end of Northern #18: Cottonwood Canyon Trail, zero trip meter and bear right through a nongated fence line.

GPS: N 39°43.59' W 110°10.18'

▼ 1.0 SO Cross through Cottonwood Creek.

▼ 2.3 SO Campsite on left at start of ascent from canyon.

▼ 4.8 SO Track on right.

GPS: N 39°42.09' W 110°13.87'

▼ 5.6 SO Start of rutted uphill section.

▼ 6.2 BR Fork in road. Left goes 0.25 miles to an overlook. Zero trip meter.

GPS: N 39°41.25' W 110°14.97'

▼ 0.0 Proceed along trail.

▼ 0.2 SO Track on left.

Northern Trail #20: Twin Hollow Trail

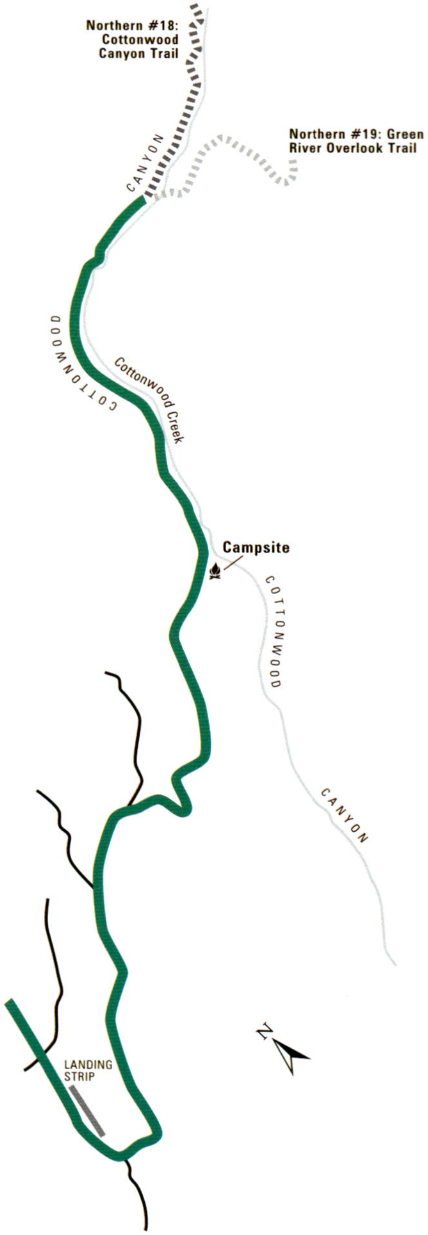

▼ 0.9 SO Track on left.

▼ 1.2 Trail dead-ends. A short walk leads to views from Flat Iron Mesa.

GPS: N 39°42.15' W 110°14.69'

Franks Canyon and Sand Wash Trail

STARTING POINT Northern #15: Nine Mile Canyon Trail
FINISHING POINT US 40, west of Myton
TOTAL MILEAGE 52.8 miles
UNPAVED MILEAGE 44.9 miles
DRIVING TIME 3 hours
ELEVATION RANGE 4,600–6,500 feet
USUALLY OPEN Year-round
DIFFICULTY RATING 3
SCENIC RATING 9
REMOTENESS RATING +1

Special Attractions

- Riverside access to the Green River.
- Driving through Franks Canyon and along Sand Wash.
- Access from the north to the eastern end of Northern #15: Nine Mile Canyon Trail.

BLM sign and Franks Canyon terrain

History

Franks Canyon and Sand Wash Trail passes near two sites that both used to serve as river crossings in days gone by. The Sand Wash ferry was developed at the only feasible crossing of the Green River between the towns of Green River, Utah, and Green River, Wyoming. Owned and operated by the Stewart family in the 1920s, the ferry was in service until the mid-1950s, when it was washed out. The Stewarts' four-room log cabin still stands at the site.

Petroglyphs in Franks Canyon

The trail following along Sand Canyon

Myton, originally known as "The Bridge," is located on what was once the only crossing of the Duchesne River, and it served as a gateway into the Uinta Basin in 1905 when the Uintah-Ouray Indian Reservation was opened up to white settlers. As settlers rushed to homestead the land, Myton became an important supply center in this otherwise remote region. The town grew and prospered for about 25 years, but the Great Depression almost killed it. Today, Myton survives as a small supply center for the nearby farmers and ranchers of the Uinta Basin.

Description

At the east end of Northern #15: Nine Mile Canyon Trail, head north into Franks Canyon. The primitive trail runs along the stony surface of the canyon floor as it crisscrosses through the wash. The tall canyon walls seem to close in on you as you drive along this impressive section of narrow track. Make sure you check the weather before driving this trail, as the canyon floods after heavy rains.

After 15.3 miles, turn right onto a 3.4-mile spur trail to the Green River. The spur trail follows the bed of Sand Wash and ends near a ranger station on the riverbank. Easy access to the water's edge makes this a popular launching spot for river rafters.

Back on the main road, the landscape becomes a flat expanse of sagebrush that is remarkably different from the rocky walls of Franks Canyon. There is extensive oil drilling in the area, and a number of side tracks jump off the main road and lead to oil wells. Navigation is easy, though, since the service roads are all much smaller than the graded two-lane road to Myton.

This last section of the road is unexciting—it travels past more mining and oil drilling—and is described only because it provides access to Myton and US 40. As its name indicates, the trail's most interesting and scenic parts are in Franks Canyon and along Sand Wash to the Green River.

View of Franks Canyon from trail

The end of the spur down Sand Wash to the Green River makes a great place for a picnic

Green River at the end of Sand Wash

Northern Trail #21: Franks Canyon and Sand Wash Trail

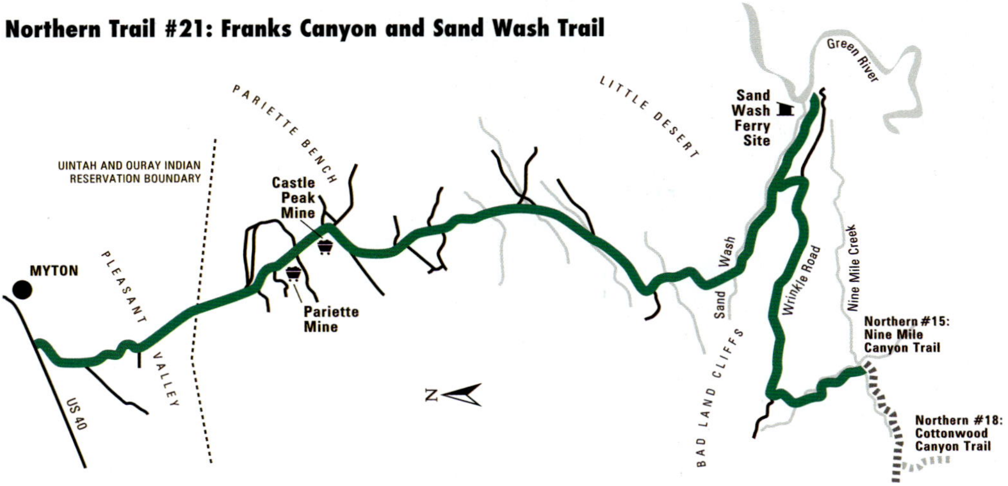

Current Road Information

BLM Price Field Office
125 South 600 West
Price, UT 84501
(435) 636-3600

BLM Vernal Field Office
170 South 500 East
Vernal, UT 84078
(435) 781-4400

Map References

BLM Price, Seep Ridge, Duchesne
USFS Ashley National Forest
USGS 1:24,000 Pinnacle Canyon, Duches Hole, Wilkin Ridge, Myton SE, Myton
1:100,000 Price, Seep Ridge, Duchesne
Utah Atlas & Gazetteer, pp. 38, 28
Utah Road & Recreation Atlas, pp. 62, 54 (incomplete)

Route Directions

▼ 0.0 At east end of Northern #15: Nine Mile Canyon Trail, zero trip meter at padlocked gate at end of canyon. Turn left onto unmarked track.
5.0 ▲ Trail ends at east end of Northern #15: Nine Mile Canyon Trail.
GPS: N 39°48.33' W 110°04.62'

▼ 0.9 SO Pass through gate.
4.0 ▲ SO Pass through gate.

▼ 4.9 BR Fork in road. Pass BLM sign on left.
0.1 ▲ BL Track enters on right (part of a delta leading back to Wrinkle Road).
GPS: N 39°50.66' W 110°05.94'

▼ 5.0 TR Intersection with Wrinkle Road. Left to Wellington-Myton Road. Zero trip meter.
0.0 ▲ Continue into Franks Canyon.
GPS: N 39°50.83' W 110°05.94'

▼ 0.0 Proceed toward Sand Wash.
10.3 ▲ TL Intersection. Turn left to Franks Canyon and zero trip meter. Straight ahead leads to Wellington-Myton Road.

▼ 8.9 SO Track on right.
1.4 ▲ SO Track on left.
GPS: N 39°50.27' W 109°57.76'

▼ 9.8 SO Track on left.
0.5 ▲ SO Track on right.

▼ 10.1 TR Intersection. Sign indicates Myton straight ahead. Turn right toward Sand Wash.
0.2 ▲ TL Intersection. Road on right is second entrance to Myton Road. Turn left toward Franks Canyon.

▼ 10.3 TR Intersection. Left is continuation of main trail to Myton. Turn right on spur road to Sand Wash. You will return to this intersection after visiting the Green River. Zero trip meter.
0.0 ▲ Continue along trail.
GPS: N 39°51.03' W 109°57.96'

Spur Trail to Sand Wash

▼ 0.0 Continue toward Sand Wash.
▼ 2.7 SO Cattle guard.
GPS: N 39°50.36' W 109°55.33'

▼ 3.3 SO Track on left to ranger station.
▼ 3.4 UT Toilets on right. Ranger station and two cabins on left. Then end at Green River and site of old Sand Wash ferry. U-turn and return to the intersection where you zeroed before.
GPS: N 39°50.42' W 109°54.74'

▼ 6.8 SO Intersection where you previously zeroed. Zero trip meter.
GPS: N 39°51.03' W 109°57.96'

Continuation of Main Trail

▼ 0.0 Continue toward Myton.
12.0 ▲ SO Track on right is continuation of main trail. Go straight on spur road to Sand Wash. You will return to this intersection after visiting the Green River. Zero trip meter.

▼ 0.3 SO Intersection.

Rock formations in Franks Canyon

11.7 ▲ SO Right goes toward Franks Canyon.

▼ 0.6 SO Cattle guard.
11.4 ▲ SO Cattle guard.

▼ 4.1 SO Track on left.
7.8 ▲ SO Track on right.

▼ 4.5 SO Track on right.
7.4 ▲ SO Track on left.

▼ 6.6 SO Cattle guard and cross through wash.
5.4 ▲ SO Cross through wash. Then cattle guard.

▼ 7.6 SO Track on left.
4.4 ▲ SO Track on right.

▼ 8.3 SO Track on left.
3.7 ▲ SO Track on right.

▼ 12.0 SO Intersection. Zero trip meter.
0.0 ▲ Continue toward Sand Wash.
GPS: N 39°57.20' W 109°59.53'

▼ 0.0 Continue toward Myton.
18.7 ▲ SO Intersection. Zero trip meter.

▼ 1.1 SO Intersection. Tracks on left and right.
17.6 ▲ SO Tracks on left and right. Follow signs to Sand Wash.
GPS: N 39°58.17' W 109°59.33'

▼ 1.6 SO Tracks on left and right.
17.1 ▲ SO Tracks on left and right.

▼ 1.7 SO Track on right.
17.0 ▲ SO Track on left.

▼ 3.7 SO Track on left.
15.0 ▲ SO Track on right.

▼ 5.2 SO Service road crosses right and left.
13.5 ▲ SO Service road crosses right and left.

▼ 6.4 SO Track on right.
12.3 ▲ SO Track on left.

▼ 6.8 BR Road on left.
11.8 ▲ BL Road on right.

▼ 7.7 TL T-intersection.
11.0 ▲ TR Intersection.

▼ 9.1 SO Road on left.
9.6 ▲ SO Road on right.
GPS: N 40°04.16' W 110°01.59'

▼ 12.1 SO Road on right.
6.6 ▲ SO Road on left.

▼ 16.5 SO Road on right.
2.1 ▲ SO Road on left.

▼ 18.7 Trail ends at US 40. Turn east for Myton.
0.0 ▲ On US 40, about 1.7 miles west of the bridge over the Duchesne River in Myton, zero trip meter and proceed along 5550 West toward Pleasant Valley, Sand Wash, and Nine Mile Canyon.
GPS: N 40°11.17' W 110°05.66'

NORTHERN REGION TRAIL #22

Reservation Ridge Trail

STARTING POINT US 191, 28 miles south of Duchesne
FINISHING POINT Northern #24: Timber Canyon Trail
TOTAL MILEAGE 17.8 miles
UNPAVED MILEAGE 17.8 miles
DRIVING TIME 1 hour
ELEVATION RANGE 8,700–9,700 feet
USUALLY OPEN Mid-May to mid-November
DIFFICULTY RATING 2
SCENIC RATING 8
REMOTENESS RATING +0

Special Attractions

- Great views as you journey through the Ashley National Forest.
- Access to a network of 4WD trails.
- Aspen viewing in the fall.

Reservation Ridge Road winds through the landscape below

History

Reservation Ridge follows along the old boundary line of the Uintah-Ouray Indian Reservation. Over the years, the reservation's boundaries have changed quite a lot, and much of the land originally set aside by Abraham Lincoln was quickly stripped away for use by white settlers. The east-west Reservation Ridge is located on West Tavaputs Plateau and lies south of the current reservation boundaries.

Description

Reservation Ridge Trail starts out along wide, maintained FR 147 and passes through the thick Engelmann, lodgepole, and aspen of Ashley National Forest. The start of the road is graded from time to time and could easily be driven by a 2WD car. Over the course of the next 4 miles it slowly deteriorates into a more typical forest road. The Avintaquin campground is located 1.1 miles into the trail on the right side and has limited facilities.

As you climb to the 6-mile point, the trail offers broad views to both the north and the south. Then the landscape gradually changes from forest to meadow and reveals more expansive views. By the time you reach the panoramic 270-degree overlook at Cat Peak, the trail is narrow and treeless.

Overall, the Reservation Ridge Trail is very scenic and has a number of excellent viewpoints. Short sections of wide shelf road look out over huge tracts of aspens that are breathtaking in autumn.

About 4 miles from the end, the trail intersects with the challenging spur

Another panoramic view from the trail

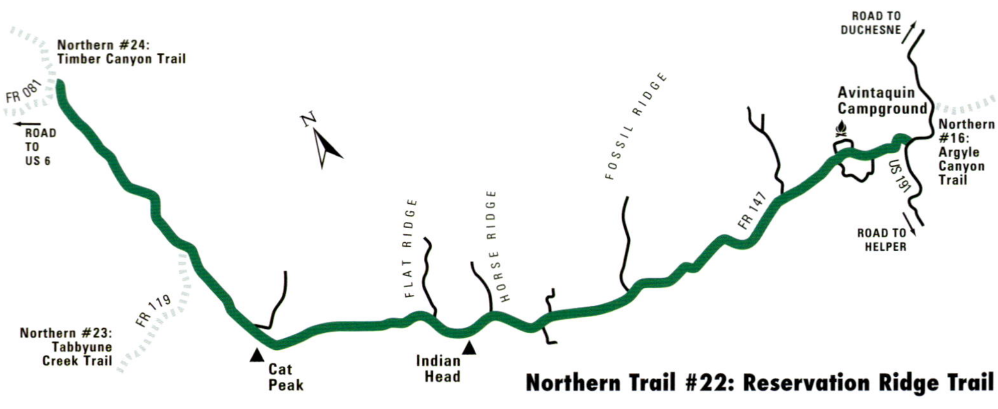

Northern Trail #22: Reservation Ridge Trail

Northern #23: Tabbyune Creek Trail, before coming to an end at Northern #24: Timber Canyon Trail.

Current Road Information

Ashley National Forest
Duchesne/ Roosevelt Ranger District
85 West Main
Duchesne, UT 84021
(435) 738-2482

BLM Price Field Office
125 South 600 West
Price, UT 84501
(435) 636-3600

Map References

BLM Price
USFS Ashley National Forest: Duchesne Ranger District
USGS 1:24,000 Gray Head Peak, Matts Summit, Kyune, Flat Ridge
1:100,000 Price
Utah Atlas & Gazetteer, pp. 27, 26
Utah Road & Recreation Atlas, pp. 53, 52

Route Directions

▼ 0.0 On US 191, 28 miles southwest of Duchesne, turn west onto FR 147 and zero trip meter. Follow sign to "Reservation Ridge Road and Avintaquin Campground."
8.1 ▲ Trail ends at US 191. Turn left for Duchesne, right for Helper.
GPS: N 39°52.71′ W 110°45.60′

▼ 0.7 SO Cross through seasonal gates.
7.4 ▲ SO Cross through seasonal gates.

▼ 0.8 SO Track on left.
7.3 ▲ SO Track on right.

▼ 1.1 BL Avintaquin Campground on right.
7.0 ▲ BR Avintaquin Campground on left.

▼ 1.3 SO Track on right.
6.7 ▲ SO Track on left.

▼ 2.4 SO Track on left.
5.7 ▲ SO Track on right.

▼ 2.5 SO Track on right.
5.6 ▲ SO Track on left.

▼ 2.7 SO Cross cattle guard.
5.4 ▲ SO Cross cattle guard.

▼ 3.1 SO Track on left.
5.0 ▲ SO Track on right.

▼ 5.7 SO Track to Fossil Ridge on right.
2.3 ▲ SO Track to Fossil Ridge on left.
GPS: N 39°52.32′ W 110°51.17′

▼ 6.0 SO Track on left, then cross cattle guard.
2.1 ▲ SO Track on right, then cross cattle guard.

▼ 6.8 SO Track on left.

1.3 ▲ SO Track on right.

GPS: N 39°52.44′ W 110°52.27′

▼ 7.1 SO Track on right.
1.0 ▲ SO Track on left.

▼ 8.1 SO Track to Horse Ridge Canyon on right. Zero trip meter.
0.0 ▲ Continue along main track.

GPS: N 39°52.84′ W 110°53.52′

▼ 0.0 Proceed along main track.
5.9 ▲ SO Track to Horse Ridge Canyon on left. Zero trip meter.

▼ 0.3 SO Cross cattle guard.
5.6 ▲ SO Cross cattle guard.

▼ 0.6 SO Track on left.
5.3 ▲ SO Track on right.

▼ 1.1 SO Track on right to Flat Ridge Trail.
4.8 ▲ SO Track on left to Flat Ridge Trail.

▼ 2.2 SO Track on left.
3.7 ▲ SO Track on right.

▼ 2.4 SO Track on right.
3.5 ▲ SO Track on left.

▼ 2.9 SO Cross cattle guard.
3.0 ▲ SO Cross cattle guard.

▼ 4.2 SO Track on left to Cat Peak.
1.7 ▲ SO Track on right to Cat Peak.

GPS: N 39°53.99′ W 110°57.47′

▼ 4.3-4.9 SO Good views on left, straight, and right of road as you travel along the ridge.
1.0-1.6 ▲ SO Good views as you travel along the ridge.

▼ 5.9 SO Track on left is Northern #23: Tabbyune Creek Trail (FR 119). Track on right. Zero trip meter.
0.0 ▲ Continue along main track.

GPS: N 39°55.46′ W 110°57.95′

▼ 0.0 Continue along main track.
3.8 ▲ SO Track on left. Northern #23: Tabbyune Creek Trail (FR 119) on right. Zero trip meter.

▼ 1.1 SO Track on right.
2.7 ▲ SO Track on left.

▼ 1.3 SO Track on right.
2.4 ▲ SO Track on left.

▼ 1.9 SO Track on right.
1.9 ▲ SO Track on left.

▼ 2.4 SO Track on right.
1.4 ▲ SO Track on left.

▼ 3.4 SO Track on right.
0.4 ▲ SO Track on left.

▼ 3.8 Trail ends at Northern #24: Timber Canyon Trail (FR 081). Continue straight for Timber Canyon, turn left for US 6.
0.0 ▲ On Northern #24: Timber Canyon Trail (FR 081), 7.9 miles from US 6 at the top of Reservation Ridge, zero trip meter and turn right.

GPS: N 39°58.48′ W 110°58.86′

NORTHERN REGION TRAIL #23

Tabbyune Creek Trail

STARTING POINT Northern #22: Reservation Ridge Trail
FINISHING POINT Uinta National Forest boundary
TOTAL MILEAGE 3.6 miles
UNPAVED MILEAGE 3.6 miles
DRIVING TIME 45 minutes (one-way)
ELEVATION RANGE 7,600–9,000 feet
USUALLY OPEN Mid-May to mid-November
DIFFICULTY RATING 5
SCENIC RATING 7
REMOTENESS RATING +0

Special Attractions

- Challenging short spur trail.
- Attractive fall colors.

A rutted section of the trail crosses through a stand of aspen

Description

On Northern #22: Reservation Ridge Trail, 14 miles from US 191, turn southwest onto the narrow dirt FR 119. Initially, quite a few stands of overhanging aspens line the road, which then give way to conifers farther down the trail. At times, the trees crowd in on the road enough to make passing impossible without one vehicle backing up a short distance.

Over the years, the road has become very rutted, mainly because shade from the trees keeps the area muddy. High clearance is a must, as some sections of road seem to stay wet all the time. After heavy rains, the road becomes impassable and should be avoided.

Most of the trail runs downhill along a mild shelf road, which allows you to use your momentum to drive through any deeper sections of mud. However, driving the return back up to Northern #22: Reservation Ridge Trail can present much greater difficulty.

Although the road continues to US 6 through private property, the trail properly ends at the boundary line of the Uinta National Forest. And remember, on this trail it's important to evaluate the road at all times: Don't go past any muddy sections that your vehicle may not be able to make it back up.

Northern Trail #23: Tabbyune Creek Trail

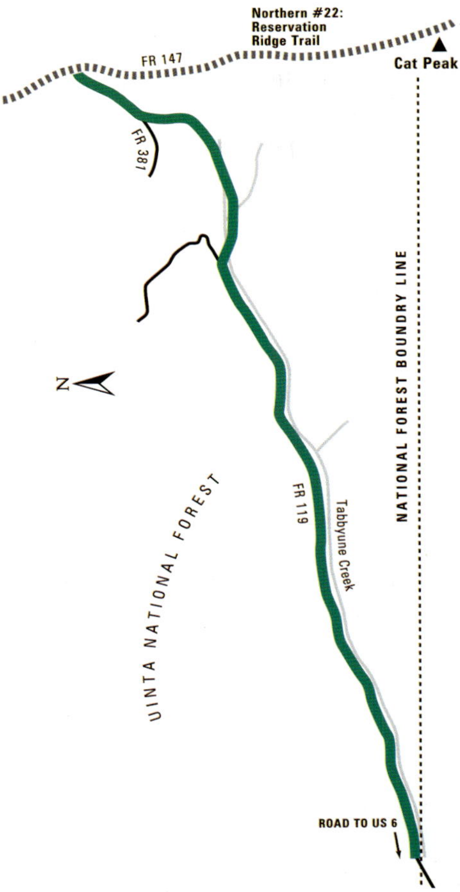

Current Road Information

Ashley National Forest
Duchesne/Roosevelt Ranger District
85 West Main
Duchesne, UT 84021
(435) 738-2482

Uinta-Wasatch-Cache National Forest
Heber-Kamas Ranger District
2460 South Hwy 40
Heber, UT 84032
(435) 654-0470

BLM Price Field Office
125 South 600 West
Price, UT 84501
(435) 636-3600

Map References

BLM Price, Nephi
USFS Ashley National Forest: Duchesne Ranger District
USGS 1:24,000 Flat Ridge, Soldier Summit
1:100,000 Price, Nephi
Utah Atlas & Gazetteer, p. 26
Utah Road & Recreation Atlas, p. 52

Route Directions

▼ 0.0 On Northern #22: Reservation Ridge Trail (FR 147), 14 miles from US 191, zero trip meter and turn onto FR 119 (Tabbyune Canyon Road).

GPS: N 39°55.46' W 110°57.95'

▼ 0.3 SO Track on right.
▼ 0.4 SO FR 381 on right.

Narrow, muddy Tabbyune Creek Trail

▼ 0.6 SO Track on left.
▼ 1.5 SO Cross through creek.
▼ 1.6 TL T-intersection.
GPS: N 39°54.70' W 110°58.97'

▼ 3.6 Seasonal closure gate. End at forest boundary.
GPS: N 39°54.00' W 111°00.93'

NORTHERN REGION TRAIL #24

Timber Canyon Trail

STARTING POINT US 6, about 0.7 miles southeast of Soldier Summit
FINISHING POINT US 40, 7.8 miles west of Duchesne
TOTAL MILEAGE 42.1 miles
UNPAVED MILEAGE 37.3 miles
DRIVING TIME 2 hours
ELEVATION RANGE 6,800–9,000 feet
USUALLY OPEN May to November
DIFFICULTY RATING 2
SCENIC RATING 8
REMOTENESS RATING +0

Special Attractions

- Attractive scenery along Timber Canyon and Strawberry River and panoramic views.
- Great fall colors.
- A network of 4WD trails to explore.

History

Soldier Summit sits at the highest point along the Denver & Rio Grande Western Railroad through Utah. When the railroad's main division point moved in 1919 from Helper to Soldier Summit, the town was soon bustling with activity. At its peak, 2,500 people called Soldier Summit home. However, due to severe winters and the inefficient cost of basing operations in Soldier Summit, the division point was moved back to Helper in 1930. As the jobs left the area, so did the people, though there are still a few residents today. The town currently consists of little more than a gas station, a couple of modern houses, many deserted buildings, and a few foundations.

Description

On US 6, about 0.7 miles southeast of Soldier Summit, head north on FR 081, a wide dirt road that runs along the Right

Cottonwoods in Timber Canyon

Fork of the White River. For the first 5 miles or so, beaver dams can be seen on the river. The road passes by quite a few stands of aspen as it runs through sagebrush and willow bottoms.

For the first 6 miles, the road is considerably rutted and bumpy and can become boggy when wet. However once the trail crosses the creek, it becomes smoother, climbing up a broad section of shelf road and offering a pleasant view over the creek.

After 7.9 miles, you reach an intersection with Northern #22: Reservation Ridge Trail. The road to Timber Canyon smooths out and follows a level ridgeline with broad views to either side. About 8.4 miles after the trail intersection, there is a section of wide shelf road that runs along a 100-foot drop-off down into Timber Canyon.

The drive through Timber Canyon is very scenic and attractive. A number of old cottonwoods, willow bottoms, and oak trees line the Strawberry River. The trail also offers many gorgeous views that are at their most beautiful in the full color of autumn.

Toward the end, the road surface becomes maintained gravel and can be driven by car. Timber Canyon Trail ends at US 40, about 8 miles west of Duchesne.

Thick sagebrush along the approach to Timber Canyon

Northern Trail #24: Timber Canyon Trail

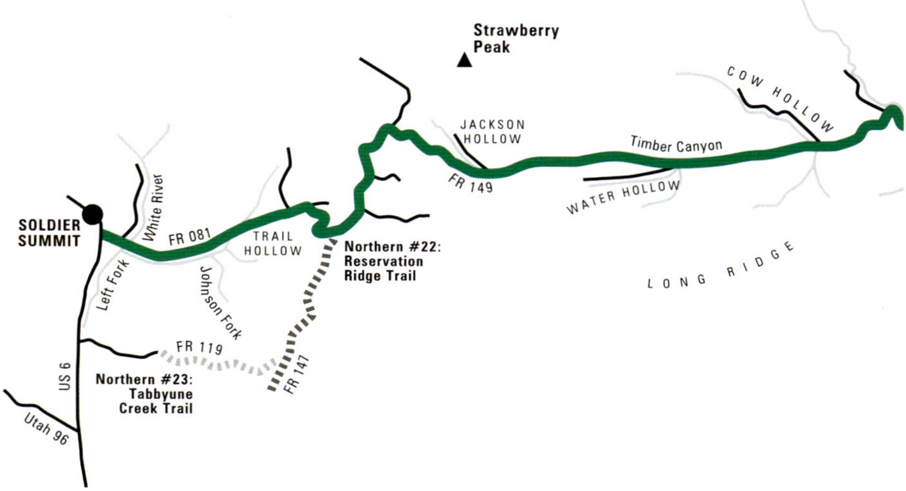

Current Road Information

Ashley National Forest
Duchesne/Roosevelt Ranger District
85 West Main
Duchesne, UT 84021
(435) 738-2482

BLM Price Field Office
125 South 600 West
Price, UT 84501
(435) 636-3600

Map References

BLM Nephi, Price, Duchesne
USFS Ashley National Forest: Duchesne Ranger District
USGS 1:24,000 Soldier Summit, Flat Ridge, Strawberry Peak, Avintaquin Canyon, Fruitland, Strawberry Pinnacles, Rabbit Gulch
1:100,000 Nephi, Price, Duchesne
Utah Atlas & Gazetteer, pp. 26, 27
Utah Road & Recreation Atlas, pp. 52, 53

Route Directions

▼ 0.0		On US 6, about 0.7 miles southeast of Soldier Summit, zero trip meter and turn onto unmarked dirt road (FR 081).
7.9 ▲		Trail ends at US 6. Turn right for Soldier Summit, left for Price.
		GPS: N 39°55.52′ W 111°04.16′
▼ 0.2	BL	Cross cattle guard. Gated road on right.
7.7 ▲	BR	Gated road on left. Cross cattle guard.
▼ 0.5	BR	Fork in road. Left goes to White River.
7.4 ▲	BL	Road on right to White River.
▼ 0.6	SO	Track on left.
7.3 ▲	SO	Track on right.
▼ 0.8	SO	Cross over Left Fork White River.
7.1 ▲	SO	Cross over Left Fork White River.
▼ 1.8	SO	Track on right to riverside campsite.
6.1 ▲	SO	Track on left to riverside campsite.
▼ 2.1	SO	Enter Uinta National Forest.
5.8 ▲	SO	Leave Uinta National Forest.
▼ 3.0	SO	Johnson Fork.
4.9 ▲	SO	Johnson Fork.
		GPS: N 39°56.34′ W 111°01.47′
▼ 4.3	SO	Track on left.
3.6 ▲	SO	Track on right.
▼ 4.5	SO	Track on left. Cross bridge over Right Fork White River.
3.4 ▲	SO	Cross bridge over Right Fork White River. Track on right.

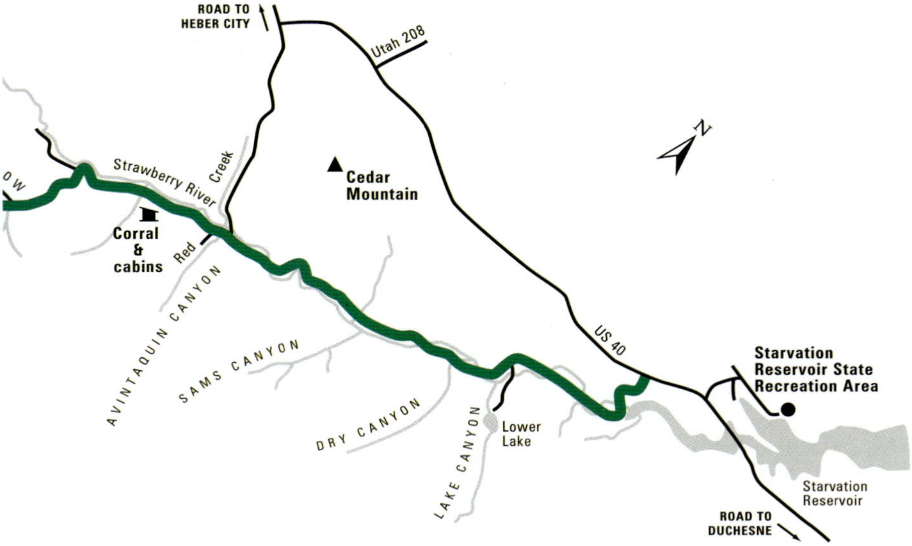

▼ 5.4 SO Track on left.
2.5 ▲ SO Track on right.

▼ 5.9 SO Track on left.
2.0 ▲ SO Track on right.
GPS: N 39°58.04' W 111°00.30'

▼ 6.0 SO Cross over creek.
1.9 ▲ SO Cross over creek.

▼ 7.1 BL Fork in road. Continue to climb.
0.8 ▲ BR Track on left.
GPS: N 39°57.99' W 110°59.30'

▼ 7.9 TL Intersection. Turn left toward Bumper Canyon, Timber Canyon, and Grassy Hollow. Zero trip meter. Right is Northern #22: Reservation Ridge Trail to US 191.
0.0 ▲ Continue toward US 6.
GPS: N 39°58.49' W 110°58.85'

▼ 0.0 Proceed toward Timber Canyon.
20.4 ▲ TR Intersection. Turn right to US 6. Straight is Northern #22: Reservation Ridge Trail to US 191.

▼ 0.2 SO Intersection. Long Ridge to the right.
20.2 ▲ SO Track on left to Long Ridge.

▼ 0.3 BL Fork in the road. Bumper Canyon and Rough Hollow to the right.
20.1 ▲ SO Road enters on left.
GPS: N 39°58.77' W 110°58.87'

▼ 1.3 SO Track on right.
19.1 ▲ SO Track on left.

▼ 1.7 SO Track on left.
18.7 ▲ SO Track on right.

▼ 2.8 TR Turn right at fork onto FR 149 toward Timber Canyon. Strawberry Peak is straight ahead.
17.5 ▲ TL Intersection. Turn left onto FR 081 to Reservation Ridge. Strawberry Peak is to the right.
GPS: N 40°00.68' W 110°59.40'

▼ 3.6 SO Track on left.
16.8 ▲ SO Track on right.

▼ 6.1 SO Track on left to Jackson Hollow.
14.3 ▲ SO Track on right to Jackson Hollow.
GPS: N 40°01.39° W 110°56.19'

▼ 7.5 SO Cross cattle guard. Track to Pine Hollow on left.
12.9 ▲ SO Track to Pine Hollow on right. Cross cattle guard.

▼ 10.5 SO Track to Water Hollow on right.
9.9 ▲ SO Track to Water Hollow on left.

▼ 12.7 SO Seasonal gate.
7.6 ▲ SO Seasonal gate.
GPS: N 40°04.91′ W 110°50.51′

▼ 12.8 SO Cross cattle guard.
7.6 ▲ SO Cross cattle guard.

▼ 13.5 SO Cross over bridge.
6.8 ▲ SO Cross over bridge.

▼ 13.6 SO Track on left to Cow Hollow.
6.8 ▲ SO Track on right to Cow Hollow.

▼ 13.8 SO Track on right to Rough Hollow.
6.6 ▲ SO Track on left to Rough Hollow.

▼ 14.4 SO Cross over creek.
6.0 ▲ SO Cross over creek.

▼ 14.5 SO Cross over creek.
5.8 ▲ SO Cross over creek.

▼ 14.7 SO Cross over creek.
5.7 ▲ SO Cross over creek.

▼ 14.8 SO Cross cattle guard.
5.6 ▲ SO Cross cattle guard.

▼ 15.3 SO Cross over creek.
5.1 ▲ SO Cross over creek.

▼ 15.6 SO Cross over creek.
4.8 ▲ SO Cross over creek.

▼ 15.7 SO Cross bridge over Strawberry River. Road on left.
4.7 ▲ SO Road on right. Cross bridge over Strawberry River.

▼ 15.8 BR Intersection. Bear right toward Duchesne.
4.6 ▲ BL Follow sign to Timber Canyon.
GPS: N 40°06.97′ W 110°48.71′

▼ 18.1 SO Corral and old cabins on right.
2.3 ▲ SO Corral and old cabins on left.

▼ 19.7 SO Track on left.
0.7 ▲ SO Track on right.

▼ 20.1 SO Road is now paved.
0.3 ▲ SO Road is now unpaved.

▼ 20.2 SO Avintaquin Canyon and Ashley to the right. Proceed straight toward Duchesne.
0.2 ▲ SO Follow sign to Strawberry River and Timber Canyon.

▼ 20.3 SO Cross bridge over Red Creek.
0.1 ▲ SO Cross bridge over Red Creek.

▼ 20.4 TR Intersection. Zero trip meter.
0.0 ▲ Continue along road.
GPS: N 40°07.72′ W 110°44.39°

▼ 0.0 Continue along unpaved road.
13.8 ▲ TL Zero trip meter at intersection and follow signs to Camelot Resort.

▼ 3.3 SO Cross bridge
10.5 ▲ SO Cross bridge.

▼ 3.7 SO Cross bridge over Strawberry River.
10.1 ▲ SO Cross bridge over Strawberry River.

▼ 4.0 SO Cross cattle guard.
9.8 ▲ SO Cross cattle guard.

▼ 4.6 SO Road on left.
9.2 ▲ SO Road on right.

▼ 5.3 SO Cross cattle guard.
8.4 ▲ SO Cross cattle guard.

▼ 5.6 SO Cross bridge over Strawberry River.
8.2 ▲ SO Cross bridge over Strawberry River.

▼ 7.8 SO Cross bridge over Strawberry River.
6.0 ▲ SO Cross bridge over Strawberry River.

▼ 8.3 SO Road on right.
5.4 ▲ SO Road on left.

▼ 11.9 SO Cross bridge over Strawberry River.
1.9 ▲ SO Cross bridge over Strawberry River.

▼ 13.8 Trail ends at US 40. Turn right for Duchesne, left for Heber City.
0.0 ▲ On US 40, 7.8 miles west of Duchesne and US 191, zero trip meter and turn onto 29500 West Street.

GPS: N 40°10.38' W 110°32.88'

NORTHERN REGION TRAIL #25

Brown's Park Trail

STARTING POINT Jones Hole Road
FINISHING POINT Jarvie Homestead
TOTAL MILEAGE 32.9 miles
UNPAVED MILEAGE 31.2 miles
DRIVING TIME 1.5 hours
ELEVATION RANGE 5,300–7,800 feet
USUALLY OPEN Year-round
DIFFICULTY RATING 1
SCENIC RATING 8
REMOTENESS RATING +0

Special Attractions

- Historic location along the old Outlaw Trail.
- John Jarvie homestead.
- The swinging bridge across the Green River.
- Scenic Crouse Canyon.

History

As early as the 1820s Brown's Park, also known as Brown's Hole, was known to fur trappers from the United States and Canada. Brown's Park sits inside a circular ring of mountains where the borders of Utah, Colorado, and Wyoming all meet. Trappers such as William H. Ashley and Baptiste Brown were among the earliest white men to discover Brown's Park, and it is believed the region was named after the latter.

In 1837, a trading post called Fort Davy Crockett was established in the region for the many trappers who made Brown's Park their winter headquarters. However, as the beaver population soon began to dwindle, many left to search for the valuable pelts in other regions.

By 1868 there were still a few residents left when news came that a transcontinental railroad was to be built just south of Brown's Park. It would follow the relatively new route through the region that had been recently discovered by famed Utah trapper and trader Jim Bridger.

With the completion of the railroad, Brown's Park became a natural home and

Jones Hole road rolls along undulating hills

The Swinging Bridge across the Green River

safe haven for outlaws, cattle rustlers, and men who lived their lives just around (and sometimes over) the limits of the law. While the railroad provided easy access to northeastern Utah, Brown's Park remained extremely isolated and naturally defensible, situated in 65 miles of mostly uncharted, mountainous terrain.

Notable local figures John Jarvie, who ran a general store and river ferry, and Charlie Crouse, a rancher and businessman, moved into Brown's Park in the 1870s and 1880s. Although not known as outlaws themselves, these men nonetheless provided food and shelter to such famed bank robbers as Butch Cassidy (who at one time worked for Crouse), Matt Warner, and Elza Lay. The bank robbers, in turn, generally treated their hosts with respect and generosity, and they became well liked by local townsfolk.

This trail passes by a number of historical landmarks in Brown's Park. In 1927, Stanley Crouse, Charlie's son, built a swinging bridge across the Green River. John Jarvie had been operating a ferry in the area since the early 1880s, but the bridge was only the second in the region to cross the Green River. The first bridge had been built just

Tombstone in the cemetery at the Jarvie homestead

Jarvis Cabin is surrounded by fantastic old cottonwood trees

Crouse Canyon

after the turn of the century by Charlie Crouse but lasted only a couple of years. The bridge proved very tenuous and collapsed less than a year later. Learning from his mistakes, the younger Crouse built a second bridge that lasted until 1950, when it again became irreparably damaged. In 1954 the BLM built a new swinging bridge with a load capacity equal to 400 sheep or a three-ton vehicle. This third swinging bridge is still in use today.

The trail comes to an end at the old Jarvie homestead. From the 1880s until his death in 1909, Jarvie lived in Brown's Park and owned a prosperous general store. He was a popular, well-liked character and a relatively well-educated man with a talent for music.

Description

To get to Brown's Park Trail from Vernal, follow the start of Northern #26: Rainbow and Island Park Trail. Leave Vernal on 500 North Street, which becomes Jones Hole Road. Rainbow and Island Park Trail turns off the paved Jones Hole Road at the 8.3-mile mark, but continue straight for another 17 miles until you reach Brown's Park Road. This intersection is the start of Brown's Park Trail.

The trail begins on a gravel country road that passes through rolling sagebrush with occasional pinyon and juniper. Although the road is easy and accessible by passenger car in dry weather, it becomes impassable in wet weather.

After 13.6 miles you reach the dramatic Crouse Canyon, which has a number of old cottonwoods and stunning rock formations. As you wind your way back and forth across the creek, the walls of the narrow canyon tower high above the trail.

After 17.3 miles, you enter Brown's Park National Wildlife Refuge and follow the Green River east into Colorado for a few miles until you reach the swinging suspen-

John Jarvie's cabin

THE WILD BUNCH AND THE OUTLAW TRAIL

Shadowed in notoriety, the Wild Bunch was a gang of outlaws whose exploits are legendary. Butch Cassidy (Robert Leroy Parker) served as the gang's head, and under his leadership the Wild Bunch was responsible for the robberies of several banks and trains throughout the West. Behind Cassidy rode such colorful characters as Kid Curry (Harvey Logan), the McCarty Brothers, the Tall Texan (Ben Kilpatrick), the Sundance Kid (Harry Longabaugh), Elza Lay (William Ellsworth), and Matt Warner (Willard Christianson). Although the gang existed before his arrival, it was Cassidy who tempered the outlaws' wild behavior and prompted them to extensively plan each hold-up. Their horses were trained to remain perfectly still in the midst of shouting, gunshots, and other disturbances. This way, when members of the Wild Bunch robbed a bank, they could sprint to their horses under a hail of gunfire without the animals becoming spooked. Other members of the gang would be stationed at various spots along the getaway route with fresh teams of horses. This enabled the robbers to keep ahead of the posses chasing them. It also allowed them to ride great distances to safety, earning the group the nickname, "long riders."

Butch Cassidy

Harry A. Longabaugh and Etta Place (taken in New York City in 1902)

The Wild Bunch. From left: Harry Longabaugh, Bill Carver, Ben Kirkpatrick, Harvey Logan, Robert LeRoy Parker

One of the outlaws' most infamous robberies took place on April 21, 1897, in Castle Gate, Utah. Along with Elza Lay and Joe Walker, Butch Cassidy robbed the Pleasant Valley Coal Company payroll of $7,000. No one was shot during the course of the robbery. After heists like these members of the Wild Bunch often sought refuge along the Outlaw Trail. However this trail did not follow a single, well-defined route. Instead, it was a difficult and ambiguous stretch of terrain that extended from Arizona, northeast through Utah, and into Wyoming. All along the trail, there were rough, less traveled roads and natural strongholds such as Hole-in-the-Wall in Wyoming and Brown's Park and Robbers Roost in Utah. These places were safe havens for outlaws on the run from posses and law enforcers.

Brown's Park—located in the northeast corner of Utah and also called Brown's Hole or Diamond Mountain—shares a bit of history with Cassidy's gang of desperados. This location was known early on as a safe refuge from the law, as it was located near the boundaries of three states (Wyoming, Utah, and Colorado), and it was often difficult to figure out who had jurisdiction. This confusion allowed the outlaws to make a quick getaway into another state. Local figures such as Charlie Crouse and John Jarvie welcomed the outlaws and warned them if a posse was on their trail. In turn, the outlaws were always very generous to their hosts in Brown's Park and never robbed them. Perhaps it was this loyalty to their friends and hosts that allowed members of the Wild Bunch to stay one step ahead of the law.

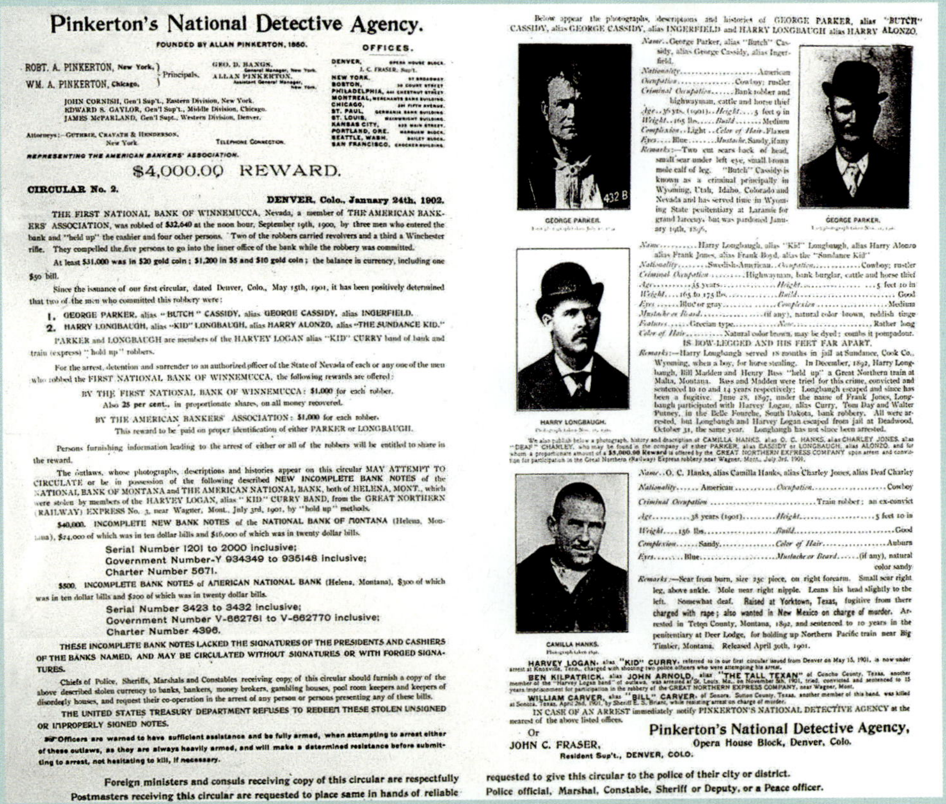
Pinkerton's National Detective Agency.

FOUNDED BY ALLAN PINKERTON, 1850.

ROBT. A. PINKERTON, New York, } Principals. WM. A. PINKERTON, Chicago.

GEO. D. BANGS, General Manager, New York.
ALLAN PINKERTON, Assistant General Manager, New York.

JOHN CORNISH, Gen'l Sup't., Eastern Division, New York.
EDWARD S. GAYLOR, Gen'l Sup't., Middle Division, Chicago.
JAMES McPARLAND, Gen'l Supt., Western Division, Denver.

Attorneys:—Guthrie, Cravath & Henderson, New York. Telephone Connection.

OFFICES.
DENVER, Opera House Block. J. C. FRASER, Sup't.
NEW YORK, 57 Broadway.
BOSTON, 30 Court Street.
PHILADELPHIA, 441 Chestnut Street.
MONTREAL, Merchants Bank Building.
CHICAGO, 201 Fifth Avenue.
ST. PAUL, Germania Bank Building.
ST. LOUIS, Wainwright Building.
KANSAS CITY, 622 Main Street.
PORTLAND, ORE. Marquam Block.
SEATTLE, WASH. Bailey Block.
SAN FRANCISCO, Crocker Building.

REPRESENTING THE AMERICAN BANKERS' ASSOCIATION.

$4,000.00 REWARD.

CIRCULAR No. 2.

DENVER, Colo., January 24th, 1902.

THE FIRST NATIONAL BANK OF WINNEMUCCA, Nevada, a member of THE AMERICAN BANKERS' ASSOCIATION, was robbed of $32,640 at the noon hour, September 19th, 1900, by three men who entered the bank and "held up" the cashier and four other persons. Two of the robbers carried revolvers and a third a Winchester rifle. They compelled the five persons to go into the inner office of the bank while the robbery was committed.

At least $31,000 was in $20 gold coin; $1,200 in $5 and $10 gold coin; the balance in currency, including one $50 bill.

Since the issuance of our first circular, dated Denver, Colo., May 15th, 1901, it has been positively determined that two of the men who committed this robbery were:

1. GEORGE PARKER, alias "BUTCH" CASSIDY, alias GEORGE CASSIDY, alias INGERFIELD.
2. HARRY LONGBAUGH, alias "KID" LONGBAUGH, alias HARRY ALONZO, alias "THE SUNDANCE KID."

PARKER and LONGBAUGH are members of the HARVEY LOGAN alias "KID" CURRY band of bank and train (express) "hold up" robbers.

For the arrest, detention and surrender to an authorized officer of the State of Nevada of each or any one of the men who robbed the FIRST NATIONAL BANK OF WINNEMUCCA, the following rewards are offered:

BY THE FIRST NATIONAL BANK OF WINNEMUCCA: $1,000 for each robber.
Also 25 per cent., in proportionate shares, on all money recovered.

BY THE AMERICAN BANKERS' ASSOCIATION: $1,000 for each robber.
This reward to be paid on proper identification of either PARKER or LONGBAUGH.

Persons furnishing information leading to the arrest of either or all of the robbers will be entitled to share in the reward.

The outlaws, whose photographs, descriptions and histories appear on this circular MAY ATTEMPT TO CIRCULATE or be in possession of the following described NEW INCOMPLETE BANK NOTES of the NATIONAL BANK OF MONTANA and THE AMERICAN NATIONAL BANK, both of HELENA, MONT., which were stolen by members of the HARVEY LOGAN, alias "KID" CURRY BAND, from the GREAT NORTHERN (RAILWAY) EXPRESS No. 3, near Wagner, Mont., July 3rd, 1901, by "hold up" methods.

$40,000. INCOMPLETE NEW BANK NOTES of the NATIONAL BANK OF MONTANA (Helena, Montana), $24,000 of which was in ten dollar bills and $16,000 of which was in twenty dollar bills.

Serial Number 1201 to 2000 inclusive;
Government Number-Y 934349 to 935148 inclusive;
Charter Number 5671.

$500. INCOMPLETE BANK NOTES of AMERICAN NATIONAL BANK (Helena, Montana), $300 of which was in ten dollar bills and $200 of which was in twenty dollar bills.

Serial Number 3423 to 3432 inclusive;
Government Number V-662761 to V-662770 inclusive;
Charter Number 4396.

THESE INCOMPLETE BANK NOTES LACKED THE SIGNATURES OF THE PRESIDENTS AND CASHIERS OF THE BANKS NAMED, AND MAY BE CIRCULATED WITHOUT SIGNATURES OR WITH FORGED SIGNATURES.

Chiefs of Police, Sheriffs, Marshals and Constables receiving copy of this circular should furnish a copy of the above described stolen currency to banks, bankers, money brokers, gambling houses, pool room keepers and keepers of disorderly houses, and request their co-operation in the arrest of any person or persons presenting any of these bills.

THE UNITED STATES TREASURY DEPARTMENT REFUSES TO REDEEM THESE STOLEN UNSIGNED OR IMPROPERLY SIGNED NOTES.

Officers are warned to have sufficient assistance and be fully armed, when attempting to arrest either of these outlaws, as they are always heavily armed, and will make a determined resistance before submitting to arrest, not hesitating to kill, if necessary.

Below appear the photographs, descriptions and histories of GEORGE PARKER, alias "BUTCH" CASSIDY, alias GEORGE CASSIDY, alias INGERFIELD and HARRY LONGBAUGH alias HARRY ALONZO.

GEORGE PARKER.

Name..George Parker, alias "Butch" Cassidy, alias George Cassidy, alias Ingerfield.
Nationality....................American
Occupation..............Cowboy; rustler
Criminal Occupation......Bank robber and highwayman, cattle and horse thief
Age..36 yrs. (1901)..*Height*....5 feet 9 in
Weight..165 lbs.....*Build*.......Medium
Complexion..Light ..*Color of Hair*..Flaxen
Eyes....Blue.......*Mustache*, Sandy, if any
Remarks:—Two cut scars back of head, small scar under left eye, small brown mole calf of leg. "Butch" Cassidy is known as a criminal principally in Wyoming, Utah, Idaho, Colorado and Nevada and has served time in Wyoming State penitentiary at Laramie for grand larceny, but was pardoned January 19th, 1896.

GEORGE PARKER.

HARRY LONGBAUGH.

Name..........Harry Longbaugh, alias "Kid" Longbaugh, alias Harry Alonzo alias Frank Jones, alias Frank Boyd, alias the "Sundance Kid"
Nationality........Swedish-American..*Occupation*............Cowboy; rustler
Criminal Occupation.........Highwayman, bank burglar, cattle and horse thief
Age...........35 years...............*Height*.................5 feet 10 in
Weight....165 to 175 lbs.............*Build*..........................Good
Eyes......Blue or gray..............*Complexion*...................Medium
Mustache or Beard................(if any), natural color brown, reddish tinge
Features......Grecian type............*Nose*......................Rather long
Color of Hair..........Natural color brown, may be dyed; combs it pompadour.
IS BOW-LEGGED AND HIS FEET FAR APART.
Remarks:—Harry Longbaugh served 18 months in jail at Sundance, Cook Co., Wyoming, when a boy, for horse stealing. In December, 1892, Harry Longbaugh, Bill Madden and Henry Bass "held up" a Great Northern train at Malta, Montana. Bass and Madden were tried for this crime, convicted and sentenced to 10 and 14 years respectively; Longbaugh escaped and since has been a fugitive. June 28, 1897, under the name of Frank Jones, Longbaugh participated with Harvey Logan, alias Curry, Tom Day and Walter Putney, in the Belle Fourche, South Dakota, bank robbery. All were arrested, but Longbaugh and Harvey Logan escaped from jail at Deadwood, October 31, the same year. Longbaugh has not since been arrested.

We also publish below a photograph, history and description of CAMILLA HANKS, alias O. C. HANKS, alias CHARLEY JONES, alias "DEAF" CHARLEY, who may be found in the company of either PARKER, alias CASSIDY or LONGBAUGH, alias ALONZO, and for whom a proportionate amount of a $5,000.00 Reward is offered by the GREAT NORTHERN EXPRESS COMPANY upon arrest and conviction for participation in the Great Northern (Railway) Express robbery near Wagner, Mont., July 3rd, 1901.

CAMILLA HANKS.

Name..O. C. Hanks, alias Camilla Hanks, alias Charley Jones, alias Deaf Charley
Nationality......American...........*Occupation*...................Cowboy
Criminal Occupation..........................Train robber; an ex-convict
Age..........38 years (1901).........*Height*....................5 feet 10 in
Weight....156 lbs..................*Build*..........................Good
Complexion......Sandy...............*Color of Hair*.................Auburn
Eyes........Blue......................*Mustache or Beard*......(if any), natural color sandy
Remarks:—Scar from burn, size 25c piece, on right forearm. Small scar right leg, above ankle. Mole near right nipple. Leans his head slightly to the left. Somewhat deaf. Raised at Yorktown, Texas, fugitive from there charged with rape; also wanted in New Mexico on charge of murder. Arrested in Teton County, Montana, 1892, and sentenced to 10 years in the penitentiary at Deer Lodge, for holding up Northern Pacific train near Big Timber, Montana. Released April 30th, 1901.

HARVEY LOGAN, alias "KID" CURRY, referred to in our first circular issued from Denver on May 15, 1901, is now under arrest at Knoxville, Tenn., charged with shooting two police officers who were attempting his arrest.

BEN KILPATRICK, alias JOHN ARNOLD, alias "THE TALL TEXAN" of Concho County, Texas, another member of the "Harvey Logan band" of outlaws, was arrested at St. Louis, Mo., on November 5th, 1901, tried, convicted and sentenced to 15 years imprisonment for participation in the robbery of the GREAT NORTHERN EXPRESS COMPANY, near Wagner, Mont.

WILLIAM CARVER, alias "BILL" CARVER, of Sonora, Sutton County, Texas, another member of this band, was killed at Sonora, Texas, April 2nd, 1901, by Sheriff E. S. Briant, while resisting arrest on charge of murder.

IN CASE OF AN ARREST immediately notify PINKERTON'S NATIONAL DETECTIVE AGENCY at the nearest of the above listed offices.

Or
JOHN C. FRASER,
Resident Sup't., DENVER, COLO.

Pinkerton's National Detective Agency,
Opera House Block, Denver, Colo.

Foreign ministers and consuls receiving copy of this circular are respectfully requested to give this circular to the police of their city or district.

Postmasters receiving this circular are requested to place same in hands of reliable Police official, Marshal, Constable, Sheriff or Deputy, or a Peace officer.

Wanted poster for Butch Cassidy and the Sundance Kid

sion bridge. Just before the bridge, a side track branches off the main road and travels for 7 miles along the Green River before coming to an abrupt end at a gate, where it is closed to motorized vehicle traffic. Just before the gate, Hoy Draw (named for the Hoy family who lived in the area in the late 1800s) goes off to the right. Although it appears as a 4WD road on most maps, it is now closed to all motorized vehicles.

The Brown's Park Trail continues over the suspension bridge and turns back west into Utah, where it eventually comes to an end at the historic Jarvie Ranch.

To begin the trail from the Jarvie Ranch end, take US 191 to Minnies Gap just over the state line into Wyoming. From here, turn east onto Basin Road or Brown's Park Road Scenic Backway. Continue along this wide, country road through Jessie Ewing Canyon (named after yet another interesting figure in Brown's Park's history) until the turnoff for the John Jarvie Ranch. Turn right toward the ranch and the start of the trail.

Current Road Information

BLM Vernal Field Office
170 South 500 East
Vernal, UT 84078
(435) 781-4400

Map References

BLM Dutch John
USGS 1:24,000 Crouse Reservoir, Hoy Mtn., Swallow Canyon, Willow Creek Butte, Clay Basin
1:100,000 Dutch John
Utah Atlas & Gazetteer, p. 21
Utah Road & Recreation Atlas, p. 47

Route Directions

▼ 0.0	On Jones Hole Road, 17 miles past the turnoff for Northern #26: Rainbow and Island Park Trail, zero trip meter and turn north onto Brown's Park Road. This is signed to Crouse Reservoir, Calder Reservoir, and Brown's Park. Then cross cattle guard.
5.5 ▲	Trail ends at Jones Hole Road. Turn

Remains of Jarvis homestead

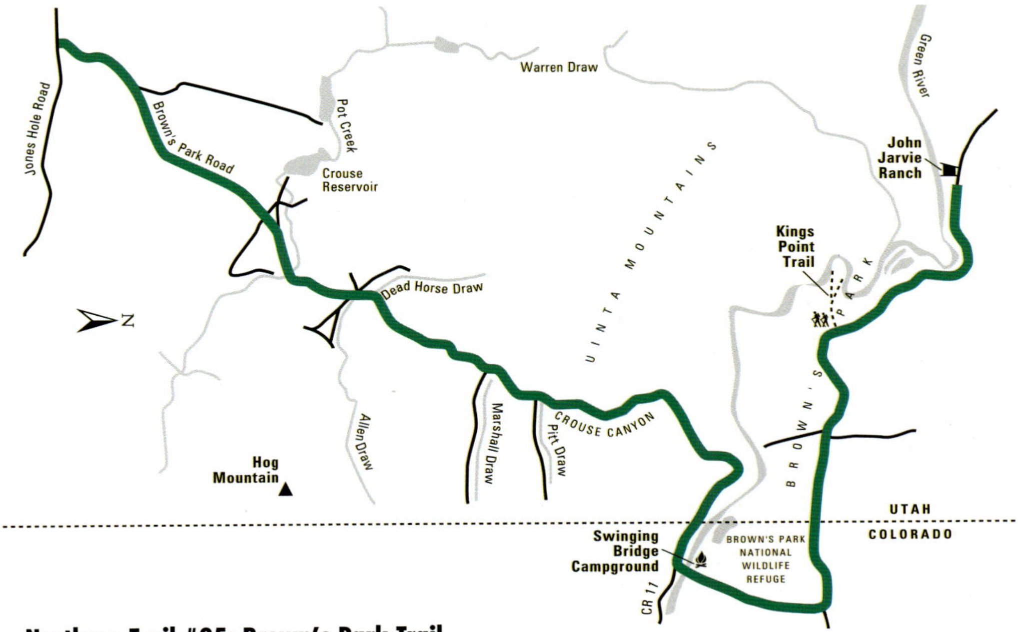

Northern Trail #25: Brown's Park Trail

right for Vernal and Northern #26: Rainbow and Island Park Trail.
GPS: N 40°39.25′ W 109°13.66′

▼ 2.1 BR Road forks. Crouse and Calder Reservoirs to the left.
3.4 ▲ BL Crouse and Calder Reservoirs to the right.
GPS: N 40°40.77′ W 109°12.61′

▼ 2.9 SO Cattle guard.
2.6 ▲ SO Cattle guard.

▼ 4.3 SO Cattle guard.
1.2 ▲ SO Cattle guard.

▼ 5.5 SO Road to Crouse Reservoir on left. Zero trip meter.
0.0 ▲ Continue along main road.
GPS: N 40°42.77′ W 109°09.82′

▼ 0.0 Continue straight.
10.9 ▲ SO Road to Crouse Reservoir on right. Zero trip meter.

▼ 0.2 SO Cattle guard.
10.7 ▲ SO Cattle guard.

▼ 1.2 SO Cross Pot Creek.
9.7 ▲ SO Cross Pot Creek.

▼ 1.6 SO Cattle guard.
9.3 ▲ SO Cattle guard.

▼ 2.5 SO Track on right to Allen Draw.
8.4 ▲ SO Track on left to Allen Draw.

▼ 3.0 BR Track on left to Dead Horse Draw.
7.8 ▲ BL Track on right to Dead Horse Draw.

▼ 3.5 SO Cattle guard.
7.4 ▲ SO Cattle guard.

▼ 4.7 SO Track on right.
6.2 ▲ SO Track on left.

▼ 5.0 SO Cattle guard.
5.8 ▲ SO Cattle guard.

▼ 5.7 SO Track on right to Marshall Draw.
5.2 ▲ SO Track on left to Marshall Draw.
GPS: N 40°46.43′ W 109°06.36′

▼ 6.7 SO Track on right to Pitt Draw.

4.1 ▲ SO Track on left to Pitt Draw.

▼ 8.1 SO Cattle guard. Enter Crouse Canyon.
2.8 ▲ SO Cattle guard. Exit Crouse Canyon.
GPS: N 40°48.23′ W 109°05.40′

▼ 9.9 SO Climb out of Crouse Canyon.
1.0 ▲ SO Descend Crouse Canyon.
GPS: N 40°49.44′ W 109°05.63′

▼ 10.9 SO Track on left to Taylor Flat. Zero trip meter.
0.0 ▲ Continue north.
GPS: N 40°49.79′ W 109°04.75′

▼ 0.0 Continue south.
3.5 ▲ SO Track on right to Taylor Flat. Zero trip meter.

▼ 0.9 SO Enter Brown's Park National Wildlife Refuge.
2.5 ▲ SO Leave Brown's Park National Wildlife Refuge.

▼ 2.5 SO Cattle guard.
1.0 ▲ SO Cattle guard.

▼ 3.5 BL Suspension bridge is on left; CR 11 is straight ahead. Zero trip meter at intersection.
0.0 ▲ Continue along trail.
GPS: N 40°49.60′ W 109°01.85′

▼ 0.0 Continue over suspension bridge.
6.7 ▲ BR Exit bridge. CR 11 on left. Zero trip meter at intersection.

▼ 0.1 SO Swinging Bridge Campground on left.
6.6 ▲ SO Swinging Bridge Campground on right. Cross the bridge.

▼ 0.3 SO Track on right.
6.4 ▲ SO Track on left.

▼ 1.3 SO Cattle guard. Leave Brown's Park National Wildlife Refuge.
5.4 ▲ SO Cattle guard. Enter Brown's Park National Wildlife Refuge.

▼ 2.8 TL Cattle guard and intersection with paved road.
3.9 ▲ TR Cattle guard and intersection with paved road.
GPS: N 40°51.96′ W 109°00.94′

▼ 4.5 SO Cross cattle guard and Utah/Colorado state line.
2.2 ▲ SO Cross Utah/Colorado state line and cattle guard.

▼ 6.2 SO Cattle guard. Old log cabin on private property is in line with cattle guard on left.
0.5 ▲ SO Cattle guard. Old log cabin on private property is in line with cattle guard on right.

▼ 6.7 SO Track on left to Swallow Canyon (1.7 miles), which has small boat launch area with public toilets. Zero trip meter.
0.0 ▲ Continue along main road.
GPS: N 40°52.13′ W 109°05.36′

▼ 0.0 Continue toward Jarvie Ranch.
6.3 ▲ SO Track on right to Swallow Canyon (1.7 miles), which has small boat launch area with public toilets. Zero trip meter.

▼ 2.0 SO Kings Point Trail on left.
4.3 ▲ SO Kings Point Trail on right.

▼ 4.7 TL Track to Jarvie historic site on left.
1.6 ▲ TR Turn right onto Brown's Park Road.

▼ 5.1 SO David's Ranch on left.
1.2 ▲ SO David's Ranch on right.

▼ 6.0 SO Bridge Hollow Recreation Area to the left.
0.2 ▲ SO Bridge Hollow Recreation Area to the right.

▼ 6.3 Trail ends at John Jarvie Ranch on left.
0.0 ▲ At historic John Jarvie Ranch, zero trip meter and proceed east toward Brown's Park Road.
GPS: N 40°53.97′ W 109°10.61′

NORTHERN REGION TRAIL #26

Rainbow and Island Park Trail

STARTING POINT Vernal
FINISHING POINT Green River in Island Park
TOTAL MILEAGE 29.4 miles
UNPAVED MILEAGE 19.7 miles
DRIVING TIME 1.25 hours (one-way)
ELEVATION RANGE 5,000–5,800 feet
USUALLY OPEN Year-round
DIFFICULTY RATING 2
SCENIC RATING 8
REMOTENESS RATING +1

Special Attractions

- McKee Spring petroglyphs.
- Green River overlooks.
- Ruple Ranch.
- Dinosaur National Monument.

History

The Rainbow and Island Park Trail runs through a part of northeastern Utah that was, millions of years ago, home to the dinosaurs, who lived in Utah throughout the Jurassic Period. The first discovery of dinosaur fossils in Utah was made in 1909 by paleontologist Earl Douglass from the Carnegie Museum in Pittsburgh, Pennsylvania, who dug up the remains of an apatosaurus (known also as brontosaurus). Since then, his quarry has become one of the most important regions in the world for dinosaur research and excavation. In 1938, 200,000 acres in Utah and Colorado were set aside as Dinosaur National Monument. The park's visitor center, constructed in 1958, was built so that from inside you can see about two thousand exposed bones in the quarry's wall.

The McKee Spring petroglyphs located along the trail are evidence of the Fremont Indian culture, which lived in Utah from about A.D. 100 to 1250. No one knows its

Green River flows below the Island Park Overlook

The old cabin at Ruple Ranch

View of Island Park track

significance, but this rock art has endured for centuries. Please do not touch the art. McKee Spring gets its name from the large McKee family that lived near Rainbow and Island Park in the late 1800s. Much to father James McKee's chagrin, his eight boys were notorious thugs in the region, even going so far as to ride around killing bucks by clubbing them on the head and leaving them for dead. However, the McKees were among the first to run cattle on Diamond Mountain, north of Green River, and so have left their name attached to many of its landmarks.

Around the same time as the McKee boys were getting into mischief, Hank and May Ruple quietly made their home in Island Park. The Ruple Ranch, established in 1883, is home to a large cottonwood tree that is thought to be the largest of its kind in the western United States. The Ruples used it to hang up saddles, bridles, and harnesses, and they enjoyed its peaceful shade. The cottonwood remains today as a distinctive landmark in Island Park.

In the late 19th century, Vernal became an important stop along the Outlaw Trail.

Petroglyphs at Dino Park

The remote Brown's Park, in the very northeastern corner of the state, served as one of the Wild Bunch's main hideouts. When members of the Wild Bunch would come into "sudden riches," it was not uncommon to see them in Vernal celebrating, stocking up on supplies, and repaying old debts.

Description

Starting out on Main Street in Vernal, the Rainbow and Island Park Trail leaves town on paved roads before turning onto a well-maintained country gravel road. Once you cross into Dinosaur National Monument, the trail becomes a sandy and red, but easy, graded dirt road.

This trail enters the national monument from the north after 19.6 miles and is very interesting, providing wonderful views over the Green River. You reach the wall of Fremont Indian petroglyphs about three-quarters of a mile after you enter the monument.

Traveling mostly through sage with scattered pinyon and juniper, you eventually come upon the Ruple Ranch buildings and the enormous cottonwood. From this point, the trail becomes somewhat more difficult and follows a single-lane, sandy track out to an overlook of the Green River Valley and the old Ruple ranchlands.

Northern Trail #26: Rainbow and Island Park T

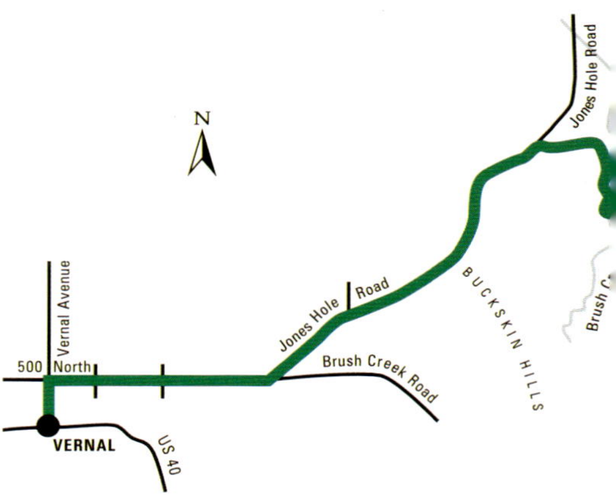

Green River from Rainbow Park Boat Launch

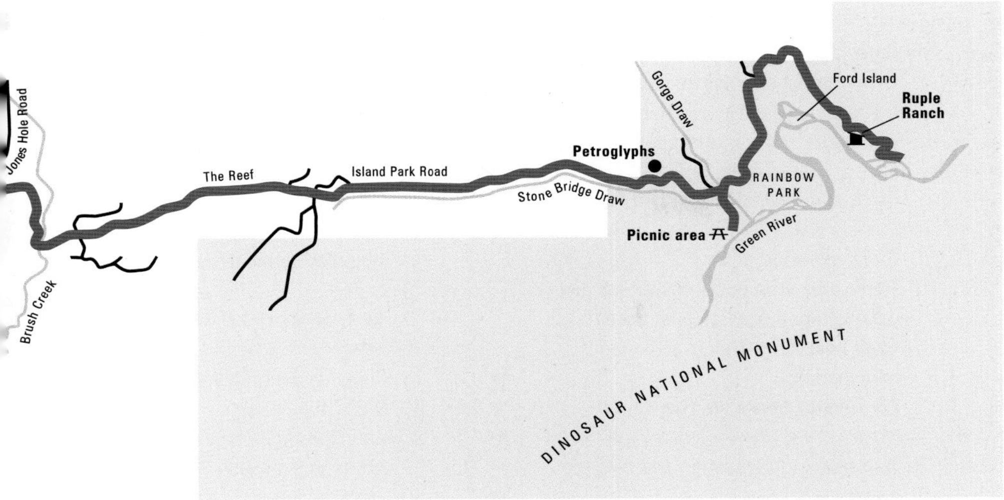

Current Road Information

BLM Vernal Field Office
170 South 500 East
Vernal, UT 84078
(435) 781-4400

Dinosaur National Monument
4545 Highway 40
Dinosaur, CO 81610
(435) 781-7700

Map References

BLM Vernal, Dutch John
USGS 1:24,000 Vernal NE, Naples, Donkey Flat, Dinosaur Quarry, Jensen Ridge, Island Park, Split Mtn., Jones Hole
1:100,000 Vernal, Dutch John
Trails Illustrated, #220 (incomplete)
Utah Atlas & Gazetteer, p. 29
Utah Road & Recreation Atlas, p. 55

Route Directions

▼ 0.0 In Vernal, on Main Street (US 40), turn north on Vernal Avenue and zero trip meter.
GPS: N 40°27.36′ W 109°31.65′

▼ 0.4 SO Ashley National Forest Office on left.
▼ 0.5 TR Turn right onto 500 North Street.
▼ 3.4 BL Bear left; road becomes Jones Hole Road. Road on right is Brush Creek Road.
▼ 8.3 TR Turn right onto unmarked road and zero trip meter.
GPS: N 40°30.52′ W 109°24.11′

▼ 0.0 Proceed east.
▼ 0.7 TR Intersection.
▼ 1.4 SO Trail is now gravel road.
▼ 1.8 BL Fork in road.
▼ 1.9 SO Cross cattle guard.
▼ 2.1 SO Track on right.
▼ 4.9 SO Cattle guard.
▼ 5.9 SO Track on left.
▼ 6.4 SO Track on left.
▼ 7.0 SO Cross over Stone Bridge Draw.
▼ 8.8 SO Cross over Stone Bridge Draw. Then track on right.
▼ 9.4 SO Cross through wash.
▼ 9.9 SO Track on left.
▼ 10.1 SO Cross through wash.
▼ 11.2 SO Cross through wash.
▼ 11.3 SO Cattle guard. Enter Dinosaur National Monument. Zero trip meter.
GPS: N 40°30.49′ W 109°12.63′

▼ 0.0 Proceed east.
▼ 0.7 SO Several panels of petroglyphs on left; look at dark parts of rock face. You can pull off trail before crossing wash.
GPS: N 40°30.49′ W 109°11.88′

▼ 1.8 BR Cross over Gorge Draw. Fork in road. Bear right on spur to Green River. Main trail continues left to Island Park. You will return to this intersection after spur to Green River.

GPS: N 40°30.32' W 109°10.73'

▼ 2.0 SO Cross over Gorge Draw.

▼ 2.6 UT Picnic area with public restrooms and parking. Road dead-ends at Green River boat ramp. Return to previous intersection.

GPS: N 40°29.73' W 109°10.41'

▼ 3.4 TR Turn right at intersection and zero trip meter.

GPS: N 40°30.32' W 109°10.73'

▼ 0.0 Continue along trail toward Island Park.

▼ 1.5 BR Intersection with loop road to overlook with spectacular view of Green River and beyond.

GPS: N 40°31.14' W 109°09.86'

▼ 1.7 BR Bear right onto Island Park Road.

▼ 2.6 SO Track on left.

▼ 3.4 SO Cattle guard.

▼ 4.4 SO Two tracks on right are 1.4-mile, 4WD loop road to the Green River. Zero trip meter.

GPS: N 40°31.74' W 109°08.95'

▼ 0.0 Continue past private track on left.

▼ 0.4 SO Cross over wash.

▼ 0.7 SO Gate into Ruple Ranch. Then track on left, which makes a 1.8-mile loop.

▼ 0.8 SO Corral on left and cabin on right. The Ruples' enormous cottonwood tree is beside road.

▼ 2.0 End of trail.

GPS: N 40°30.84' W 109°07.35'

Island Park Overlook

View from Echo Park road

NORTHERN REGION TRAIL #27

Echo Park and Yampa Bench Trail

STARTING POINT US 40 in Utah, 12.3 miles east of Jensen
FINISHING POINT US 40 in Colorado, 28.5 miles east of Utah state line
TOTAL MILEAGE 81.4 miles
UNPAVED MILEAGE 68.2 miles
DRIVING TIME 4 hours
ELEVATION RANGE 5,200–8,100 feet
USUALLY OPEN May to November
DIFFICULTY RATING 2
SCENIC RATING 10
REMOTENESS RATING +1

Special Attractions

- Travel through part of Dinosaur National Monument.
- Petroglyphs by the Fremont Indians.
- Spectacular views overlooking the Yampa River.
- Sand Canyon and Echo Park.
- Chew Ranch and Baker cabin.

History

The earliest known white men to pass through Echo Park were fur trappers (William H. Ashley, for example, came through in the 19th century) but the rock art displayed along the canyon walls shows that the region was inhabited by Indians at least 600 years earlier. Echo Park was named during John Wesley Powell's 1869 expedition of the Colorado Plateau, and in 1883, Patrick Lynch was the first man to homestead in the canyon.

Just before the trail passes the panel of petroglyphs, it comes to the remains of the old Chew Ranch. Born in England, Jack Chew moved to America with his family and grew up in southern Utah. Around the age of 12, Chew ran away from home and met up with the McCarty gang. A band of notorious outlaws and cattle rustlers, the McCarty gang demonstrated an unexpected soft side when they allowed Jack to live with them for the next 10 years, during which Jack learned about horses, cattle, and life in the Utah wilderness. He eventually started his own family and settled down in northeastern Utah on what is now known as the Chew Ranch.

By 1912, the Chews had left their ranch

Yampa River in Echo Park Hole

Wash on Yampa Bench road

Site of petroglyphs near Chew Ranch

up to the Yampa Plateau. The trail then briefly crosses into Colorado, returns to Utah, and then returns to Colorado for the rest of the trail.

After 11.7 miles, you reach the national monument information center; turn north here onto paved Harpers Corner Drive. About 7.4 miles along Harpers Corner Drive, Canyon Overlook is to the right. The land here drops away quickly along the faultline between the Yampa and Red Rocks continental plates. Over millions of years, one of the Weber sandstone plates fell away from the other and was then carved out even further by the Yampa River. The result is this narrow river canyon 2,600 feet below the overlook.

About 5.5 miles farther up the road there is an overlook into the valley where three faults come together. Shortly thereafter, turn east onto Echo Park Road and begin the descent into the iron-red valley. Originally

Chew Ranch

and moved across to Pats Hole in Colorado. Pats Hole sits at the meeting of the Yampa and Green Rivers. In the days of the Outlaw Trail, members of the Wild Bunch found this place to be the best river crossing on their way in and out of Brown's Park to the north.

The Baker cabin is another historic site along the trail and is located about 150 yards off the main trail along a disused vehicle track. The cabin, stables, and corral were built in 1918 and abandoned in the 1930s.

Description

On US 40, about 12 miles east of Jensen and 1.2 miles east of Utah 45, turn north onto CR 16S (Blue Mountain Road) and head toward Dinosaur National Monument. The first section of the trail follows a graded county road that soon turns east and travels through dense pinyon and juniper about a mile south of the 2,000-foot cliffs that rise

Baker cabin

The Green River from Harding Hole Overlook

used by the Chew family, this steep road had no switchbacks, forcing the homesteaders to hitch horses to the rear of their wagons to act as brakes. The road is not as difficult to negotiate these days and can be driven by passenger cars as well as SUVs; however, it should not be driven by large vehicles or ones towing trailers. Avoid the road when it is wet; the red clay becomes thick and greasy and is impassable.

About 5 miles from the turn onto Echo Park Road, the red scenery gives way to buff-colored sandstone as you enter Sand Canyon. The road surface in the canyon becomes sandy, but remains easy to drive. After 7.4 miles along Echo Park Road, a 3.8-mile spur trail leads down another beautiful sandstone canyon to the 800-foot Steamboat Rock at the confluence of the Green and Yampa Rivers. This Echo Park landmark stands at the old outlaw river crossing known as Pats Hole.

Along the spur to Pats Hole and Echo Park is the Chew Ranch and the Fremont Indian petroglyphs. At the end, there is a developed campground and a boat launch for white-water rafting on the Green River. Fees and noncommercial river permits are required for rafting; for information, call (970) 374-2468.

After returning to the main trail, you begin a 1,000-foot ascent onto Yampa Bench, which winds through a number of canyons and draws. Even though the road here is periodically graded, it does have a few washouts and occasional rough spots. This section of the route is more remote, and the scenery, though somewhat varied, consists mostly of sagebrush, pinyon, and juniper. The highlights along the Yampa Bench are the high overlooks above the twisting canyons of the Yampa River. The old Baker cabin sits about 150 yards off the main road up an old, abandoned vehicle track that still serves as a walking path.

Although the drive along the Echo Park and Yampa Bench Trail takes about four hours nonstop, you could easily spend a few

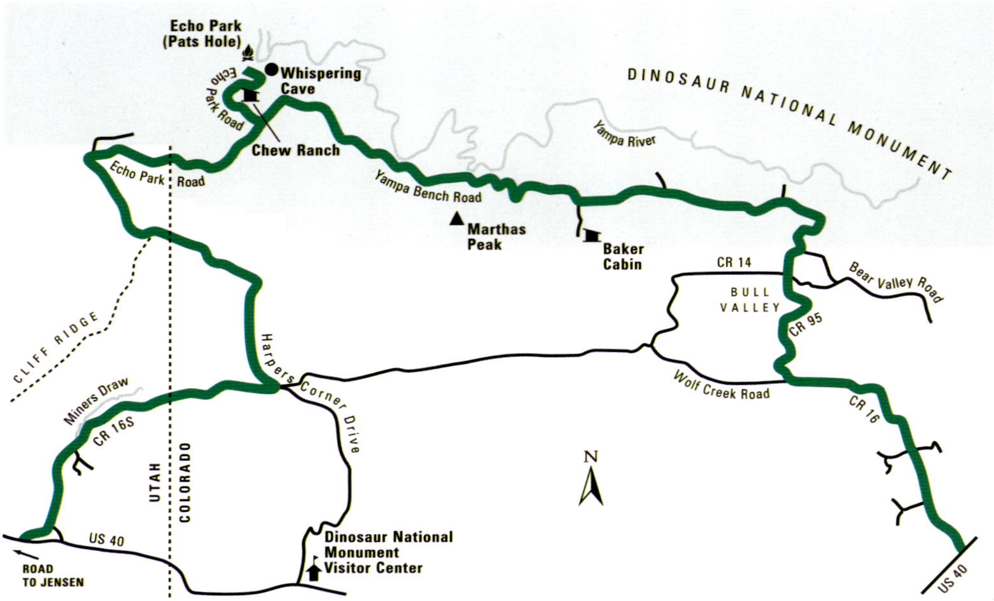

Northern Trail #27: Echo Park and Yampa Bench Trail

days exploring the side canyons, camping along the river, and relaxing at some of the many overlooks. The trail eventually ends at US 40 in Colorado.

Current Road Information

Dinosaur National Monument
4545 E. Highway 40
Dinosaur, CO 81610-9724
(435) 781-7700

Map References

BLM Vernal, Rangely, Dutch John, Canyon of Lodore
USGS 1:24,000 Cliff Ridge, Snake John Reef, Plug Hat Rock, Hells Canyon, Stuntz Reservoir, Jones Hole, Tanks Peak, Haystack Rock, Skull Creek
1:100,000 Vernal, Rangely, Dutch John, Canyon of Lodore
Trails Illustrated, #220 (incompete)
Utah Atlas & Gazetteer, p. 29 (incomplete)
Utah Road & Recreation Atlas, p. 63 (incomplete)

Route Directions

▼ 0.0		On US 40, about 12.3 miles east of Jensen, zero trip meter and turn north onto CR 16S (Blue Mountain Road).
11.7 ▲		Trail ends at US 40; turn right for Jensen, left for Colorado.
		GPS: N 40°17.25' W 109°08.40'
▼ 1.0	SO	Track on right. Then cross over Cliff Creek.
10.7 ▲	SO	Cross over Cliff Creek. Then track on left.
▼ 1.7	SO	Track on left.
10.0 ▲	SO	Track on right.
▼ 4.0	SO	Corral on left. Then cross Miners Draw.
7.7 ▲	SO	Cross Miners Draw. Then corral on right.
▼ 7.3	SO	Cattle guard.
4.4 ▲	SO	Cattle guard.
▼ 11.7	TL	Cattle guard, then turn left onto paved Harpers Corner Drive and zero trip meter. Dinosaur National Monument

information center is to the left.
0.0 ▲ Continue along unpaved road.
GPS: N 40°21.76′ W 108°58.97′

▼ 0.0 Continue along paved road.
13.2 ▲ TR Turn right onto CR 16S (Blue Mountain Road). Zero trip meter.

▼ 0.6 SO Cattle guard.
12.6 ▲ SO Cattle guard.

▼ 0.7 SO Seasonal gate.
12.5 ▲ SO Seasonal gate.

▼ 2.0 SO Marker #12 for Wolf Creek Fault.
11.2 ▲ SO Marker #12 for Wolf Creek Fault.

▼ 2.3 SO Marker for good wildlife viewing area.
10.9 ▲ SO Marker for good wildlife viewing area.

▼ 4.2 SO Marker #14 notes that this is highest point along Harpers Corner Drive.
9.0 ▲ SO Marker #14 notes that this is highest point along Harpers Corner Drive.

▼ 4.6 SO Cattle guard.
8.6 ▲ SO Cattle guard.

▼ 7.4 SO Canyon Overlook on right. Picnic area and nature trail.
5.8 ▲ SO Canyon Overlook on left. Picnic area and nature trail.

▼ 9.3 SO Cross state line into Utah.
3.9 ▲ SO Cross state line into Colorado.

▼ 11.7 SO View right of Douglas Mountain and Zenobia Peak (9,006 feet).
1.5 ▲ SO View left of Douglas Mountain and Zenobia Peak (9,006 feet).

▼ 12.0 SO Corral on left; used in spring and fall for cattle and sheep.
1.2 ▲ SO Corral on right; used in spring and fall for cattle and sheep.

▼ 12.9 SO Marker notes meeting point of Yampa, Red Rock, and Mitten Park Faults. From overlook you can see Echo Park Road.
0.3 ▲ SO Parking area and view back onto Echo Park Road.

▼ 13.2 TR Turn right onto Echo Park Road. Then cross cattle guard. Zero trip meter.
0.0 ▲ Continue along main road.
GPS: N 40°28.62′ W 109°05.84′

▼ 0.0 Descend into canyon.
7.4 ▲ TL Turn left onto paved Harpers Corner Drive. Zero trip meter.

▼ 3.2 SO Cross cattle guard.
4.2 ▲ SO Cross cattle guard.

▼ 4.9 SO Entering Sand Canyon.
2.5 ▲ SO Leaving Sand Canyon.

Remains of Baker homestead

▼ 7.4 SO Straight is spur trail to Pats Hole and Echo Park. Main trail continues right on Yampa Bench Road. Zero trip meter. You will return to this intersection.
0.0 ▲ Continue along route.
GPS: N 40°29.38′ W 108°59.37′

Spur Trail to Pats Hole

▼ 0.0 Proceed north toward Pats Hole.
7.6 ▲ SO At intersection of Yampa Bench Road and Echo Park Road, zero trip meter and continue straight ahead.

▼ 1.2 SO Chew Ranch buildings on right and left.
6.4 ▲ SO Chew Ranch buildings on right and left.
GPS: N 40°29.97′ W 109°00.47′

▼ 1.3 SO Cross Pool Creek ford.
6.2 ▲ SO Cross Pool Creek ford.

▼ 1.7 SO Log structure on left.
5.9 ▲ SO Log structure on right.

▼ 2.7 SO Ford.
4.9 ▲ SO Ford.
GPS: N 40°30.68′ W 108°59.33′

▼ 2.8 SO Petroglyphs about 35 feet above creek on left. Pullover area on right.
4.8 ▲ SO Petroglyphs about 35 feet above creek on right. Pullover area on left.

▼ 3.2 SO Whispering Cave on right.
4.4 ▲ SO Whispering Cave on left.

▼ 3.3 SO Ford.
4.2 ▲ SO Ford.

▼ 3.4 SO Ford.
4.2 ▲ SO Ford.

▼ 3.6 SO Road on left.
4.0 ▲ SO Road on right.

▼ 3.7 SO Ford.
3.9 ▲ SO Ford.

▼ 3.8 UT Pats Hole and Echo Park. Boat launch area, public toilets, and camping. Return to previous intersection where you zeroed trip meter.
3.8 ▲ UT Pats Hole and Echo Park. Boat launch area, public toilets, and camping. Return to previous intersection where you zeroed trip meter.
GPS: N 40°31.19′ W 108°59.39′

▼ 7.6 TL At intersection of Yampa Bench Road and Echo Park Road, zero trip meter and turn left onto Yampa Bench Road (CR 14N).
0.0 ▲ Continue toward Pats Hole.
GPS: N 40°29.38′ W 108°59.37′

Continuation of Main Trail

▼ 0.0 Continue along Yampa Bench Road.
6.4 ▲ TR Turn right for spur trail to Pats Hole and Echo Park. Main trail continues left on Echo Park Road. Zero trip meter. You will return to this intersection.

▼ 1.0 SO Cross through wash.
5.4 ▲ SO Cross through wash.

▼ 2.7 SO Cattle guard.
3.7 ▲ SO Cattle guard.

▼ 3.8 SO Track on right.
2.6 ▲ SO Track on left.

▼ 5.7 SO Cross through wash.
0.7 ▲ SO Cross through wash.

▼ 5.9 SO Cross through wash.
0.5 ▲ SO Cross through wash.
GPS: N 40°28.13′ W 108°54.62′

▼ 6.3 SO Cross through wash.
0.1 ▲ SO Cross through wash.

▼ 6.4 SO Castle Park Overlook on left. Zero trip meter.
0.0 ▲ Continue toward Echo Park Road.
GPS: N 40°28.01′ W 108°54.13′

▼ 0.0 Continue along Yampa Bench Road.
2.7 ▲ SO Castle Park Overlook on right. Zero trip meter.

▼ 0.9 SO Cattle guard.
1.8 ▲ SO Cattle guard.

▼ 1.1 BR Road forks. Left is private road to Mantle Ranch. Then cross through wash.
1.6 ▲ BL Cross through wash. Then road forks. Right is private road to Mantle Ranch.
GPS: N 40°27.50′ W 108°53.33′

▼ 2.7 SO Track on left to Harding Hole Overlook. Zero trip meter.
0.0 ▲ Continue along main trail.
GPS: N 40°27.73′ W 108°51.73′

▼ 0.0 Continue along main trail.
1.2 ▲ SO Track on right to Harding Hole Overlook. Zero trip meter.

▼ 1.2 SO Wagon Wheel Point Overlook on left. For best views, walk about 250 yards. Zero trip meter.
0.0 ▲ Continue along trail.
GPS: N 40°27.59′ W 108°50.64′

▼ 0.0 Continue along trail.
15.2 ▲ SO Wagon Wheel Point Overlook on right. For best views, walk about 250 yards. Zero trip meter.

▼ 1.6 SO Cross through wash.
13.6 ▲ SO Cross through wash.

▼ 4.5 SO Closed track on right to Baker cabin, stables, and corrals.
10.7 ▲ SO Closed track on left to Baker cabin, stables, and corrals.
GPS: N 40°27.04′ W 108°47.60′

▼ 7.2 SO Track on left.
8.0 ▲ SO Track on right.

▼ 8.5 SO Track on left.
6.7 ▲ SO Track on right.

▼ 12.1 SO Cattle guard.
3.1 ▲ SO Cattle guard.

▼ 15.2 SO Cattle guard. Leave Dinosaur National Monument. Zero trip meter.
0.0 ▲ Continue along main trail.
GPS: N 40°25.69′ W 108°39.36′

▼ 0.0 Continue along main trail.
15.9 ▲ SO Enter Dinosaur National Monument and cross cattle guard. Zero trip meter.

▼ 0.1 BR Bear right onto CR 95. CR 14N continues straight.
15.8 ▲ BL Bear left onto CR 14N.
GPS: N 40°25.65′ W 108°39.30′

▼ 1.2 TR T-intersection.
14.7 ▲ TL Road on left.
GPS: N 40°24.87′ W 108°39.73′

▼ 1.3 BL Road on right is CR 14. Continue on CR 95.
14.6 ▲ BR Road on left is CR 14. Continue along CR 95.

▼ 6.3 SO Cattle guard.
9.6 ▲ SO Cattle guard.

▼ 6.5 TL Turn left onto CR 16, Wolf Creek Road.
9.4 ▲ TR Turn right onto CR 95.
GPS: N 40°21.65′ W 108°40.06′

▼ 6.7 SO Cattle guard.
9.2 ▲ SO Cattle guard.

▼ 9.8 SO Road on left.
6.1 ▲ SO Road on right.

▼ 15.9 Cattle guard. Trail ends at US 40. Turn right for Utah and Jensen.
0.0 ▲ On US 40, about 28.5 miles east of the Utah/Colorado state line, zero trip meter and turn north onto CR 16.
GPS: N 40°16.67′ W 108°33.54′

NORTHERN REGION TRAIL #28

Rainbow and Watson Ghost Towns Trail

STARTING POINT Northern #29: Dragon Ghost Town Trail
FINISHING POINT Utah 45, the American Gilsonite Company, Bonanza Mines
TOTAL MILEAGE 60.5 miles
UNPAVED MILEAGE 55.8 miles
DRIVING TIME 3 hours
ELEVATION RANGE 5,000–8,400 feet
USUALLY OPEN Year-round
DIFFICULTY RATING 2
SCENIC RATING 8
REMOTENESS RATING +1

Special Attractions

- Extremely remote trail that when linked with Central #25: Book Cliffs Loop (which can be found in *Utah Trails: Central Region*) forms a connection between Vernal and Green River, Moab, and Grand Junction.
- The historic ghost towns of Rainbow and Watson.
- Gilsonite mines at Rainbow.

History

By the beginning of the 20th century, commercial gilsonite (which is almost exclusively found in eastern Utah's Uinta Basin) had become an important mineral in such products as paints, inks, storage batteries, and asphalt. However, the region's gilsonite mines were soon producing more of the mineral than could be shipped out of this remote desert area.

The most efficient way to ship large amounts of gilsonite was by rail. The mining companies attempted to contract with the Union Pacific and the Rio Grande Western to build a rail line from Mack, Colorado, to the mines in Utah, but both companies refused. As a result, the Barber Asphalt Company decided to build the Uintah Railway itself.

Originally, the line extended only as far as Dragon, but when the mining operations began to move north, the railway followed. First it was extended to Watson and then an additional few miles to Rainbow. All three towns relied almost completely on gilsonite and the Uintah Railway for their survival.

Another ghost town that appears along the trail is White River, which has also been known as White River Crossing and Ignatio. This small settlement was established after the cost of extending the railroad to Vernal

Weathered structure at Watson Ghost Town

The gilsonite vein at Rainbow Ghost Town

Some of the cabins at Watson Ghost Town

Old dugout at Rainbow Ghost Town

was deemed prohibitive. The railroad built a toll road instead, with a ferry crossing the Green River and a bridge over the White River. At the bridge, White River functioned as a little more than a stage stop along the route and as a home for workers and guards. The cost of a trip from Vernal all the way to Dragon with freight wagons varied from $2.50 to $3.50, depending upon the number of teams and wagons in the outfit. In 1935, the toll-road company went out of business and the property was transferred to the county for maintenance. Today, there is not much left of this old stage stop except the skeleton of the bridge that many years ago spanned the width of the White River.

Description

This trail heads northeast from Northern #29: Dragon Ghost Town Trail, passing through the remote desert country of eastern Utah's Uintah County. Keep your eye out for deer and elk, animals common to the area. Driving through the thick pinyon and juniper of the region's desert landscape, it is hard to imagine how such towns as Rainbow and Watson once thrived along the Uintah Railway.

The trail proceeds through a number of gas fields along a broad, maintained dirt road. Most of the side trails that branch off from the main road lead to natural gas wells. The drive itself is not very difficult except for areas of thick, powder-fine sand. In some patches, the sand can be up to 8 to 10 inches deep and vehicles can kick up blinding clouds of dust. After rains, the trail is often impassable, as the entire region can become boggy and full of mud holes.

After 42 miles, you reach a short spur trail to the ghost town of Rainbow. Before it was played out, a major gilsonite vein ran through town; the channel looks like someone took a slice out of the ridge. For a nice view of the area, take a side road about 0.1 miles past downtown Rainbow to the communications tower. From here you can see old, wooden mining structures in the gilsonite vein as well as many other buildings and foundations. If you take the short road opposite the one to the communications tower, you reach a crest that offers another good view of the old gilsonite vein.

After Rainbow, the ruins of Watson sit 3.7 miles up the road. The site is heavily overgrown. However, a quick search reveals collapsing buildings and foundations that date back to Watson's heyday as a terminus along the Uintah Railway.

After another 5 miles, the trail intersects with Northern #29: Dragon Ghost Town Trail, which heads south back to Central #25: Book Cliffs Loop. The remains of the White River stage stop are another 5.5 miles past the trail intersection.

Just a couple of miles past White River, the trail proper finishes in front of the Bonanza Mines Office of the American Gilsonite Company. There are no services in Bonanza, so do not count on refueling there. However, you can reach Vernal quickly if you continue north on paved Utah 45.

Current Road Information

BLM Moab Field Office
82 East Dogwood
Moab, UT 84532
(435) 259-2100

BLM Vernal Field Office
170 South 500 East
Vernal, UT 84078
(435) 781-4400

Map References

BLM Vernal, Seep Ridge, Westwater
USGS 1:24,000 Bonanza, Southam Canyon, Weaver Ridge, Rainbow, Archy Bench SE, Cooper Canyon, Bates Knolls, Pine Spring Canyon, Seep Canyon, PR Spring
1:100,000 Vernal, Seep Ridge, Westwater
Utah Atlas & Gazetteer, pp. 29, 39
Utah Road & Recreation Atlas, pp. 55, 63

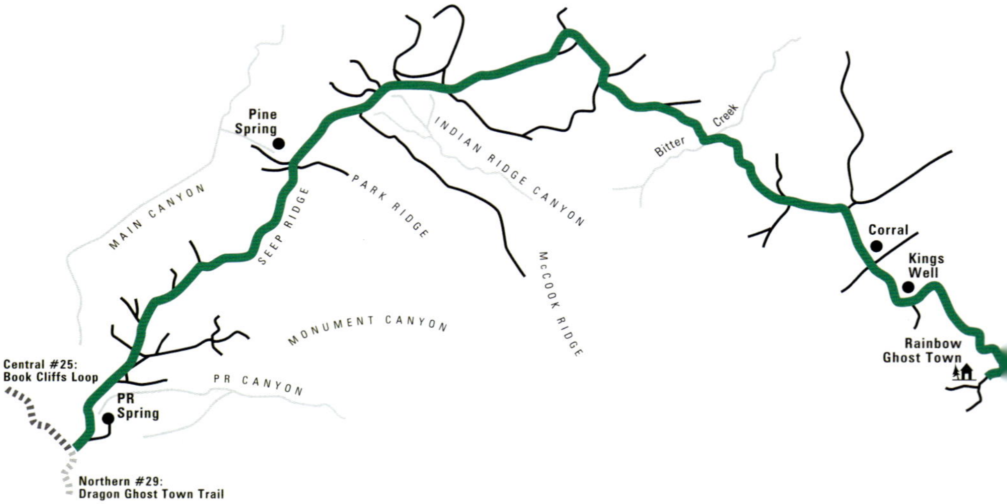

Northern Trail #28: Rainbow and Watson Ghost Towns Trail

Route Directions

▼ 0.0		On Northern #29: Dragon Ghost Town Trail, 38.6 miles from I-70, zero trip meter and proceed toward Seep Ridge Road, PR Junction, Indian Ridge, Pine Springs, and Ouray.
11.7 ▲		Trail ends at the southern end of Northern #29: Dragon Ghost Town Trail; either direction leads to I-70.
		GPS: N 39°27.14′ W 109°16.43′
▼ 0.4	SO	Corral on right. Track on right to PR Spring.
11.3 ▲	SO	Track on left to PR Spring. Corral on left.
▼ 1.5	SO	Enter Uintah County.
10.2 ▲	SO	Enter Grand County.
▼ 2.4	SO	Track on left.
9.3 ▲	SO	Track on right.
▼ 3.7	SO	Cattle guard and corral. Track on right to Monument Ridge. Then track on left.
7.9 ▲	SO	Track on right. Then track on left to Monument Ridge. Cross cattle guard with corral on left.
		GPS: N 39°29.31′ W 109°19.18′
▼ 5.9	SO	Track on left.
5.8 ▲	SO	Track on right.
▼ 7.1	SO	Track on left.
4.6 ▲	SO	Track on right.
▼ 8.0	SO	Track crosses road.
3.7 ▲	SO	Track crosses road.
▼ 11.3	SO	Track on right.
0.4 ▲	SO	Track on left.
▼ 11.6	SO	Corral on left. Track on right.
0.1 ▲	SO	Track on left. Corral on right.
▼ 11.7	SO	Intersection. Road on left to Pine Spring Canyon and Main Canyon. Stock pond on left. Zero trip meter.
0.0 ▲		Continue along main road.
		GPS: N 39°34.55′ W 109°24.06′
▼ 0.0		Continue along main road.
2.5 ▲	SO	Intersection. Road on right to Pine Spring Canyon and Main Canyon. Stock pond on right. Follow sign to Book Cliff Divide. Zero trip meter.

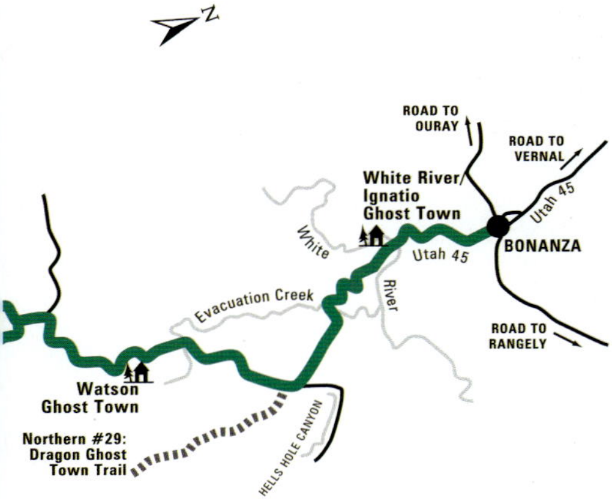

▼ 0.5 SO Track on left.
1.9 ▲ SO Track on right.

▼ 1.2 SO Track on left.
1.3 ▲ SO Track on right.

▼ 1.3 SO Cross cattle guard. Corral on right.
1.2 ▲ SO Corral on left. Cross cattle guard.

▼ 2.5 SO Intersection. Right to Indian Ridge Road and McCook Ridge. Zero trip meter.
0.0 ▲ Continue toward PR Spring.
GPS: N 39°36.55' W 109°25.29'

▼ 0.0 Continue toward Ouray.
7.1 ▲ SO Intersection. Left to Indian Ridge Road and McCook Ridge. Zero trip meter.

▼ 1.0 SO Track on right. Then road to Crow Roost Canyon on left.
6.1 ▲ SO Road to Crow Roost Canyon on right. Then track on left.

▼ 1.4 SO Track to Wood Canyon and Willow Creek on left.
5.6 ▲ SO Track to Wood Canyon and Willow Creek on right.
GPS: N 39°37.73' W 109°25.85'

▼ 2.0 SO Track on right.
5.1 ▲ SO Track on left.

▼ 2.7 SO Corral on left at intersection.
4.4 ▲ SO Corral on right at intersection.
GPS: N 39°38.71' W 109°25.26'

▼ 4.3 SO Track on right.
2.7 ▲ SO Track on left.

▼ 4.8 SO Track on left.
2.3 ▲ SO Track on right.

▼ 6.7 SO Intersection.
0.3 ▲ SO Intersection.

▼ 7.1 TR Turn right toward Kings Well and Bonanza. Zero trip meter.
0.0 ▲ Continue toward Book Cliffs.
GPS: N 39°42.05' W 109°26.38'

▼ 0.0 Continue toward Bonanza.
10.8 ▲ TL Intersection. Zero trip meter.

▼ 0.3 SO Track on right.
10.5 ▲ BR Track on left.

▼ 0.7 BL Track on right.
10.0 ▲ BR Track on left.

▼ 2.3 SO Cattle guard.
8.5 ▲ SO Cattle guard.

▼ 7.3 SO Cross over Bitter Creek.
3.5 ▲ SO Cross over Bitter Creek.
GPS: N 39°45.22' W 109°21.28'

▼ 8.4 BL Track on right.
2.3 ▲ BR Track on left.

▼ 10.8 SO Tracks on left and right. Zero trip meter.
0.0 ▲ Continue on main road.
GPS: N 39°46.62' W 109°18.41'

▼ 0.0 Continue on main road.
10.0 ▲ SO Tracks on right and left. Zero trip meter.

One of the structures remaining at Watson Ghost Town

▼ 0.8 SO Track on right.
9.2 ▲ SO Track on left.

▼ 1.0 SO Track on left.
9.0 ▲ SO Track on right.

▼ 1.5 BR Track on left to West Asphalt and Bitter Creek. Bear right toward Rainbow and Bonanza.
8.5 ▲ SO Track enters on right.

GPS: N 39°47.80' W 109°17.76'

▼ 1.6 SO Track on left.
8.4 ▲ BL Road forks. Right goes to West Asphalt and Bitter Creek. Bear left toward Seep Ridge Road.

▼ 1.7 SO Track on right.
8.3 ▲ SO Track on left.

▼ 1.8 SO Track on right.
8.2 ▲ SO Track on left.

▼ 2.1 SO Track on right.
7.9 ▲ SO Track on left.

▼ 3.2 SO Track on right.
6.8 ▲ SO Track on left.

▼ 3.3 SO Corral on left. Tracks on left and right.
6.7 ▲ SO Tracks on left and right. Corral on right.

GPS: N 39°48.11' W 109°15.80'

▼ 3.8 SO Track on right.
6.2 ▲ SO Track on left.

▼ 4.2 SO Track on left.
5.8 ▲ SO Track on right.

▼ 5.3 SO Kings Well.
4.7 ▲ SO Kings Well.

GPS: N 39°48.70' W 109°13.96'

▼ 5.7 SO Track on right.
4.3 ▲ SO Track on left.

▼ 9.5 SO Gas well on right.
0.5 ▲ SO Gas well on left.

▼ 10.0 TR Intersection. Turn right on spur road to Rainbow. Zero trip meter. You will return to this intersection. Main trail continues straight.
0.0 ▲ Continue along main road.

GPS: N 39°50.87' W 109°11.28'

Spur Trail to Rainbow

▼ 0.0 Proceed toward Rainbow.
▼ 0.5 SO Rainbow town site. Gilsonite mining structure on right.
▼ 0.6 SO Road on right to radio tower and overlook of gilsonite mine and vein. Road on left to a crest where a deep gilsonite vein can be viewed clearly across the valley.
▼ 0.7 UT Old dugout dwelling on the right. Turn around at the cattle guard and return to main road.

GPS: N 39°50.58' W 109°10.97

▼ 1.4 TR Intersection with the main road. Zero trip meter.

GPS: N 39°50.87' W 109°11.28'

Continuation of Main Trail

▼ 0.0 Continue along main road.
8.6 ▲ TL Intersection. Turn left on spur trail to Rainbow. Zero trip meter. You will return to this intersection. Main trail continues straight.

▼ 0.5 SO Track to Asphalt Wash on left.
8.1 ▲ BL Asphalt Wash road on right. Bear left on main road toward Rainbow and Kings Well.

▼ 3.7 SO Town site of Watson. Ruins are in the overgrowth. Park along a short track on left.
4.9 ▲ SO Town site of Watson. Ruins are in the overgrowth. Park along a short track on right.

GPS: N 39°52.80' W 109°09.34'

▼ 3.8 SO Cross through Evacuation Creek, which can be deep.
4.8 ▲ SO Cross through Evacuation Creek, which can be deep.

▼ 3.9 SO Short track on right to various log and stone structures, part of Watson.
4.7 ▲ SO Short track on left to various log and stone structures, part of Watson.

▼ 6.5 SO Track on right.
2.1 ▲ SO Track on left.

▼ 8.6 SO Intersection. Right is Northern #29: Dragon Ghost Town Trail; road also leads to Baxter Pass, Colorado. Zero trip meter.
0.0 ▲ Continue along main route.

GPS: N 39°55.69' W 109°07.43'

▼ 0.0 Continue along main route.
3.7 ▲ SO Intersection. Left is Northern #29: Dragon Ghost Town Trail; road also leads to Baxter Pass, Colorado. Zero trip meter.

▼ 0.1 SO Corral on right.
3.6 ▲ SO Corral on left.

THE MORMON IMMIGRATION

In 1820, 14-year-old Joseph Smith journeyed into the woods of upstate New York in order to find the answer to a lingering religious question and experienced the first in a series of spiritual epiphanies. An angel named Moroni appeared to him, telling him that he was a prophet and revealing hidden scriptures on golden tablets, which Smith translated from an unknown language. In 1830, Smith published these revealed writings as the Book of Mormon, and along with six other men, he formed the Church of Christ, later known as the Church of Jesus Christ of Latter-day Saints (LDS).

Brigham Young

Because of religious opposition, Smith and his growing number of followers left New York for Kirtland, Ohio, a year later. Shortly after, in 1832, a young follower named Brigham Young was baptized into the faith and quickly moved up the ranks of the church.

The Mormons experienced increasing animosity from settlers in Ohio, so even as their church grew there, they established new settlements in Missouri. In 1835, Brigham Young was appointed to the Council of the Twelve Apostles, the highest governing group in the church.

In 1838, Missouri issued an "extermination order" against the Mormons. This animosity toward church members came from exaggerated rumors of violence and the fear among original settlers that they would lose control of the area to the increasing number of Mormons. With harassment continuing in Ohio, the church moved to Nauvoo, Illinois, where things improved only temporarily. Here as well, non-Mormon settlers eventually began to persecute and even kill church members, mostly over their espousal of religious superiority and of polygamy. While jailed in Carthage, Illinois, in 1844, Joseph Smith and one of his followers were murdered by a furious mob.

Shortly before Smith's assassination, he had commissioned Young to lead an expedition west in order to find a place where the church could build a community free of persecution. He did this, and in April of 1847, Young, now the president of the Church of Latter-day Saints, led a large group of followers on a 111-day journey to find their new home. When Young arrived in the Salt Lake Valley near Emigrant Canyon on July 24, 1847, he declared to his people, "This is the right place."

Often referred to as one of the most significant colonizers in U.S. history, Brigham Young began his expansion in 1849 by moving 30 families south of the Salt Lake Valley. Young's idea was to establish communities along each of the eight major Utah streams. Any region that contained a water source was open for colonization.

During the next 20 years, over 80,000 Mormons immigrated to the Utah Territory, while approximately 6,000 perished along the way. Young endeavored to find places to live for arriving families as well as to establish livelihoods for his followers. Throughout this time, Young continually expanded the Mormon colonies to such areas as the Sanpete Valley and Little Salt Lake Valley in southern Utah.

In 1850, the Mormon leader helped found Parowan, the first iron enterprise of the LDS. Until this time, most Mormon colonies had been farming and livestock communities. The founding of Parowan began a trend of establishing mining towns based on natural resources, such as coal, silver, lead, and zinc.

Under the leadership of Brigham Young, the LDS devised two main types of colonization: direct and nondirect. The direct method was the most popular, and it consisted of establishing colonies with the full planning and guidance of the church. Religious leaders organized, formed, and financially backed the community, deciding which families would go, what their livelihoods would be, and any other long-term goals of the town. In contrast, nondirect settlements occurred when individual families ventured out in small groups to establish their own communities. They were not under the guidance of the LDS and did not receive any financial aid. However, the church encouraged nondirect settlements, especially for younger families.

When the transcontinental railroad was completed in 1869, it allowed for larger numbers of settlers to immigrate than ever before, and Young and the church welcomed this growth. However, in the early 1870s, overpopulation emerged as an obstacle for Utah settlers. Consequently, many families began migrating to the outlying states of Nevada, Arizona, Colorado, Idaho, and Wyoming.

Perhaps as a result of this rapid growth, the U.S. government began to view the Mormons as a threat. In 1857, President James Buchanan sent 3,000 soldiers from Fort Leavenworth to infiltrate the Salt Lake Valley in what became known as the Utah War. There was no bloodshed during the "war," and the army ultimately succeeded in its mission—the removal of Brigham Young as leader of the territory and the appointment of a new, non-Mormon governor.

In the two decades spanning 1858 to 1877, the Mormons managed to establish 205 additional settlements. Areas such as Bear Lake, Cache Valley, Pahvant Valley, and the valleys along the Sevier, Virgin, and Muddy Rivers blossomed with Mormon communities. Despite the popularity of the LDS in Utah, the federal government continued to keep a tight hold on the territory. In 1887, Congress passed legislation that unincorporated the church, made voting for women illegal, and strongly enforced the law against polygamy. The new laws forced church leaders to renounce their doctrine encouraging plural marriages, which had been in effect since 1843.

During the early 1900s, very few regions in Utah did not have Mormon settlements, and church leaders changed their focus from colonization to building up previously established communities. The public view of the LDS has changed through the years from one of apprehension to one of acceptance. The growth of the church continues today in Utah as well as in many countries around the world.

▼ 0.2 SO Track on right to Hells Hole Canyon and Weaver Ridge.
3.5 ▲ SO Track on left to Hells Hole Canon and Weaver Ridge.

▼ 3.0 SO Cross bridge over Evacuation Creek.
0.7 ▲ SO Cross bridge over Evacuation Creek.

▼ 3.4 SO Track on right.
0.3 ▲ SO Track on left.

▼ 3.7 TR Intersection with Utah 45. Southam Canyon and Asphalt Wash to the left. Zero trip meter.
0.0 ▲ Continue along road.

GPS: N 39°57.54' W 109°09.74'

▼ 0.0 Continue on paved Utah 45.
4.7 ▲ TL Turn left onto unpaved road toward Book Cliffs, Rainbow Junction, and Baxter Pass. Zero trip meter.

▼ 1.4 SO Track to White River (Ignatio) on left.
3.3 ▲ SO Track to White River (Ignatio) on right.

GPS: N 39°58.53' W 109°10.37'

▼ 1.8 SO Cross bridge over the White River. Site of White River (Ignatio) stage stop is on left.
2.9 ▲ SO Cross bridge over the White River. Site of White River (Ignatio) stage stop is on right.

▼ 4.4 SO Intersection. Rangely to the right and Ouray to the left.
0.3 ▲ SO Intersection. Rangely to the left and Ouray to the right.

GPS: N 40°00.82' W 109°10.20'

▼ 4.7 Trail ends at the American Gilsonite Company, Bonanza Mines Office, on Utah 45. Continue north on Utah 45 to reach Vernal.
0.0 ▲ On Utah 45 in Bonanza, zero trip meter in front of the American Gilsonite Company and proceed south.

GPS: N 40°01.13' W 109°10.33'

NORTHERN REGION TRAIL #29

Dragon Ghost Town Trail

STARTING POINT Northern #28: Rainbow and Watson Ghost Towns Trail
FINISHING POINT Northern #28: Rainbow and Watson Ghost Towns Trail
TOTAL MILEAGE 64.4 miles
UNPAVED MILEAGE 64.4 miles
DRIVING TIME 3 hours
ELEVATION RANGE 5,500–8,600 feet
USUALLY OPEN Year-round
DIFFICULTY RATING 2
SCENIC RATING 8
REMOTENESS RATING +1

Special Attractions

- Extremely remote region.
- Dragon, a historic gilsonite mining and railroad site.
- Connects with Northern #28: Rainbow and Watson Ghost Towns Trail and Central #25: Book Cliffs Loop (which can be found in *Utah Trails: Central Region*) to form a route from Vernal to Green River and Moab.

History

In 1885, Sam Gilson discovered a pocket of a black, oil-based mineral in Uintah County in what appeared to be the shape of a black dragon. The mineral came to be called gilsonite in honor of the man who both found it and promoted it as a commercially usable material. The mine where the ore was discovered soon became known as the Black Dragon Mine. Though it was established in the late 1800s, the Black Dragon Mine only became a major producer of gilsonite after 1904, when the Uintah Railway connected it to Mack, Colorado.

The mining town of Dragon quickly grew as more and more people were needed to work in the mine and the railyard. During its brief life span, Dragon was home to one of the Uinta Basin's finest hotels, a public school, and a public library. Though it did not have a reputation as a lawless town, outlaws from the Wild Bunch made frequent stops in Dragon. Due to its remoteness (especially before the Uintah Railway was built), Dragon served as a safe resting point for Butch Cassidy, Elza Lay, and other outlaws.

However, Dragon's days were numbered. In 1908, a fire started in the Black Dragon Mine that supposedly lasted for two years. By this time, much of the mining had been moved north to such towns as Rainbow and Watson. Then, in 1911, the railway terminus was extended north 10 miles to the town of Watson, and slowly Dragon faded away. For a time it survived as a supply depot on the way to Vernal, but by the 1920s, it was pretty much abandoned.

Description

Although the remote Dragon Ghost Town Trail has many interesting attractions, one of its most appealing aspects is its location in the middle of nowhere. With the exception of a limited amount of mining in the region, the terrain through which the trail proceeds seems void of human influence or interference.

The trail begins along the north end of Northern #28: Rainbow and Watson Ghost Towns Trail, 10 miles after the turnoff to Rainbow, and heads south. The wide, dusty, maintained road to Dragon moves through grassy terrain dotted with pinyon and juniper. The trail's biggest obstacle, in fact, is its large amount of dust, which when kicked up by a passing vehicle can form a blinding

Powder-fine dust billows up behind the vehicles along this trail

One of the structures remaining at Dragon Ghost Town

cloud. When wet, these areas of powder-fine sand turn into mud holes, and if the area has just seen rain or melting snow, you should save this trail for another day, as it can become impassable.

After 8.6 miles, you come to a spur trail leading to the town site of Dragon, which has a number of old buildings still standing and foundations lying beneath the brush. From here, an interesting side road extends west from the town into Dragon Canyon. This canyon road winds through narrow gaps between shaley, sagebrush-covered hills. About 0.9 miles up Dragon Canyon on the left, you can look across the creek to a bluff where the old Dragon cemetery was located. About 0.1 miles later, look to the right to see the very conspicuous trench where a reef of gilsonite has been mined. About 3.5 miles up Dragon Canyon there is a gate where the trail peters out. Turn around and head back past Dragon to the main road.

From here, the main trail follows along sections of road that seem to have been dug into the ground. At times it feels like driving through a pipeline, as dense brush on either side rises above ground, seeming to wall you in. Make sure to stay alert through these areas because at times there can be considerable traffic associated with the mines.

About 10.4 miles after the turnoff to Dragon, you traverse Atchee Ridge and the desert shrub country becomes thick with pinyon and juniper. The road deteriorates along this section and becomes rougher and more narrow. This is more of a forest road than the mining road earlier in the trail.

Around Rat Hole Ridge and Canyon, 12 to 15 miles farther, the trail passes through significant stands of aspen that are somewhat uncharacteristic of the region. As you descend into Bitter Creek Canyon from Rat Hole Ridge, there are sections of narrow shelf road with rocky patches. Bitter Creek Canyon is a long narrow valley with a reasonably flat bottom and steep sides. This coniferous valley lined with aspens provides quite a nice change of scenery from the previous desert country.

Disused White River bridge

Deer and elk inhabit the valley and use Bitter Creek as a life-sustaining water source.

Near the south end of the trail, you drive along County Line Ridge and Overlook Ridge, which provide spectacular views southeast over the plains from the top of the Book Cliffs. The trail ends at Central #25: Book Cliffs Loop. More information about this trail can be found in *Utah Trails: Central Region.*

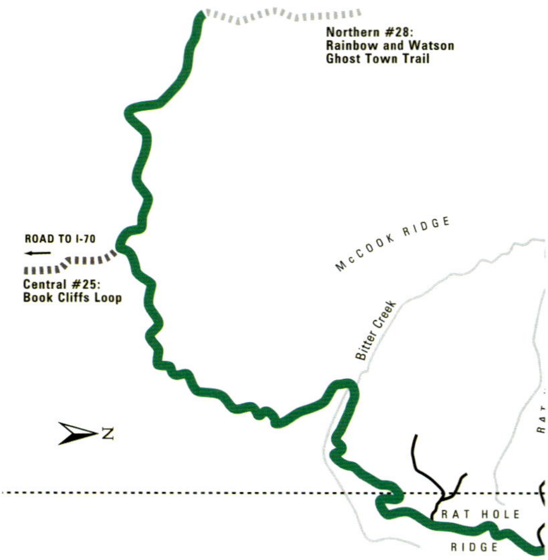

Current Road Information

BLM Moab Field Office
82 East Dogwood
Moab, UT 84532
(435) 259-2100

BLM Vernal Field Office
170 South 500 East
Vernal, UT 84078
(435) 781-4400

Map References

BLM Seep Ridge, Westwater
USGS 1:24,000 Weaver Ridge, Dragon, Rainbow, Burnt Timber Canyon, Davis Canyon, Rat Hole Ridge, San Arroyo Ridge
1:100,000 Seep Ridge, Westwater
Utah Atlas & Gazetteer, pp. 29, 39
Utah Road & Recreation Atlas, pp. 55, 63

Route Directions

▼ 0.0 On Northern #28: Rainbow and Watson Ghost Towns Trail, 3.7 miles from Utah 45, zero trip meter and turn south onto road toward Baxter Pass.
8.6 ▲ Trail ends at Northern #28: Rainbow and Watson Ghost Towns Trail. Turn north for Utah 45, south for Central #25: Book Cliffs Loop (which can be found in *Utah Trails: Central Region*).
GPS: N 39°55.69' W 109°07.43'

▼ 3.3 SO Track on left.
5.3 ▲ SO Track on right.

▼ 3.6 SO Track on left is mining operation.
5.0 ▲ SO Track on right is mining operation.

▼ 4.4 SO Track on left to Rabbit Mountain.
4.2 ▲ SO Track on right to Rabbit Mountain.
GPS: N 39°52.19' W 109°06.34'

▼ 5.3 SO Track on left.
3.3 ▲ SO Track on right.

▼ 6.9 SO Track on left to Park Canyon. Then cross cattle guard.
1.7 ▲ SO Cross cattle guard. Then track on right to Park Canyon.
GPS: N 39°50.40' W 109°07.60'

▼ 7.2 SO Cross bridge over Evacuation Creek.
1.3 ▲ SO Cross bridge over Evacuation Creek.

▼ 7.8 SO Track on right. Then cross through wash.
0.8 ▲ SO Cross through wash. Track on left.

▼ 8.6 SO Continue straight on spur trail to Dragon. Track on right is continuation of main trail to Three Mile Canyon and Atchee Ridge. After visiting Dragon the route will return to this intersection. Zero trip meter.

Northern Trail #29: Dragon Ghost Town Trail

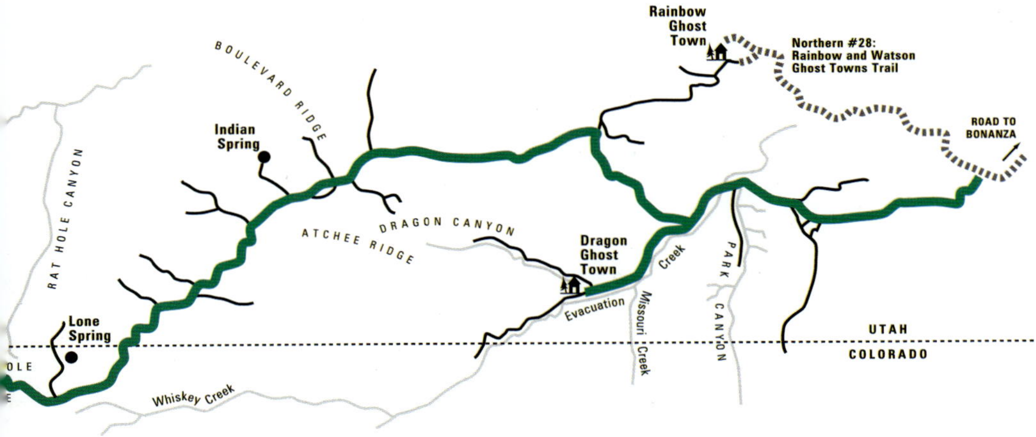

0.0 ▲ Continue along route.

GPS: N 39°49.47′ W 109°06.29′

Spur Trail to Dragon

▼ 0.0 Continue toward Dragon.

▼ 2.2 SO Pass Mid-American Pipeline Company Dragon Station on left. Track on left to Missouri Creek.

▼ 3.3 UT Site of Dragon. Tracks on left and right. Right track goes 3.5 miles up Dragon Canyon. Return to main trail after exploring canyon.

GPS: N 39°47.14′ W 109°04.37′

▼ 6.6 Turn toward Atchee Ridge and Three Mile Canyon, zero trip meter.

GPS: N 39°49.47′ W 109°06.29′

Continuation of Main Trail

▼ 0.0 Continue along route.

10.4 ▲ TR Intersection. Zero trip meter. Turn right on spur trail to Dragon. Straight is continuation of main trail. After visiting Dragon the route will return to this intersection.

▼ 4.4 BL Fork in road. Bear left toward Boulevard Ridge and Rat Hole Ridge. Rainbow and Bonanza are to the right.

6.0 ▲ SO Track enters on left.

GPS: N 39°47.40′ W 109°09.16′

▼ 4.5 BL Road on right.

5.9 ▲ TR Straight continues to Rainbow and Bonanza. Turn right toward Three Mile Canyon and Evacuation Creek.

▼ 7.0 SO Cattle guard.

3.4 ▲ SO Cattle guard.

▼ 7.4 SO Tracks on right.

3.0 ▲ SO Tracks on left.

GPS: N 39°45.09′ W 109°08.42′

▼ 8.8 SO Track on right.

1.5 ▲ SO Track on left.

▼ 10.1 SO Track on right.

0.3 ▲ SO Track on left.

▼ 10.4 SO Track on right to Big Park, Cooper Canyon, and McCook Ridge Junction.

Zero trip meter.
0.0 ▲ Continue toward Three Mile Canyon.

GPS: N 39°42.48' W 109°08.54'

▼ 0.0 Continue toward Atchee Ridge.
11.8 ▲ SO Track on left to Big Park, Cooper Canyon, and McCook Ridge Junction. Zero trip meter.

▼ 0.5 SO Track on left.
11.3 ▲ SO Track on right.

▼ 0.9 SO Track on left.
10.9 ▲ SO Track on right.

▼ 1.3 SO Boulevard Ridge to the right.
10.5 ▲ SO Boulevard Ridge to the left.

GPS: N 39°41.64' W 109°07.79'

▼ 1.4 SO Cross cattle guard.
10.4 ▲ SO Cross cattle guard.

▼ 3.4 SO Track on right to Indian Spring.
8.4 ▲ SO Track on left to Indian Spring.

▼ 3.6 SO Track on left and right. Right goes to Augusi Ridge.
8.2 ▲ SO Track on left and right. Left goes to Augusi Ridge.

▼ 4.6 SO Track on left.
7.2 ▲ SO Track on right.

▼ 5.8 SO Track to Moonshine Ridge on right. Then cross cattle guard.
6.0 ▲ SO Cross cattle guard. Track to Moonshine Ridge on left.

GPS: N 39°38.99' W 109°04.90'

▼ 6.2 SO Track on right to Moonshine Ridge.

Old Dragon gilsonite vein and mine ruins

5.6 ▲ SO Track on left to Moonshine Ridge.

▼ 6.4 SO Track on left.
5.4 ▲ SO Track on right.

▼ 9.7 SO Cross cattle guard.
2.1 ▲ SO Cross cattle guard.

▼ 10.0 SO Track on left.
1.8 ▲ SO Track on right.

▼ 10.3 SO Track on left to Whiskey Creek Canyon.
1.5 ▲ SO Track on right to Whiskey Creek Canyon.

▼ 11.6 SO Old building on right.
0.2 ▲ SO Old building on left.

▼ 11.8 SO Track on left to Cripple Cowboy Ranch. Track on right to Lone Spring. Zero trip meter.
0.0 ▲ Continue along main road.

GPS: N 39°35.40′ W 109°01.34′

▼ 0.0 Proceed toward McCook Ridge and Bitter Creek.
19.9 ▲ SO Track on left to Lone Spring. Cripple Cowboy Ranch on right. Zero trip meter.

▼ 0.5 BL Road forks. Rat Hole Canyon to the right.
19.3 ▲ BR Road to Rat Hole Canyon on left.

▼ 1.9 SO Track on left.
18.0 ▲ SO Track on right.

▼ 2.3 SO Track on right.
17.6 ▲ SO Track on left.

▼ 3.1 SO Track on right to Rat Hole Ridge.
16.7 ▲ SO Track on left to Rat Hole Ridge.

▼ 3.4 SO Track on left.
16.4 ▲ SO Track on right.

▼ 5.6 SO Cross state line into Utah.
14.3 ▲ SO Cross state line into Colorado.

GPS: N 39°32.25′ W 109°03.03′

▼ 7.7 SO Cattle guard.
12.1 ▲ SO Cattle guard.

▼ 7.9 SO Track on left to Cripple Cowboy Ranch.
12.0 ▲ SO Track on right to Cripple Cowboy Ranch.

▼ 9.1 SO Track on right.
10.8 ▲ SO Track on left.

▼ 9.3 SO Cross over Bitter Creek.
10.6 ▲ SO Cross over Bitter Creek.

GPS: N 39°31.51′ W 109°05.95′

▼ 9.4 SO Cross cattle guard.
10.5 ▲ SO Cross cattle guard.

▼ 13.3 SO Cross cattle guard.
6.6 ▲ SO Cross cattle guard.

▼ 13.5 SO Track on left.
6.3 ▲ SO Track on right.

▼ 19.7 TL Cross cattle guard. Then turn left at intersection toward Divide and Ouray. McCook Ridge is to the right.
0.2 ▲ TR Proceed toward Overlook Ridge, Bitter Creek, Fatty Canyon, and Atchee Ridge. Cross cattle guard.

▼ 19.9 TR Intersection. Track on left leads 31.4 miles to I-70. Straight ahead goes to radio tower. Turn right and zero trip meter in middle of intersection.
0.0 ▲ Continue north, following signs to Atchee Ridge and McCook Ridge.

GPS: N 39°26.59′ W 109°09.84′

▼ 0.0 Continue toward PR Spring and Ouray.
7.1 ▲ TL Intersection. Road on right goes to radio tower. Straight ahead leads 31.4 miles to I-70. Turn left and zero trip meter in middle of intersection.

▼ 0.5 SO Intersection. Road on left to East Canyon. Proceed straight along Seep Ridge Road.
6.6 ▲ SO Road on right to East Canyon.

GPS: N 39°26.87′ W 109°10.27′

▼ 1.4 SO Track on right.
5.6 ▲ SO Track on left.

▼ 2.7 SO Track on right.
4.4 ▲ SO Track on left.

▼ 3.0 SO Track on right.
4.0 ▲ SO Track on left.

▼ 3.6 SO Gas well on left.
3.5 ▲ SO Gas well on right.

▼ 4.4 SO Tracks on left and right.
2.7 ▲ SO Tracks on right and left.
GPS: N 39°26.77' W 109°13.91'

▼ 5.0 BR Road and radio tower on left.
2.0 ▲ BL Road and radio tower on right.

▼ 5.5 SO Cattle guard. Corral and track on right.
1.6 ▲ SO Corral and track on left. Cattle guard.

▼ 6.1 SO Road on right to South Canyon and Sweetwater Canyon.
1.0 ▲ SO Road on left to South Canyon and Sweetwater Canyon.

▼ 6.5 SO Track on right to Black Horse Canyon; it ends in 6 miles.
0.5 ▲ SO Track on left to Black Horse Canyon; it ends in 6 miles.
GPS: N 39°26.91' W 109°15.90'

▼ 7.1 Trail ends at intersection with Northern #28: Rainbow and Watson Ghost Towns Trail. Go straight to drive that trail north to Utah 45. Track on left, signed to Winter Ridge Junction, eventually leads 37.8 miles to I-70.
0.0 ▲ Trail starts at the end of Northern #28: Rainbow and Watson Ghost Towns Trail at intersection with Book Cliffs Ridge Road. Zero trip meter and proceed southeast toward McCook Ridge.
GPS: N 39°27.14' W 109°16.43'

NORTHERN REGION TRAIL #30

Sawtooth Mountain Trail

STARTING POINT US 50, 0.6 miles west of mile marker 53
FINISHING POINT Marjum Canyon Road, 25.1 miles west of US 50
TOTAL MILEAGE 27.1 miles
UNPAVED MILEAGE 27.1 miles
DRIVING TIME 4 hours
ELEVATION RANGE 4,500–8,000 feet
USUALLY OPEN Year-round
DIFFICULTY RATING 3
SCENIC RATING 7
REMOTENESS RATING +2

Special Attractions

- Mining remains in North Canyon.
- Chance to travel some remote, little-used desert tracks.
- Views of Lake Sevier, the House Range, and Tule Valley.

History

One of the major features on this trail is Sevier Lake, presently the third largest body of water in Utah. Sevier Lake is part of the ancient inland sea of Lake Bonneville, which covered 20,000 square miles of the Great Basin. Sevier Lake is situated on a southern tongue of the old lake. Until recently, the lake was slowly diminishing in size, but with higher than usual runoff in the past few years, it has expanded and become a permanent year-round body of water. Under normal conditions, the lake is dry for part of each year. The lake is the drainage for the Sevier River, and both the lake and the river have no outlet to the sea, ending as they do in the Great Basin.

The lake has undergone several name changes. Originally it was named Laguna de Miera after a cartographer with the 1776 Domínguez-Escalante Expedition. Then it was known as Ashley Lake, after William Ashley, a fur trapper in the region in the 1820s. Next it became Nicollet Lake, after Joseph Nicollet, a French geologist who surveyed the region with Captain J. H. Simpson in the 1850s. Finally, it became known as Sevier Lake, after the river that drains into it.

The Sevier River takes its name not from American general John Sevier, but is a corruption of the Spanish word *severo,* which means "severe." The Spanish, the first non-Indian visitors to the region, called the river "Rio Severo" because of its dangerous passages.

The trail hugs the eastern flank of the House Range and then ascends into the range itself along a spur trail into North Canyon. The House Range was named in 1856 by Captain J. H. Simpson while he was surveying the western desert for the government. While still many miles away, he noted, "The range of mountains [is] quite remarkable on account of its well-defined stratification and the resemblance of portions of its outline to domes, minarets, houses, and other structures...I call it the House Range."

The Spanish mined the House Range extensively; in North Canyon, later miners found hand tools in an old tunnel, and another tunnel led to a series of rooms interconnected with ladders, where they found leather ore buckets and more hand tools for digging. This site is now caved in.

The range contains some of the oldest known animal fossils in Utah, and there are several sites that will be of interest to rock hounds. You can collect trilobites and remnants of ancient sponge reefs. The Warm Springs Resource Area map (see below) notes several sites as well as sites for collecting gemstones and minerals.

Description

This trail follows some very little used tracks in extremely remote desert country within the Warm Springs Resource Area. You are unlikely to see other travelers, and if you break down, help will be a long time coming. Local ranchers use these trails to varying degrees, and the part of the trail that runs up North Canyon is better traveled, but travelers should be well prepared and self-sufficient; carry additional fuel, food, and water. A detailed regional map is strongly recommended. You can obtain a free map of the Warm Springs Resource Area, which shows the area's major tracks, from the Fillmore BLM office.

Looking along the trail to Sawtooth Mountain

Old mining truck

The trail passes along the southern end of the House Range, which has striking, rugged escarpments and towering peaks 4,000 feet above the Tule Valley. The trail starts in the grassy plains, where harsh conditions and alkaline soil allow only a few salt-tolerant plants to survive. As the trail ascends, you pass through scattered pinyon, juniper, and sagebrush, and at the top, there are even small stands of aspens.

Navigation is difficult—there are no signs and many small tracks. A GPS is invaluable in this terrain, as vehicle tracks can quickly become overgrown or new ones pushed through, rendering the directions hard to follow.

The trail leaves US 50 approximately 30 miles west of Delta and begins as a small graded dirt road; you eventually loop back to US 50 on Marjum Canyon Road. Over the first 7 miles, the route makes several turns onto unmarked dirt roads, which get smaller and narrower until, at its least-used point, the trail is a narrow two-track with grass growing in the middle. A wise safety precaution is to check your vehicle's undercarriage at regular intervals to ensure that seeds and dry material are not collecting underneath, where they could be ignited by the heat from your exhaust.

The trail travels partway into Candland Canyon, and then it connects with a graded gravel spur trail up North Canyon. On the spur trail, once you cross North Canyon Creek, the trail standard becomes rougher with a short, moderately steep ledgy climb up the canyon. At the placer mines, there are many small tracks leading off among the remains. There are some interesting old buildings and vehicles lying derelict in the grass, and the original open pit mine is being revegetated and restored to a natural state. It is worth exploring some of the dead-end tracks leading off from the mines and into the Amasa Valley toward Pine Peak. The spur trail ends at a panoramic viewpoint of Sevier Lake and Miller Canyon. Sevier Lake is particularly beautiful from here on a clear day. The striking blue color of the lake and still conditions can make perfect mirror images in the shallow water. The trail continues, but it is steep and appears mainly to be used by ATVs.

From the viewpoint, retrace your path down North Canyon and continue northeast on the main trail to Marjum Canyon Road. This major gravel road will quickly take you back to US 50.

Although open year-round, snow or heavy rain can close the trail on occasion.

Current Road Information

BLM Fillmore Field Office
95 East 500 North
Fillmore, UT 84631
(435) 743-3100

Map References

BLM Tule Valley
USGS 1:24,000 Long Ridge SW, Long Ridge Reservoir, Miller Cove, Notch Peak
1:100,000 Tule Valley
Utah Atlas & Gazetteer, pp. 41, 31
Utah Road & Recreation Atlas, pp. 65, 57

Route Directions

▼ 0.0		On US 50, 0.6 miles west of mile marker 53, turn northwest on unmarked small graded dirt road and zero trip meter.
4.2 ▲		Trail ends at US 50. Turn left for Delta, right for Ely, Nevada.
		GPS: N 39°06.35' W 113°08.67'
▼ 1.2	SO	Cross through fence line on rise.
3.0 ▲	SO	Cross through fence line on rise.
▼ 4.2	TR	Unsigned T-intersection. Zero trip meter.
0.0 ▲		Continue toward US 50.
		GPS: N 39°07.86' W 113°12.93'
▼ 0.0		Continue north.
3.7 ▲	TL	Unsigned junction; zero trip meter.
▼ 0.2	SO	Exclosure on left.
3.5 ▲	SO	Exclosure on right.
▼ 0.3	TL	Turn left onto unmarked, ungraded, less-used small two-track.
3.4 ▲	TR	Turn right onto unmarked larger track.
		GPS: N 39°08.11' W 113°12.87'
▼ 1.7	BL	Fork.
2.0 ▲	SO	Fork.
		GPS: N 39°08.47' W 113°14.36'
▼ 3.1	SO	Cross through wash.
0.6 ▲	SO	Cross through wash.
▼ 3.7	TR	Intersection. Turn right onto unmarked, ungraded two-track and zero trip meter.
0.0 ▲		Continue east.
		GPS: N 39°08.69' W 113°16.68'
▼ 0.0		Continue north.
2.9 ▲	TL	Intersection. Turn left onto unmarked, ungraded two-track and zero trip meter.
▼ 0.2	SO	Cross through small wash.
2.7 ▲	SO	Cross through small wash.
▼ 0.5	SO	Cross through small wash.
2.4 ▲	SO	Cross through small wash.
▼ 0.6	SO	Enclosure on left.
2.3 ▲	SO	Enclosure on right.
▼ 1.4	SO	Enter creek wash.
1.5 ▲	SO	Exit creek wash.

Northern Trail #30: Sawtooth Mountain Trail

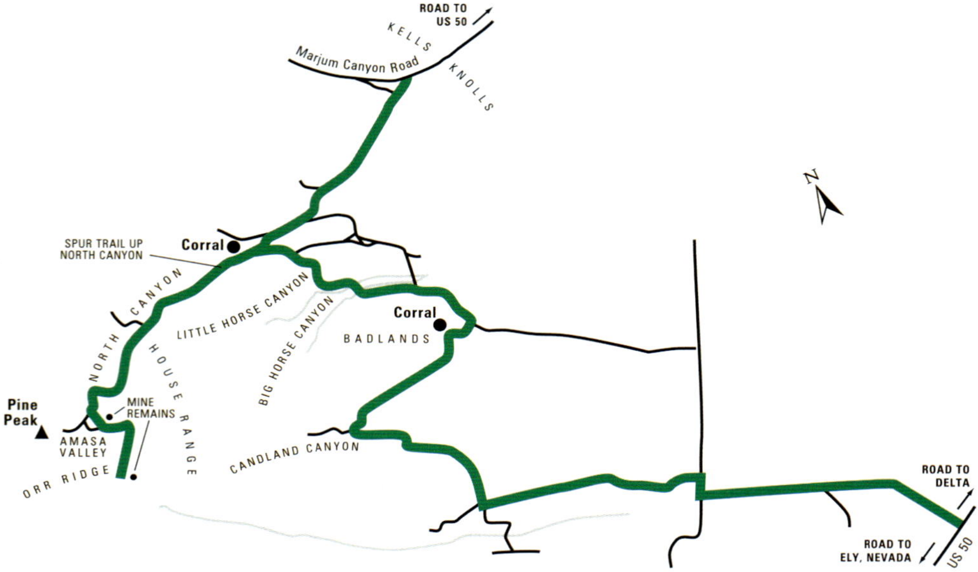

▼ 1.5 SO Exit creek wash to the right.
1.4 ▲ SO Enter creek wash.

▼ 1.9 TR Unmarked T-intersection.
1.0 ▲ TL Unmarked junction.
GPS: N 39°09.87' W 113°17.68'

▼ 2.1 SO Enter creek wash.
0.8 ▲ SO Exit creek wash.

▼ 2.3 SO Exit creek wash.
0.6 ▲ SO Enter creek wash.

▼ 2.5 SO Cross through wash.
0.4 ▲ SO Cross through wash.

▼ 2.9 TR T-intersection. Left goes up Candland Canyon and dead-ends. Zero trip meter.
0.0 ▲ Continue southeast on lesser-used trail.
GPS: N 39°10.31' W 113°18.49'

▼ 0.0 Continue up slightly better used trail.
2.7 ▲ TL Straight goes up Candland Canyon and dead-ends. Zero trip meter.

▼ 0.3 SO Track on left, then cross through wash.
2.4 ▲ SO Cross through wash, then track on right.

▼ 1.5 SO Cross through small wash.
1.2 ▲ SO Cross through small wash.

▼ 2.0 SO Cross through small wash.
0.7 ▲ SO Cross through small wash.

▼ 2.2 TR Corral on left.
0.5 ▲ TL Turn left before corral.
GPS: N 39°11.17' W 113°16.31'

▼ 2.4 SO Cross through wash.
0.3 ▲ SO Cross through wash.

▼ 2.5 SO Cross through wash.
0.2 ▲ SO Cross through wash.

▼ 2.7 TL Unmarked T-intersection. Zero trip meter.
0.0 ▲ Continue southwest.
GPS: N 39°11.29' W 113°15.84'

▼ 0.0 Continue northwest.
4.0 ▲ TR Unmarked junction. Zero trip meter.

View from the saddle between North Canyon and Amasa Valley

▼ 0.3 SO Cross through two small washes.
3.7 ▲ SO Cross through two small washes.

▼ 1.0 SO Track on left and track on right.
3.0 ▲ SO Track on left and track on right.
GPS: N 39°11.94' W 113°16.56'

▼ 1.3 SO Cross through wash.
2.7 ▲ SO Cross through wash.

▼ 1.8 SO Cross through wash.
2.2 ▲ SO Cross through wash.

▼ 1.9 BR Track on left goes up Big Horse Canyon.
2.1 ▲ BL Track on right goes up Big Horse Canyon.
GPS: N 39°12.12' W 113°17.56'

▼ 2.2 SO Cross through small wash.
1.8 ▲ SO Cross through small wash.

▼ 2.7 BR Track on left goes up Little Horse Canyon.
1.3 ▲ BL Track on right goes up Little Horse Canyon.
GPS: N 39°12.43' W 113°18.21'

▼ 3.3 SO Cross through wash.
0.7 ▲ SO Cross through wash.

▼ 3.4 SO Track on right.
0.6 ▲ BR Track on left.
GPS: N 39°13.00' W 113°18.58'

▼ 3.8 SO Track on right.
0.2 ▲ SO Track on left.

▼ 4.0 TL Unmarked T-intersection. Turn left onto spur trail up North Canyon and zero trip meter. You will return to this intersection after completing the spur trail.
0.0 ▲ From end of North Canyon spur trail, bear right (southeast) at unmarked junction to continue along main trail toward US 50.
GPS: N 39°13.12' W 113°19.20'

Spur Trail Up North Canyon

▼ 0.0 Continue on graded gravel road up North Canyon.
GPS: N 39°13.12' W 113°19.20'

▼ 0.6 SO Cross through wash.
▼ 0.8 SO Track on left.
▼ 1.0 SO Track on right.
▼ 1.1 SO Enter wash.
▼ 1.8 SO Exit wash.
▼ 2.2 SO Cattle guard.
▼ 2.5 SO Cross through wash, then track on right.
▼ 2.6 SO Cross through wash.
▼ 3.0 SO Track on left.
▼ 3.1 SO Track on left, campsite, and small corral.
GPS: N 39°11.93' W 113°22.08'

▼ 3.3 SO Cross through wash.
▼ 3.5 SO Old mine workings on right.
▼ 3.6 SO Enter wash and start to climb.
▼ 3.8 SO Leave wash; rough rocky climb.
▼ 4.1 BL Fork at saddle. Pine Peak is ahead to the southwest.
GPS: N 39°11.69' W 113°22.84'

▼ 4.2 SO Remains of placer mines: cabins, trucks, and diggings. Zero trip meter at intersection. More remains are on left.
GPS: N 39°11.60' W 113°22.84'

▼ 0.0 Continue south.
▼ 0.1 BL Track on right, then bear left at fork and cross over creek.
GPS: N 39°11.53' W 113°22.84'

▼ 0.2 BL Fork.
▼ 0.3 TL Faint crossroads.
GPS: N 39°11.36' W 113°22.78'

▼ 0.4 SO Track on left.
▼ 0.5 SO Track on right and left.
▼ 0.9 BR Fork.
GPS: N 39°11.23' W 113°22.27'

▼ 1.2 SO Track on left.
▼ 1.3 SO Old mine workings on left.
GPS: N 39°10.92' W 113°22.45'

▼ 1.4 SO Track on right.
▼ 1.5 UT Spur trail ends at viewpoint over Miller

Canyon and Lake Sevier. Trail continues, but used mainly by ATVs. From here, return to main trail and continue.
GPS: N 39°10.79' W 113°22.45'

Continuation of Main Trail

▼ 0.0 From end of North Canyon spur trail, bear left (northeast) at unmarked junction to continue along main trail.
3.9 ▲ TR Unmarked junction. Turn right onto spur trail up North Canyon and zero trip meter. You will return to this intersection after completing the spur trail.

▼ 0.2 SO Track on right.
3.7 ▲ SO Track on left.

▼ 0.9 SO Cross through wash.
3.0 ▲ SO Cross through wash.

▼ 1.1 SO Cross through wash.
2.8 ▲ SO Cross through wash.

▼ 1.2 SO Cross through wash.
2.7 ▲ SO Cross through wash.

▼ 1.3 SO Corral on left.
2.6 ▲ SO Corral on right.
GPS: N 39°13.61' W 113°17.79'

▼ 1.5 SO Track on left.
2.4 ▲ SO Track on right.

▼ 3.3 SO Cross through wash.
0.6 ▲ SO Cross through wash.

▼ 3.9 Trail ends at Marjum Canyon Road. Kells Knolls, small round hillocks, are on right and left. Turn right to rejoin US 50, near Delta, in 25 miles.
0.0 ▲ On Marjum Canyon Road, 25.1 miles west of US 50, turn left immediately after Kells Knolls. Intersection is unmarked.
GPS: N 39°14.90' W 113°15.40'

NORTHERN REGION TRAIL #31

Confusion Range Trail

STARTING POINT US 50, 47 miles west of Delta
FINISHING POINT Utah 21, 25 miles west of Milford
TOTAL MILEAGE 49.1 miles
UNPAVED MILEAGE 49.1 miles
DRIVING TIME 3.5 hours
ELEVATION RANGE 4,600–6,000 feet
USUALLY OPEN Year-round
DIFFICULTY RATING 3
SCENIC RATING 9
REMOTENESS RATING +2

Special Attractions

- Ghost town of Ibex.
- Rockhounding for trilobites at Fossil Mountain.
- Rockhounding at zebra stone quarry.
- Desert scenery around Sevier Lake and the Confusion Range.

History

With its enclosed valleys, jagged peaks, and haphazard and rugged topography, the Confusion Range is well named. Blind Valley, so-named because of its isolated, enclosed geography, is a major valley bordered on the east by the Barn Hills and on the west by the Confusion Range. The Barn Hills contain a natural, deep valley that is completely enclosed. Jack Watson, who grazed his cattle there around 1910, named the Barn Hills—since he reckoned that when contained in this depression, his cattle were so safe they might as well be in a barn! The valley is called The Barn on topographic maps, and originally the Barn Hills were called the Ibex Hills.

The Wah Wah Mountains to the south take their name from the springs of the same name, located near Wallace Peak on the eastern edge of the range. *Wah wah* is an Indian word meaning good clear water. The springs were owned by Lydia and Edwin Squire, who sold them to Samuel Newhouse to supply his mining town on the far side of the

Barn Hills in the foreground at the start of Blind Valley

valley, located below San Francisco Peak. In the Wah Wah Valley, the Wah Wah hardpan is created by water from the springs draining and drying out across the valley each year.

To confuse ghost town hunters, there are two ghost towns called Ibex located less than 50 miles apart. The Ibex ghost town on this trail is the more southerly of the two (the more well-known one is north in the Drum Mountains). Ibex was an old mining and stockman's trading center. It may have gained its name from local animals that were bred from desert bighorn sheep and the Indian's captive goats; their horns were gradually curved like the African ibex. There are also petroglyphs in the area that seem to depict such animals. Ibex had housing, corrals, a post office, and a boardinghouse. The settlement lasted into the 1900s, but it gradually declined as the miners and sheepherders moved on. Most of the buildings are gone now; the most enduring remains are those of the stone dam walls built by settlers across the mouth of a narrow canyon to conserve precious water to the best advantage. The dams are a short hike up the small canyon. There are also remains of collapsed corrals and several dumps of tin cans.

The Confusion Range, too, has its tales of lost gold and missed opportunity. In 1870, a geologist, Frank Lane, was prospecting around the Confusion Range when he lost his way. In his desperate search for water, he came across some small holes in the rocks filled with stagnant puddles. The water saved his life, and as he drank the holes dry, he saw in the bottoms small nuggets of gold. He collected nearly 30 pounds of gold before thirst forced him out of the range; he headed across the Sevier Desert to Cove Fort near the present intersection of I-15 and I-70. A few months later he tried to return to the site of his find, but in three years of hunting he was never able to locate it.

Today, the BLM collects sagebrush seeds there each fall and uses them to revegetate portions of the Utah landscape damaged by fires or erosion.

Description

This long and varied trail travels over a mixture of maintained graded roads and little-used two-track roads to penetrate some of the valleys in the Confusion Range. The entire region is very remote, and travelers should be self-sufficient; carry extra food, water, and clothing. In addition, make sure you have a detailed regional map, since navigation can be tricky, especially over the latter part of the trail around Middle Park and Lawson Cove. The BLM at Fillmore provides a free vehicle travel map of the Warm Springs Recreation Area, which includes all the tracks on this route.

Just prior to the start of the trail, fossil hunters may enjoy a stop at Skull Rock Pass on US 50 (GPS: N 39°01.93' W113°20.48'). Where the highway has been cut through on the pass, Ordovician period fossils can be found in the shale on both sides of the road.

The trail proper starts 47 miles west of Delta, 0.8 miles west of mile marker 39. The trail leaves US 50 and follows the easy-going, graded Blackham Canyon Road for the first few miles. Then you reach the long, north-south Blind Valley, with its wide, flat sandy bottom, in the Confusion Range. After 11.5 miles from the start, a left-hand, half-mile spur takes you to the remains of Ibex. There is little left of the ghost town these days, just the old series of dams, some foundations, fencing, and old tins. The site is pretty, set in a rock alcove, and there are some pleasant campsites.

Just after the turnoff for Ibex is the turnoff for a fossil-littered canyon on the north side of Fossil Mountain. If you drive a short distance to the mouth of the canyon and walk around the opening, you can find many marine invertebrate fossils in the rocks

Old dam wall at Ibex Ghost Town

Northern Trail #31: Confusion Range Trail

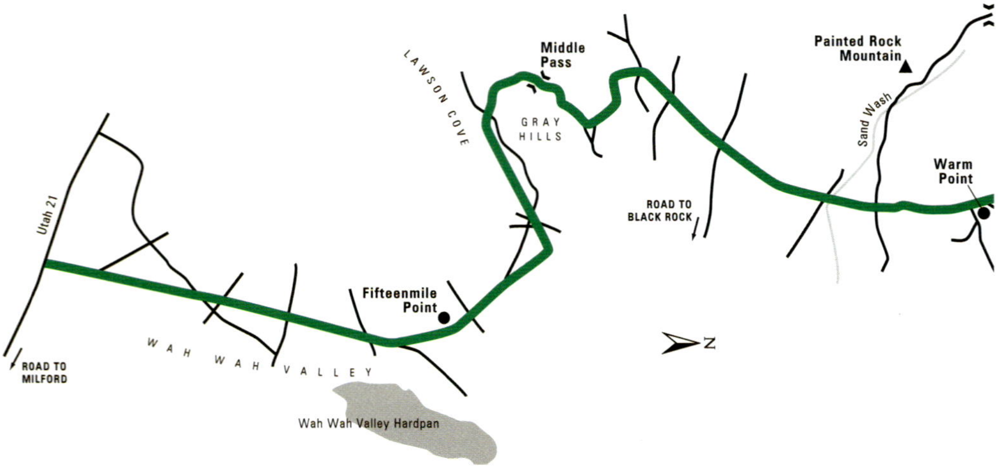

and slate. This site contains 13 fossil groups and a great variety of specimens. To the uninitiated, many of them look like clam shells and wood lice! Before you enter the canyon, there are some very pleasant vehicle campsites on the trail, that have soft sand for your tent and limited shade.

Continuing south, you pass Warm Point and head across the arid Tule Valley. The distinctive white Crystal Peak, another favorite rockhounding area, is visible to the north. The trail gets smaller and less defined as it approaches Middle Pass, a gentle grassy saddle in the Gray Hills. About 9.7 miles after the Crystal Peak turnoff, the trail drops to enter Lawson Cove, where rock hounds will find a bonus—just west of the trail is a vein of the distinctive Utah zebra rock, with its alternate bands of black and white.

From Lawson Cove, the trail is better defined as it heads southeast to join the graded gravel road leading past the Wah Wah hardpan (normally dry). It passes through the yards at Wah Wah Ranch to finish on Utah 21, 25 miles west of Milford.

Current Road Information

BLM Fillmore Field Office
95 East 500 North
Fillmore, UT 84631
(435) 743-3100

Map References

BLM Tule Valley, Wah Wah Mountains North, Wah Wah Mountains South

USGS 1:24,000 Hell 'n Moriah Canyon, The Barn, Warm Point, Fifteenmile Point, Grassy Cove, Wah Wah Cove, Wallaces Peak
1:100,000 Tule Valley, Wah Wah Mountains North, Wah Wah Mountains South

Utah Atlas & Gazetteer, p. 41
Utah Road & Recreation Atlas, pp. 64, 64

Route Directions

▼ 0.0		On US 50, 0.8 miles west of mile marker 39, turn southwest onto the graded dirt road, following sign to Blind Valley. Zero trip meter.
3.9 ▲		Trail ends at US 50. Turn right for Delta, left for Ely, Nevada.
		GPS: N 39°01.73' W 113°22.70'
▼ 0.4	SO	Intersection.
3.5 ▲	SO	Intersection.
▼ 0.8	BL	Track on right.
2.7 ▲	SO	Track on left.
		GPS: N 39°01.15' W 113°23.33'
▼ 1.4	SO	Track on left.
2.5 ▲	SO	Track on right.

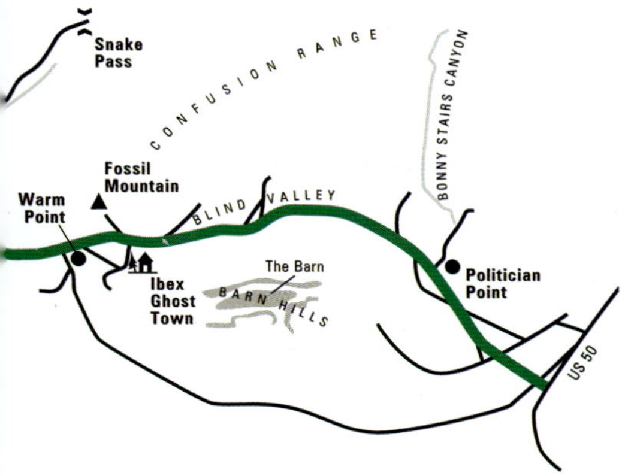

▼ 2.1 TR Intersection at north end of Barn Hills.
1.8 ▲ TL Intersection at north end of Barn Hills.
GPS: N 39°00.18′ W 113°24.02′

▼ 3.4 SO Track on left. Politician Point on right.
0.5 ▲ SO Track on right. Politician Point on left.
GPS: N 38°59.65′ W 113°25.42′

▼ 3.9 SO Track on right to Blackham Canyon. Zero trip meter.
0.0 ▲ Continue toward US 50.
GPS: N 38°59.42′ W 113°25.96′

▼ 0.0 Continue toward Blind Valley.
7.6 ▲ SO Track on left to Blackham Canyon. Zero trip meter.

▼ 0.2 SO Cross through two washes.
7.4 ▲ SO Cross through two washes.

▼ 0.6 SO Track on left.
7.0 ▲ SO Track on right.

▼ 1.0 SO Cross through wash.
6.6 ▲ SO Cross through wash.

▼ 1.4 SO Cross over wash, followed by track on right to Bonny Stairs Canyon. Trail crosses wash many times in next 2.3 miles.
6.2 ▲ SO Track on left to Bonny Stairs Canyon, then cross over wash.
GPS: N 38°58.52′ W 113°27.09′

▼ 3.7 SO Entering Blind Valley.
3.9 ▲ SO Leaving Blind Valley. Trail crosses over wash many times in next 2.3 miles.
GPS: N 38°56.60′ W 113°27.90′

▼ 4.4 SO Track on right; then second faint track on right.
3.2 ▲ SO Faint track on left; then second track on left.

▼ 4.6 SO Track on left.
3.0 ▲ SO Track on right.
GPS: N 38°55.81′ W 113°27.53′

▼ 7.6 BR Fork, directly in front of conical hillock. Fossil Mountain is prominent on right. Track on left to Ibex ghost town (0.5 miles). Zero trip meter.
0.0 ▲ Continue north along Blind Valley.
GPS: N 38°53.12′ W 113°27.05′

▼ 0.0 Continue toward Fossil Mountain.
4.4 ▲ SO Track on right to Ibex ghost town (0.5 miles). Zero trip meter.

▼ 0.1 BL Right fork goes short distance into canyon north of Fossil Mountain. Fossils can be found around mouth of canyon.
4.3 ▲ SO Track on left goes short distance into canyon north of Fossil Mountain. Fossils can be found around mouth of canyon.
GPS: N 38°53.10′ W 113°27.08′

▼ 0.5 SO Cross through wash. Fossil Mountain is directly right.
3.9 ▲ SO Cross through wash. Fossil Mountain is directly left.

▼ 1.2 SO Track on right.
3.2 ▲ SO Track on left.

▼ 1.4 SO Track on left to Ibex ghost town. Warm Point on left.
3.0 ▲ SO Track on right to Ibex ghost town. Warm Point on right.
GPS: N 38°51.94′ W 113°26.95′

▼ 1.6 SO Intersection. Road on left to Tule Valley.
2.8 ▲ SO Intersection. Road on right to Tule Valley.
GPS: N 38°51.82' W 113°26.90'

▼ 1.7 SO Track on left.
2.7 ▲ SO Track on right.

▼ 2.5 SO Track on right.
1.9 ▲ SO Track on left.

▼ 4.4 SO Major intersection. Road on left to Tule Valley, right to Snake Pass. Zero trip meter.
0.0 ▲ Continue north.
GPS: N 38°49.34' W 113°27.07'

▼ 0.0 Continue south.
4.6 ▲ SO Major intersection. Road on right to Tule Valley, left to Snake Pass. Zero trip meter.

▼ 1.4 SO Track on right.
3.2 ▲ SO Track on left.

▼ 1.5 SO Cross through Sand Wash.
3.1 ▲ SO Cross through Sand Wash.

▼ 4.5 SO Track on right. Crystal Mountain is visible on right.
0.1 ▲ SO Track on left. Crystal Mountain is visible on left.
GPS: N 38°45.59' W 113°28.83'

▼ 4.6 SO Major intersection. Road on left to Black Rock, right to Crystal Peak. Zero trip meter.
0.0 ▲ Continue north on more-used trail.
GPS: N 38°45.46' W 113°28.98'

▼ 0.0 Continue south on less-used trail.
3.8 ▲ SO Major intersection. Road on right to Black Rock, left to Crystal Peak. Zero trip meter.

▼ 0.1 SO Cross through deep wash.
3.7 ▲ SO Cross through deep wash.

▼ 1.4 SO Cross through deep wash.
2.4 ▲ SO Cross through deep wash.

▼ 1.7 SO Cross through deep wash.
2.1 ▲ SO Cross through deep wash.

▼ 3.0 SO Cross through wash.
0.8 ▲ SO Cross through wash.

▼ 3.4 SO Cross through wash.
0.4 ▲ SO Cross through wash.

▼ 3.8 TL Unmarked small intersection. Zero trip meter.
0.0 ▲ Continue north.
GPS: N 38°42.85' W 113°31.50'

▼ 0.0 Continue east.
5.9 ▲ TR Unmarked small junction. Zero trip meter.

▼ 0.8 SO Cross through wash.
5.1 ▲ SO Cross through wash.

▼ 1.4 SO Cross through wash.
4.5 ▲ SO Cross through wash.

▼ 1.5 BR Main track goes left. Bear right on lesser-used faint trail.
4.4 ▲ BL Track on right. Trail is now slightly better used.

▼ 2.0 TR Track on left. Join more-used track.
3.9 ▲ TL Turn left on lesser-used faint trail.
GPS: N 38°42.08' W 113°30.05'

▼ 3.0 SO Track on left. Trail follows wash. Gray Hills are on left.
2.9 ▲ SO Track on right. Trail follows wash. Gray Hills are on right.
GPS: N 38°41.48' W 113°30.85'

▼ 4.2 SO Slight grassy rise is Middle Pass. Trail descends to Lawson Cove.
1.7 ▲ SO Slight grassy rise is Middle Pass. Trail descends.
GPS: N 38°40.67' W 113°31.53'

▼ 4.8 SO Track on left.
1.1 ▲ SO Track on right.

▼ 5.0 BL Track on right, then cross through wash.

0.9 ▲	BR	Cross through wash, then track on left.
		GPS: N 38°39.93' W 113°31.24'
▼ 5.3	SO	Cross through fence line.
0.6 ▲	SO	Cross through fence line.
▼ 5.9	TL	Unmarked T-intersection. Immediately on right are diggings in a vein of zebra rock. Turn left onto larger, graded dirt road and zero trip meter.
0.0 ▲		Continue northwest.
		GPS: N 38°39.59' W 113°30.37'
▼ 0.0		Continue east.
4.2 ▲	TR	Unmarked junction. Immediately ahead are diggings in a vein of zebra rock. Turn right onto smaller ungraded trail and zero trip meter.
▼ 3.3	SO	Faint tracks on right and left.
0.9 ▲	SO	Faint tracks on right and left.
▼ 4.2	TR	Unmarked intersection. Zero trip meter.
0.0 ▲		Continue on graded dirt road.
		GPS: N 38°41.19' W 113°25.93'
▼ 0.0		Continue on good, graded dirt road.
5.3 ▲	TL	Unmarked intersection. Zero trip meter.
▼ 2.8	SO	Track on right.
2.5 ▲	SO	Track on left.
▼ 3.3	SO	Track on right.
2.0 ▲	SO	Track on left.
▼ 4.4	SO	Cattle guard. Wah Wah Valley hardpan on left.
0.9 ▲	SO	Cattle guard. Wah Wah Valley hardpan on right.
▼ 5.3	TR	Join graded gravel road. Road on left to Wah Wah Well. Zero trip meter.
0.0 ▲		Continue on smaller gravel road.
		GPS: N 38°37.05' W 113°22.96'
▼ 0.0		Continue on larger gravel road.
9.4 ▲	BL	Straight on to Wah Wah Well. Turn left at sign for Lawson Cove and zero trip meter.
▼ 0.5	SO	Track on right.
8.9 ▲	SO	Track on left.
▼ 1.0	SO	Cattle guard, then track on left along fence line.
8.4 ▲	SO	Track on right along fence line, then cattle guard.
▼ 2.7	SO	Track on right.
6.7 ▲	SO	Track on left.
▼ 4.0	SO	Tracks on right and left.
5.4 ▲	SO	Tracks on right and left.
▼ 4.4	SO	Track on right.
5.0 ▲	SO	Track on left.
▼ 4.6	SO	Tracks on right and left.
4.8 ▲	SO	Tracks on right and left.
		GPS: N 38°32.95' W 113°24.43'
▼ 8.2	SO	Cattle guard.
1.2 ▲	SO	Cattle guard.
▼ 8.9	SO	Pass through Wah Wah Ranch property and yards.
0.5 ▲	SO	Pass through Wah Wah Ranch property and yards.
▼ 9.4		Trail ends at Utah 21. Turn left for Milford.
0.0 ▲		On Utah 21, 25 miles west of Milford, turn north onto graded gravel road at sign for Wah Wah Ranch and zero trip meter.
		GPS: N 38°28.76' W 113°25.90'

NORTHERN REGION TRAIL #32

Frisco Peak Trail

STARTING POINT Utah 21, 7.8 miles west of Milford
FINISHING POINT Frisco Peak
TOTAL MILEAGE 11.8 miles
UNPAVED MILEAGE 11.8 miles
DRIVING TIME 45 minutes (one-way)
ELEVATION RANGE 5,100–9,600 feet
USUALLY OPEN May to November
DIFFICULTY RATING 5
SCENIC RATING 9
REMOTENESS RATING +0

Special Attractions

- Narrow, moderately difficult 4WD spur trail.
- Panoramic views from Frisco Peak.

History

From the top of Frisco Peak, you can see the remains and tailings of the ghost town of Newhouse. Newhouse sprang into existence in 1900 when Samuel Newhouse purchased the Cactus Mine. He established a model city for his workers, building them houses, a café, a store, and a dance hall. Newhouse was as sober as nearby Frisco was rowdy. The only saloon was deliberately built one mile outside of town, so that it didn't exert any undue influence on the good citizens of Newhouse. When the railroad arrived, that too had to stop south of town. Samuel Newhouse died before his dream city could be completed, but his brother Matt continued in his shoes until 1910, when the ore in the mines ran out.

The mines at Newhouse dug up a total of $3.5 million worth of gold, silver, and copper. The Cactus Mill in town processed the ore, which was then shipped by railroad to market. The town survived for a short time after the ore ran out. The Cactus Café and boardinghouse served sheepherders and ranchers, and there was a shearing shed there until the 1930s. The railroad disappeared shortly after, because there was no more wool to collect. The Cactus Mill was purchased in 1914 for salvage, and many of the homes were moved to Milford in the 1920s.

A switchback as the trail ascends toward Frisco Peak

The launch pad for hang gliders

In 1922, Newhouse achieved a modicum of notoriety when it provided the setting for the silent movie *The Covered Wagon.*

En route to Frisco Peak, the trail crosses Moorehouse Canyon, at the head of which is Moorehouse Springs. The springs and canyon are named after Charles Moorehouse, who carted water from the springs to sell to the miners at Frisco. The trail then travels along Sawmill Canyon. In the 1870s, a sawmill was built there to provide timber for mines in the region, including the nearby Golden Reef and the mines of Frisco.

Description

This spur trail climbs steadily to one of the highest points in the region, Frisco Peak at 9,660 feet in the San Francisco Range. From Utah 21, the trail begins as an unmarked, graded dirt road, and it quickly crosses the sagebrush benches on the eastern side of the San Francisco Range. After 6.2 miles, you reach the intersection with Northern #33: Frisco Ghost Town Trail, and after 8.7 miles, you pass the tailings piles of the Golden Reef Mine as the trail climbs up Sawmill Canyon. From the mine, the trail climbs steeply. The surface is loose and lumpy, but is generally fairly good. The most difficult section is the switchbacks that snake up toward the ridge. The trail is narrow, and the highest portions are mostly shelf roads. There are adequate passing places, but you should be prepared to back up if you meet an oncoming vehicle. The road is suitable for any high-clearance SUV.

As the trail climbs, it passes out of the juniper and sagebrush and encounters larger pines. The views get better the farther up you go. From the peak, there is a 360-degree view. To the north is the San Francisco Range, the Wah Wah Valley, the Wah Wah Hardpan, and Lake Sevier. To the northwest is the Confusion Range and the Wah Wah Mountains, which extend to the south. To the south are the Blue Mountains. Looking down from the peak to the southwest, you can see the remains of Newhouse.

At the peak there are communications towers and two hang glider launch sites (Level IV skills required). The visitors book for the launch area seems to have more entries from four-wheelers than from hang gliders.

Northern Trail #32: Frisco Peak Trail

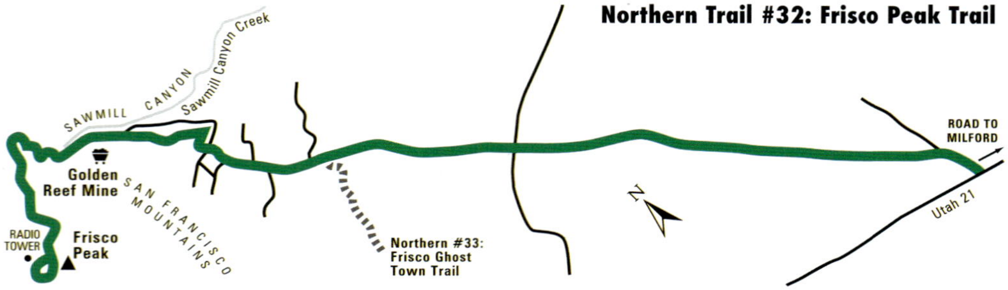

Current Road Information

BLM Cedar City Field Office
176 East D.L. Sargent Drive
Cedar City, UT 84721
(435) 865-3002

Maps References

BLM Wah Wah Mountains South, Wah Wah Mountains North
USGS 1:24,000 Milford NW, High Rock, Frisco Peak
1:100,000 Wah Wah Mountains South, Wah Wah Mountains North
Utah Atlas & Gazetteer, p. 41
Utah Road & Recreation Atlas, p. 65

Route Directions

▼ 0.0 On Utah 21, 7.8 miles west of Milford, turn northwest on unmarked graded dirt road and zero trip meter.
GPS: N 38°26.36' W 113°09.16'

▼ 0.1 SO Cross through wash.
▼ 0.3 BL Track on right.
▼ 4.4 SO Tracks on right and left.
▼ 6.2 SO Track on left is Northern #33: Frisco Ghost Town Trail.
GPS: N 38°30.23' W 113°14.27'

▼ 6.5 SO Track on right.
▼ 6.6 SO Track on right.
▼ 7.0 SO Track on left.
▼ 7.3 SO Tracks on right and left.
▼ 8.0 SO Track on left.
▼ 8.7 SO Tailings pile of Golden Reef Mine on left. Track on left to remains of mine, then track on right to Horse Spring. Zero trip meter.
GPS: N 38°31.75' W 113°15.80'

▼ 0.0 Continue into Sawmill Canyon; trail follows along Sawmill Canyon Creek.
▼ 0.5 SO Track on left.
▼ 2.2 SO Track on left.
▼ 2.8 SO Communications dish on right.
▼ 2.9 SO Start of loop around communications towers on peak.
▼ 3.0 SO Hang gliding launch pads on left and best views from the peak.
GPS: N 38°31.20' W 113°17.14'

▼ 3.1 End of loop. Retrace your steps back to Utah 21.
GPS: N 38°31.19' W 113°17.11'

NORTHERN REGION TRAIL #33

Frisco Ghost Town Trail

STARTING POINT Utah 21 at Frisco Historical Marker
FINISHING POINT Northern #32: Frisco Peak Trail
TOTAL MILEAGE 5.9 miles
UNPAVED MILEAGE 5.7 miles
DRIVING TIME 1 hour
ELEVATION RANGE 5,100–6,800 feet
USUALLY OPEN Year-round
DIFFICULTY RATING 3
SCENIC RATING 8
REMOTENESS RATING +1

Special Attractions

- Frisco ghost town, cemetery, and charcoal kilns.

History

Frisco, in its heyday, was one of the wildest and richest silver towns in Utah. Nestled in the shadow of the San Francisco Mountains, Frisco came into being in 1875 after two old prospectors, Jim Ryan and Sam Hawkes, accidentally stumbled upon a vein of nearly pure silver. According to one story, each day as the two miners left their camp, they passed by the same boulder. One day, Jim took a pick to it and discovered silver. They called their stake the Bonanza and almost immediately sold it for the princely sum of $25,000. The new owners found that the initial vein was the tip of the iceberg and that it contained a very high grade of silver ore. It was so soft it could be pared with a knife, and since the parings curled like an animal horn, they called their mine the Horn Silver.

It wasn't long before the silver lode changed hands again. The new owners were thrilled to receive the incredible sum of $5 million for the mine from Jay Cooke. However, Cooke didn't make out badly either, for he eventually unearthed $50 million in ore in what was perhaps the world's richest, single silver vein.

Frisco became the quintessential mining boomtown, and when Cooke managed to get a railroad into Frisco from Milford in 1880, the town really took off. At its peak in the early 1880s, Frisco had 23 saloons, a newspaper, boardinghouses, and stores—as well as brothels, gambling halls, and even opium dens—and a population of 6,000. The biggest problem was getting water to the town (which may have accounted for the number of saloons!). At times water was trucked in and sold door to door by the bucketful. The town was riotous, and murders were a daily occurrence. When a new, no-nonsense sheriff was brought in from Nevada to try to bring order to the town, he killed six people during his first night on the job—just to show he meant business!

The Horn Silver Mine was joined by other mines in the district. The Carbonate, Comet, Grand Republic, Hoodoo, and others sprang up, many with their own mills and charcoal kilns to run them. They never made as much money as the Horn Silver, but they turned a fair profit.

Frisco came to an end almost as abruptly as it began. The Horn Silver was a somewhat unconventional open pit mine, 900 feet deep, that was supported by a tangle of wooden supports; the miners had been so eager to get the silver that safety had been almost a secondary consideration. Inevitably, the mine caved in. In 1885, as the miners were changing shifts, the mine abruptly subsided. Amazingly, no one was hurt or killed, but the tons of rock crashing into the pit made the ground shake so violently that windows broke 20 miles away in Milford.

Frisco didn't last long after that. A few families stayed to pick over the mines, and a new shaft was drilled down to the silver vein. The town eventually produced another $20 million from the new shaft, but by 1920, the town was deserted. Some of the outlying mines are sporadically worked today. Frisco is one of Utah's most intact ghost towns, and it is a fascinating place to visit. Its beehive charcoal kilns are listed in the National Register of Historic Places, and a number of its faded downtown buildings still creak and whisper under the blazing sun.

Description

This trail begins with a short, 1.6-mile tour through Frisco and its mining remains. In this section, the graded dirt road is suitable for passenger cars, and the short distances between features make it ideal for a walking tour. However, some areas of Frisco are posted as private property; respect the signs and view these areas from the boundary.

The tour starts from the historical marker and picnic shelter on Utah 21, 13.5 miles west of Milford. Turn west on the graded gravel road. After 0.4 miles, the tour passes within 0.1 miles of the old overgrown cemetery, with its many iron-fenced graves and others marked only by small mounds. The numerous graves of infants and small children are testimony to the hard life and conditions in these mining camps. The trail then passes within 0.2 miles of the King David Mine. The famous Horn Silver Mine is south

Old kilns at Frisco Ghost Town

of the King David. This is private property; please don't go past the gate. The tour then passes by the charcoal kilns, which have been fenced. These are in generally good condition; note the slightly different shapes of each kiln and the blackened stone inside.

The trail then passes around some of the standing cabins, plus the old vault, before returning to paved Utah 21. The old railroad grade that ran through the town can be seen in several places. Hiking around some of the old ruins reveals more old mines and mining remnants. Take care, though—there are many sharp objects to catch a tire and many holes buried in the grass. Other small, and often overgrown, trails lead to some of the outlying mines on the hillsides.

Once the trail returns to Utah 21, you drive 0.2 miles before turning north along an unmarked dirt track. The trail from this point warrants a 3 rating and should only be driven by SUVs. In addition, the trails are unmarked, so follow the directions carefully; there are many dead ends and it is easy to make a wrong turn. The route winds along in the juniper and sagebrush, climbing slightly over the southern flank of San Francisco Peak, before reaching the Carbonate Mine, one of the outlying silver mines from Frisco. There are some old buildings and mining equipment here, but the area is posted against trespassers. From the Carbonate Mine, the trail is narrow and passes by the fenced Coyote Springs, and then it ends at Northern #32: Frisco Peak Trail.

Current Road Information

BLM Cedar City Field Office
176 East D.L. Sargent Drive
Cedar City, UT 84721
(435) 865-3002

Map References

BLM Wah Wah Mountains South, Wah Wah Mountains North
USGS 1:24,000 Frisco, High Rock, Milford NW
1:100,000 Wah Wah Mountains South, Wah Wah Mountains North
Utah Atlas & Gazetteer, p. 41
Utah Road & Recreation Atlas, p. 65

Route Directions

▼ 0.0		On Utah 21, 13.5 miles west of Milford, turn west onto graded gravel road at historical marker for Frisco and zero trip meter.
1.6 ▲		Trail ends at historical marker for Frisco on paved Utah 21. Turn left for Milford.
		GPS: N 38°27.17' W 113°15.54'
▼ 0.4	TR	Straight goes 0.1 miles to cemetery.
1.2 ▲	TL	T-intersection. Track on right goes 0.1 miles to cemetery.
		GPS: N 38°27.06' W 113°15.99'
▼ 0.6	SO	Intersection. Track on left goes 0.2 miles to King David Mine. Immediately after intersection, bear right at fork.
1.0 ▲	SO	Track on right immediately before intersection. Track on right at intersection goes 0.2 miles to King David Mine.
		GPS: N 38°27.20' W 113°15.99'
▼ 0.9	SO	Intersection.
0.7 ▲	SO	Intersection.
▼ 1.0	SO	Track on right.
0.6 ▲	SO	Track on left.
▼ 1.1	SO	Track on left goes 0.1 miles to charcoal kilns.
0.5 ▲	SO	Track on right goes 0.1 miles to charcoal kilns.
▼ 1.2	TR	Intersection. Remnants of town buildings scattered around crossroads.
0.4 ▲	TL	Intersection. Remnants of town buildings scattered around crossroads.
		GPS: N 38°27.61' W 113°15.55'
▼ 1.3	SO	Intersection.
0.3 ▲	SO	Intersection.
▼ 1.5	BR	Swing right toward paved road.
0.1 ▲	SO	Track on right.
▼ 1.6	TL	Join paved Utah 21 and zero trip meter.
0.0 ▲		Continue west on gravel track.
		GPS: N 38°27.60' W 113°15.13'

King David Mine buildings

Northern Trail #33: Frisco Ghost Town Trail

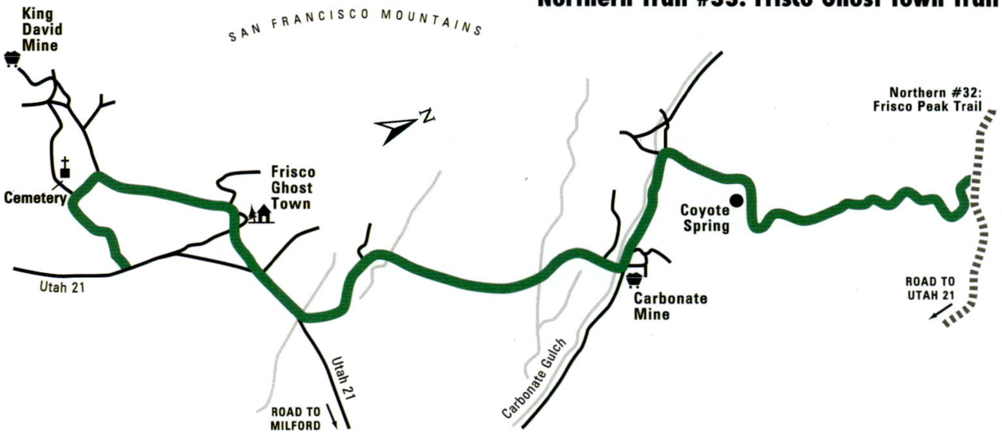

▼ 0.0 Continue northeast on Utah 21.
1.9 ▲ TR Turn onto gravel track and zero trip meter.

▼ 0.2 TL Turn onto gravel track opposite mile marker 63.
1.7 ▲ TR Turn onto paved Utah 21.
GPS: N 38°27.67' W 113°14.93'

▼ 0.4 SO Sheds and corral on left, then track on left.
1.5 ▲ SO Track on right, then sheds and corral on right.

▼ 0.5 SO Track on left.
1.4 ▲ SO Track on right.

▼ 0.6 SO Cross through wash.
1.3 ▲ SO Cross through wash.

▼ 0.7 SO Cross through wash.
1.2 ▲ SO Cross through wash.

▼ 1.0 SO Cross through wash, then five-way junction. Go straight, heading northeast (two tracks on left, one on right).
0.9 ▲ SO Five-way junction. Go straight, heading southwest (two tracks on right, one on left), then cross through wash.
GPS: N 38°28.26' W 113°14.83'

▼ 1.1 SO Track on left.
0.8 ▲ SO Track on right.

▼ 1.2 SO Cross through wash.
0.7 ▲ SO Cross through wash.

▼ 1.3 BL Faint track on right.
0.6 ▲ BR Faint track on left.

▼ 1.4 SO Cross through wash.
0.5 ▲ SO Cross through wash.

▼ 1.5 SO Enter wash.
0.4 ▲ SO Exit wash.

▼ 1.6 SO Exit wash.
0.3 ▲ SO Enter wash.

▼ 1.7 SO Cross through wash, then pass underneath powerlines. Track on left underneath powerlines.
0.2 ▲ SO Pass underneath powerlines. Track on right underneath powerlines, then cross through wash.

▼ 1.8 SO Cross through wash.
0.1 ▲ SO Cross through wash.

▼ 1.9 TL T-intersection at Carbonate Mine (private property). Zero trip meter.
0.0 ▲ Continue on smaller trail.
GPS: N 38°28.89' W 113°14.58'

▼ 0.0 Continue on better-used trail.
2.4 ▲ TR Turn right opposite the Carbonate Mine and zero trip meter.

▼ 0.1 SO Track on right to Carbonate Mine.
2.3 ▲ SO Track on left to Carbonate Mine (private property).

▼ 0.4 SO Track on right.
2.0 ▲ SO Track on left.

▼ 0.5 TR Track on left, then turn right on track to right, climbing away from wash.
1.9 ▲ BL Bear left at track on left, followed by track on right. Follow along wash.

▼ 0.6 BR Small track on left, then bear right, followed by track on right.
1.8 ▲ BL Track on left, then bear left at second track.

▼ 0.9 SO Coyote Spring on right, fenced spring and cattle tank.
1.5 ▲ SO Coyote Spring on left, fenced spring and cattle tank.

GPS: N 38°29.42′ W 113°14.70′

▼ 1.7 SO Cross through wash.
0.7 ▲ SO Cross through wash.

▼ 1.9 SO Cross through wash.
0.5 ▲ SO Cross through wash.

▼ 2.4 Trail ends at T-intersection with Northern #32: Frisco Peak Trail. Turn left for Frisco Peak, right for Utah 21.
0.0 ▲ On Northern #32: Frisco Peak Trail, 6.2 miles from Utah 21, turn west onto small, unsigned trail and zero trip meter.

GPS: N 38°30.23′ W 113°14.27′

NORTHERN REGION TRAIL #34

Soldier Pass Trail

STARTING POINT Utah 21 at Milford
FINISHING POINT Utah 21 near Beaver
TOTAL MILEAGE 17.8 miles
UNPAVED MILEAGE 17.1 miles
DRIVING TIME 1 hour
ELEVATION RANGE 4,900–7,388
USUALLY OPEN April to November
DIFFICULTY RATING 1
SCENIC RATING 8
REMOTENESS RATING +0

Special Attractions

- Easy scenic pass through the Mineral Mountains.
- Access to rockhounding areas.
- Granite Peak.

History

Soldier Pass is the highest point on the road that goes from Adamsville to Milford over the Mineral Mountains. The route was first blazed by soldiers stationed at Fort Cameron, who needed faster access to Milford on the other side of the range. Fort Cameron was positioned two miles from Beaver on the North Beaver River. The fort was one of many built to protect the citizens during the Indian Wars of the 1850s.

Adamsville, on the east side of the pass was originally called Wales, after the Welsh people who had settled it. It was known as the Beaver Iron Works for a while, before finally changing its name to Adamsville after its founder, David B. Adams.

Description

This very pretty drive connects the towns of Milford and Beaver via the 7,388-foot Soldier Pass, which winds through a gap in the Mineral Mountains, a range that is 28 miles long and averages 5 miles wide. Its major peak is Granite Peak (9,578 feet) in the center of the range. The Mineral Mountains also contain deposits of obsidian, a dark natural glass formed from cooling lava; the Indians of southwestern Utah used obsidian as an important trade item.

Northern Trail #34: Soldier Pass Trail

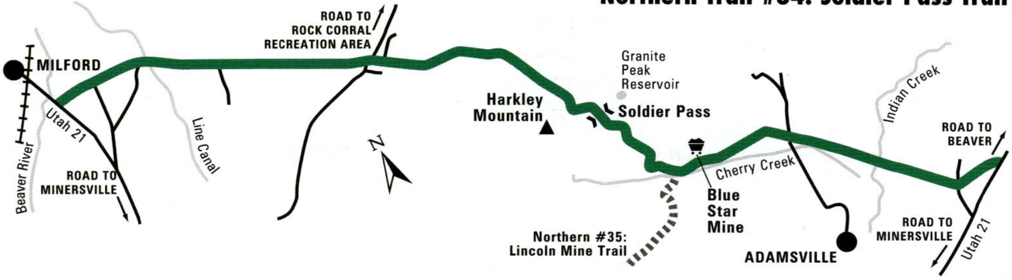

The trail starts at Milford, on the southeast edge of town, and heads east. The road is graded gravel for the first part as it makes a beeline for the Mineral Mountains. At the base of the mountains, a graded road goes to a popular rockhounding spot, the Rock Corral Recreation Area.

From here, the road standard drops slightly and it becomes narrower and slightly sandy. However, in good weather and with a little care, you can easily traverse this road in a passenger vehicle. The road climbs and winds around the western side of Soldier Pass. To the south is Harkley Mountain, and to the north is Granite Peak, which you can't miss: It has prominent bare granite slabs, standing rocks and boulders, and exposed slopes. In June 1996, a massive wildfire destroyed over 600 acres of vegetation on both sides of Soldier Pass.

From the top of the pass, there are good views into the Parowan Valley to the east and over to the lower end of the Sevier Plateau and the Tushar Mountains. Looking west you can see the Escalante Desert and the Wah Wah Mountains.

The eastern side of the pass drops swiftly, following Cherry Creek to run out along the sage-covered benches into the Parowan Valley. You intersect with Northern #35: Lincoln Mine Trail, and another track leads north to the Blue Star Mine.

The trail ends on Utah 21, 4 miles west of Beaver.

Current Road Information

BLM Cedar City Field Office
176 East D.L. Sargent Drive
Cedar City, UT 84721
(435) 865-3002

Map References

BLM Beaver, Wah Wah Mtns. South
USGS 1:24,000 Milford, Ranch Canyon, Cave Canyon, Adamsville, Beaver
1:100,000 Beaver, Wah Wah Mtns. South
Utah Atlas & Gazetteer, pp. 50, 49
Utah Road & Recreation Atlas, pp. 74, 73

The start of the trail looking toward the Mineral Mountains

Route Directions

▼ 0.0 On Utah 21 just southeast of Milford, 0.9 miles southeast of railroad crossing, turn east on paved road at BLM sign for Rock Corral Recreation Area and zero trip meter.

5.2 ▲ Trail ends on Utah 21, 1 mile southeast of downtown Milford. Turn right for Milford, left for Minersville.

GPS: N 38°22.79' W 113°00.10'

▼ 0.3 SO Cattle guard.

4.9 ▲ SO Cattle guard.

▼ 0.7 TR Intersection. Road is now graded gravel.

4.5 ▲ TL Intersection. Road is now paved.

GPS: N 38°22.97' W 112°59.44'

The east side of Soldier Pass looking toward Adamsville

▼ 1.4 SO Track on right.

3.8 ▲ SO Track on left.

▼ 1.7 SO Tracks on right and left.

3.5 ▲ SO Tracks on left and right.

▼ 2.7 SO Track on left.

2.5 ▲ SO Track on right.

▼ 3.2 SO Track on left.

2.0 ▲ SO Track on right.

▼ 5.2 SO Three-way junction; take middle road. Track on left goes to Rock Corral Recreation Area. Zero trip meter.

0.0 ▲ Continue straight toward Milford.

GPS: N 38°21.59' W 112°54.51'

▼ 0.0 Trail climbs toward Soldier Pass.

4.7 ▲ SO Three-way junction. Continue straight. Track on right goes to Rock Corral Recreation Area. Zero trip meter.

▼ 0.3 SO Track on left.

4.4 ▲ SO Track on right.

▼ 0.9 SO Track on left, then track on right.

3.8 ▲ SO Track on left, then track on right.

▼ 1.4 SO Track on right, cattle guard, then second track on right.

3.3 ▲ SO Track on left, cattle guard, then second track on left.

▼ 2.1 SO Track on left. Harkley Mountain on right, Granite Peak on left.

2.6 ▲ SO Track on right. Harkley Mountain on left, Granite Peak on right.

▼ 2.4 SO Track on left.

2.3 ▲ SO Track on right.

▼ 2.6 SO Track on right, then cross through wash.

2.1 ▲ SO Cross through wash, then track on left.

▼ 2.8 SO Tracks on right and left.

1.9 ▲ SO Tracks on left and right.

▼ 3.5 SO Track on left.

1.2 ▲ SO Track on right.

▼ 4.0 SO Track on right.
0.7 ▲ SO Track on left.

▼ 4.7 SO Cattle guard. Top of Soldier Pass. Zero trip meter.
0.0 ▲ Trail descends from pass.
GPS: N 38°19.35' W 112°50.73'

▼ 0.0 Trail descends from pass.
1.9 ▲ SO Cattle guard. Top of Soldier Pass. Zero trip meter.

▼ 0.8 SO Track on right.
1.1 ▲ SO Track on left.

▼ 1.2 SO Track on left.
0.7 ▲ SO Track on right.

▼ 1.6 SO Two tracks on right.
0.3 ▲ SO Two tracks on left.

▼ 1.9 SO Track on right is Northern #35: Lincoln Mine Trail. Zero trip meter.
0.0 ▲ Continue along Cherry Creek.
GPS: N 38°18.14' W 112°49.90'

▼ 0.0 Continue along Cherry Creek.
1.9 ▲ SO Track on left is Northern #35: Lincoln Mine Trail. Zero trip meter.

▼ 0.5 SO Cross through wash. Track on left to Blue Star Mine.
1.4 ▲ SO Track on right to Blue Star Mine. Cross through wash.
GPS: N 38°18.10' W 112°49.32'

▼ 0.7 SO Cattle guard.
1.2 ▲ SO Cattle guard.

▼ 0.9 SO Track on right, then track on left.
1.0 ▲ SO Track on right, then track on left.

▼ 1.1 SO Tracks on left and right.
0.8 ▲ SO Tracks on right and left.

▼ 1.6 SO Track on left.
0.3 ▲ SO Track on right.

▼ 1.9 BL Graded dirt road on right to Adamsville. Cross cattle guard and zero trip meter.
0.0 ▲ Continue toward Soldier Pass.
GPS: N 38°18.07' W 112°47.78'

▼ 0.0 Continue southeast.
4.1 ▲ SO Cross cattle guard, then graded dirt road on left to Adamsville. Zero trip meter.

▼ 0.1 SO Track on left.
4.0 ▲ SO Track on right.

▼ 1.4 SO Tracks on left and right.
2.7 ▲ SO Tracks on right and left.

▼ 2.3 SO Track on right.
1.8 ▲ SO Track on left.

▼ 2.6 SO Track on right.
1.5 ▲ SO Track on left.

▼ 3.1 SO Track on right, then track on left on left-hand bend.
1.0 ▲ SO Track on right on right-hand bend, then track on left.

▼ 3.5 SO Track on right.
0.6 ▲ SO Track on left.

▼ 4.1 Cattle guard, then trail ends at Utah 21. Turn left for Beaver, right for Minersville.
0.0 ▲ On Utah 21, 4.1 miles west of I-15 underpass at Beaver, turn west on unmarked, gravel Soldier Pass Road. Zero trip meter.
GPS: N 38°16.32' W 112°43.72'

NORTHERN REGION TRAIL #35

Lincoln Mine Trail

STARTING POINT Northern #34: Soldier Pass Trail
FINISHING POINT Utah 21, 0.2 miles east of Minersville
TOTAL MILEAGE 8.7 miles
UNPAVED MILEAGE 8.7 miles
DRIVING TIME 1 hour
ELEVATION RANGE 5,300–7,200 feet
USUALLY OPEN May to November
DIFFICULTY RATING 5
SCENIC RATING 7
REMOTENESS RATING +0

Special Attractions

- The old Spanish Lincoln Mine.
- Moderately challenging 4WD trail.

History

The Lincoln Mine is perhaps one of the oldest mines in America. It was first chiseled out by the Spanish, possibly in the 18th century, and it was later discovered in 1858 by Mormon bishop James Rollins, who found old Spanish hand tools and workings inside the ancient Mineral Mountains shaft.

At the time, the Mormons were mobilizing for a possible war with the United States—Colonel Johnston's army had camped outside Salt Lake City in 1857 under orders of President Buchanan—and they desperately needed lead to make bullets. Thinking the old Spanish vein was a lead mine, the Mormons began making bullets from the ore—only to discover that the bullets were nearly pure silver!

A small mining camp sprang up around the mines, which were named after Bishop Rollins, and the population grew to around 500. The Mormons built smelters to process the ore, but they were inefficient. Although they succeeded in extracting some of the lead, the more profitable silver ended up in the slag heaps. Miners from the nearby settlement of Minersville built more efficient smelters and were the first to successfully extract silver.

Many gentile miners were drawn to the promising area, and they quickly outnumbered the Mormons. They voted to change the mine's name to the Lincoln Mine in honor of President Abraham Lincoln. However, in 1900, the Lincoln Mine was bought by a British company, and like the owners of the Kimberly Mine in the nearby Tushar Mountains the overseas company soon went bankrupt because of inefficiencies. Many of the smaller outlying mines flooded, and the Lincoln Mine was abandoned. However, more recently, rising silver prices have led some to try extracting the ore once again from this historic mine.

Description

This short, challenging trail connects Northern #34: Soldier Pass Trail to Utah 21 across the southern tip of the Mineral Mountains. For the most part, the trail is not maintained, but it is well used by vehicles. The fine granitic road surface gives way periodically to several large washouts—to negociate these requires good clearance and

Start of the unmaintained section of the trail during a suprise snowstorm

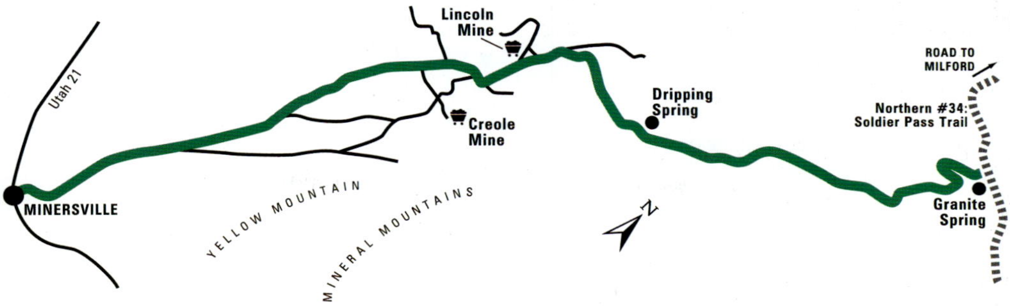

Northern Trail #35: Lincoln Mine Trail

wheel articulation. Most stock SUVs will be able to handle it, though extra long vehicles or those with running boards or lower clearance may find it difficult. A short section on the northern side of the saddle can be brushy and might cause some minor scratches on your vehicle.

The trail leaves Soldier Pass Trail at an unmarked junction 1.9 miles southeast of Soldier Pass. It immediately crosses through Cherry Creek and winds up toward the saddle. From the saddle it descends, passing Dripping Spring and then fording Lincoln Gulch. After you pass the Lincoln Mine, the trail standard improves, changing to roughly graded dirt. You pass other mine workings and a pretty reed-fringed dam fed from a spring, before descending to finish on Utah 21.

Other turns around the Lincoln Mine lead to other mines, such as the Harriet and the Creole Mines and many old shafts and adits.

Current Road Information

BLM Cedar City Field Office
176 East D.L. Sargent Drive
Cedar City, UT 84721
(435) 865-3002

Map References

BLM Beaver
USGS 1:24,000 Minersville, Cave Canyon, Adamsville
1:100,000 Beaver
Utah Atlas & Gazetteer, pp. 49, 50
Utah Road & Recreation Atlas, p. 73

Route Directions

▼ 0.0		On Northern #34: Soldier Pass Trail, 1.9 miles southeast of Soldier Pass, turn southwest on unmarked small dirt track and zero trip meter. Trail immediately crosses through Cherry Creek.
5.5 ▲		Cross through Cherry Creek, then trail ends at Northern #34: Soldier Pass Trail. Turn left for Milford, right for Beaver.
		GPS: N 38°18.14' W 112°49.90'
▼ 0.1	SO	Granite Spring on left.
5.4 ▲	SO	Granite Spring on right.
▼ 0.4	SO	Small track on right on left-hand bend.
5.1 ▲	SO	Small track on left on right-hand bend.
		GPS: N 38°17.90' W 112°50.15'
▼ 1.0	SO	Track on right.
4.5 ▲	SO	Track on left.
▼ 1.5	BR	Track on left.
4.0 ▲	BL	Track on right.
▼ 1.6	SO	Track on left.
3.9 ▲	SO	Track on right.
▼ 2.1	SO	Saddle. Trail descends.
3.4 ▲	SO	Saddle. Trail descends.
		GPS: N 38°17.11' W 112°51.32'
▼ 3.1	SO	Dripping Spring on right.
2.4 ▲	SO	Dripping Spring on left.
		GPS: N 38°16.55' W 112°52.07'

▼ 4.0 BR Old track on left; this is a washed-out creek crossing.
1.5 ▲ SO Old track on right.

▼ 4.1 SO Cross over wash.
1.4 ▲ SO Cross over wash; previous crossings are washed out.
GPS: N 38°16.62′ W 112°52.90′

▼ 4.3 SO Track on right.
1.2 ▲ BR Track on left.
GPS: N 38°16.56′ W 112°53.00′

▼ 4.4 SO Track on right.
1.1 ▲ SO Track on left.

▼ 4.6 BL Two tracks on right to Lincoln Mine. Trail is now roughly graded.
0.9 ▲ BR Two tracks on left to Lincoln Mine. Trail is now ungraded dirt.

▼ 4.8 SO Tracks on right and left.
0.7 ▲ SO Tracks on right and left.

▼ 4.9 SO Track on left.
0.6 ▲ BL Track on right.
GPS: N 38°16.12′ W 112°53.23′

▼ 5.0 SO Track on right.
0.5 ▲ SO Track on left.

▼ 5.1 SO Track on right.
0.4 ▲ SO Track on left.

▼ 5.2 SO Track on right.
0.3 ▲ SO Track on left.

▼ 5.3 SO Cross through creek.
0.2 ▲ SO Cross through creek.

▼ 5.4 SO Track on left before dam.
0.1 ▲ SO Track on right.

▼ 5.5 SO Track on left to dam, then second track on left. Zero trip meter.
0.0 ▲ Continue north.
GPS: N 38°15.82′ W 112°53.70′

▼ 0.0 Continue south.
3.2 ▲ SO Track on right, then second track on right to dam. Zero trip meter.

▼ 0.1 BL Track on right to mining remains, then second track on right.
3.1 ▲ SO Track on left, then second track on left to mining remains.

▼ 0.3 SO Tracks on right and left.
2.9 ▲ SO Tracks on right and left.
GPS: N 38°15.55′ W 112°53.96′

▼ 1.1 SO Track on left.
2.1 ▲ SO Track on right.

▼ 1.9 SO Track on left.
1.3 ▲ SO Track on right.

▼ 3.0 SO Track on right to gauging station.
0.2 ▲ BR Track on left to gauging station.

▼ 3.1 SO Tracks on right and left.
0.1 ▲ SO Tracks on right and left.

▼ 3.2 Cattle guard, then trail ends at Utah 21, 0.2 miles east of Minersville.
0.0 ▲ On Utah 21, 0.2 miles east of Minersville, turn north onto graded dirt road, cross cattle guard, and zero trip meter.
GPS: N 38°13.16′ W 112°55.12′

Photo Credits

Unless otherwise indicated in the following list of acknowledgments (which is organized by page number), all photographs were taken by Peter Massey and are copyrighted by Adler Publishing Company, Inc., or by Peter Massey.

78 Utah State Historical Society; **88** Utah State Historical Society **156** (upper left, upper right and bottom) Utah State Historical Society; **157** Utah State Historical Society; **184** Utah State Historical Society; **195-221** Bushducks—Maggie Pinder and Donald McGann.

Cover photography: Peter Massey

Trail Index

colorado and california trails

backroad & 4-wheel drive trail guides

Colorado Trails–Southwest Region
48 of the region's best scenic backroads and four-wheel drive trails. It covers Silverton, Animas Forks, Ouray, Durango, Telluride, Lake City, and Creede.
ISBN: 978-1-930193-07-9; Price: $29.95

Colorado Trails–Central Region
47 scenic backroads and 4-wheel drive trails near Georgetown, Breckenridge, Leadville, Fairplay, Buena Vista, Aspen, Crested Butte, and Salida.
ISBN 978-1-930193-51-2; Price $29.95

Colorado Trails–Front Range Region
42 scenic backroads and 4-wheel drive trails along the Front Range including trails near Fort Collins, Boulder, Idaho Springs, Denver, Colorado Springs, Cañon City, and Rocky Mountain
National Park.
ISBN 978-1-930193-50-5; Price $29.95

California Trails–Northern Sierra 55 off-road routes located near the towns of Sacramento (east), Red Bluff (east), Truckee, South Lake Tahoe, Sonora, Susanville, Chico, Oroville, Yuba City, Placerville, Stockton (east), Jackson, and Sonora.
ISBN 978-1-930193-23-9; Price $29.95

California Trails–High Sierra 50 trails located near the towns of Fresno (north), Oakhurst, Lone Pine, Bishop, Bridgeport, Coulterville, Mariposa, and Mammoth Lakes.
ISBN 978-1-930193-21-5; Price $29.95

California Trails–North Coast 47 routes located near the towns of Sacramento, Redding (west), Red Bluff, Clear Lake, McCloud, Mount Shasta, Yreka, Crescent City, and Fort Bidwell.
ISBN 978-1-930193-22-2; Price $29.95

California Trails–Central Mountains 52 trails located near the towns of Big Sur, Fresno, San Luis Obispo, Santa Barbara, Bakersfield, Mojave, and Maricopa.
ISBN 978-1-930193-19-2; Price $29.95

California Trails–South Coast 50 trails located near the towns of Los Angeles, San Bernardino, San Diego, Salton Sea, Indio, Borrego Springs, Ocotillo and Palo Verde.
ISBN 978-1-930193-24-6; Price $29.95

California Trails–Desert 51 off-road routes located near the towns of Lone Pine (east), Panamint Springs, Death Valley area, Ridgecrest, Barstow, Baker and Blythe.
ISBN 978-1-930193-20-8; Price $29.95